Opinion polls

Political Analyses

Series editors: Bill Jones, Michael Clarke and Michael Moran

Roland Axtmann
*Liberal democracy into the twenty-first century: globalization,
integration and the nation-state*

Lynn Bennie, Jack Brand and James Mitchell
How Scotland votes: Scottish parties and elections

John Burton
Violence explained: the sources of conflict, violence and crime and their prevention

Stuart Croft
Strategies of arms control: a history and typology

E. Franklin Dukes
Resolving public conflict: transforming community and governance

Brendan Evans and Andrew Taylor
From Salisbury to Major: continuity and change in Conservative politics

Michael Foley
The politics of the British constitution

Michael Foley and John E. Owens
Congress and the Presidency: institutional politics in a separated system

Opinion polls

History, theory and practice

Nick Moon

Manchester University Press
Manchester and New York
distributed exclusively in the USA by St. Martin's Press

Published by Manchester University Press
Oxford Road, Manchester M13 9NR, UK
and Room 400, 175 Fifth Avenue, New York, NY 10010, USA
http://www.man.ac.uk/mup

Distributed exclusively in the USA by
St. Martin's Press, Inc., 175 Fifth Avenue, New York, NY 10010, USA

Distributed exclusively in Canada by
UBC Press, University of British Columbia, 6344 Memorial Road,
Vancouver, BC, Canada V6T 1Z2

British Library Cataloguing-in-Publication Data
A catalogue record for this book is available from the British Library

Library of Congress Cataloging-in-Publication Data applied for

ISBN 0 7190 4223 2 *hardback*
       0 7190 4224 0 *paperback*

First published 1999

06 05 04 03 02 01 00 99   10 9 8 7 6 5 4 3 2 1

Typeset in Photina
by Servis Filmsetting Ltd, Manchester
Printed in Great Britain
by Biddles Ltd, Guildford and King's Lynn

To the two Johns, Barter and O'Brien,
without whose teaching I would not have been asked to write this book

Contents

Figures and tables

Figures

Tables

Series editors' foreword

The *Politics Today* series has been running successfully since the late 1970s, aimed mainly at an undergraduate audience. After over a decade in which a dozen or more titles have been produced, some of which run to multiple copies, MUP thought it time to launch a new politics series, aimed at a different audience and a different need.

The *Political Analyses* series was prompted by the relative dearth of research-based political science series which persists despite the fecund source of publication ideas provided by current political developments. In the UK we observe, for example: the rapid evolution of Labour politics as the party seeks to find a reliable electoral base; the continuing development of the post-Thatcher Conservative Party; the growth of pressure-group activity and lobbying in modern British politics; and the irresistible moves towards constitutional reform of an arguably outdated state.

Abroad, there are even more themes upon which to draw, for example: the ending of the Thatcher–Reagan axis; the parallel collapse of communism in Europe and Russia; and the gradual retreat of socialism from the former heartlands in Western Europe.

This series seeks to explore some of these new ideas to a depth beyond the scope of the *Politics Today* series – while maintaining a similar direct and accessible style – and to serve an audience of academics, practitioners and the well-informed reader as well as undergraduates. The series has three editors: Bill Jones and Michael Moran, who concentrate on domestic topics, and Michael Clarke, who attends to international issues.

Acknowledgements

To the extent that most of this book derives from my career on the supplier side of survey research, acknowledgements are most of all due to my employer, NOP Research, for paying me while I had the fun of doing all this research; and to the clients who paid NOP to carry out the surveys.

On the client side Peter Kellner stands out on grounds of longevity (about nine years); variety (at least five different media clients); and reasonableness (a relatively rare commodity among clients). He was also kind enough to read some of the book and make helpful comments. Others who deserve thanks for commissioning the polls from which the examples in the book are drawn are David Tytler, Robin Oakley, Alan Cochrane and Richard Heller from the *Mail/Mail on Sunday*; David Smith and the late Tony Bambridge from the *Sunday Times*; Peter Wilby from the *Independent on Sunday*; Robin McGregor and Bill Bush from the BBC; and Greg Cook from the Labour Party.

Within NOP I was taught my trade by two real experts, John Barter (who also read some of the book and made very useful comments) and John O'Brien; and was allowed to get on with it in my own sweet way by a number of tolerant bosses: Charles Ilsley, Ivor Stocker and Rockey Morrison. Equally importantly, much of the real work on the surveys was done by those who have been part of the NOP polling team during my years in charge of it: Janet English, Pete Doe, Richard Glendinning, Darren Marshall, Marie Davison, Elaine Winter, Rezina Chowdhury and my remarkable secretary, Angela Bass. Statisticians Paul Harris and Corrine Moy have always done all the hard sums for me, and done their best to overcome my aversion to formulae.

One of the nice things about survey research is that it is a pretty open profession. In most industries, if you come with an entirely new technique which will enable you to work more effectively, or produce better results, the first thing you do is patent it to ensure you are the only one to benefit from it. In market research the first thing you do is to give a paper at the Market Research Society Conference, telling everyone else how to do it. Through this spirit of openness,

I have been helped by my competitors, particularly Bob Worcester of MORI, Bob Wybrow of Gallup, and Nick Sparrow of ICM; and also those in other organisations, especially Iain Noble of Hound-Dog Research, Colm O'Muircheartaigh of the LSE and Roger Jowell of SCPR.

Although I fancy myself a bit of an expert on polling, I am not an expert on politics, and avoided a few howlers with help from various co-members of the infamous Pebble Club, especially Michael Thrasher and Colin Rallings of the University of Plymouth, and David Cowling of no fixed abode. Any remaining errors are entirely David's fault.

For filling in the very large gaps in my knowledge about polling in America I am grateful to a number of people, many of whom who gave up their time in an election campaign to explain their methods to me; in particular Warren Mitofsky, Kathy Francovic, Humphrey Taylor, Ed Lazarus, Stan Greenberg and Mick Couper.

Last, but by no means least, huge thanks are due to my wife Anne, for tolerating me spending hours writing this book, when I should have been rewiring the kitchen or putting up shelves in the children's bedrooms, and to Stephanie and Zoe for missing out a lot on their turn on the computer.

List of abbreviations

ACORN	A Classification of Residential Neighbourhoods
AGB	Audits of Great Britain
AMSO	Association of Market Survey Organizations
APOPO	Association of Professional Opinion Polling Organisations
ASL	Audience Selection Ltd
BARB	Broadcasters' Audience Research Board
BBC	British Broadcasting Corporation
BES	British Election Study
BHPS	British Household Panel Study
BIPO	British Institute of Public Opinion
BMP	formerly Boase Massimi Pollitt, now known as BMP
BMRB	British Market Research Bureau
CATI	computer-assisted telephone interviewing
CNN	Cable News Network
ESOMAR	European Society for Opinion and Market Research
ESRC	Economic and Social Research Council
GHS	General Household Survey
HEA	Health Education Authority
HEMS	Health Education Monitoring Survey
HTV	Harlech Television
ICM	now just a company name
ITC	Independent Television Commission
ITN	Independent Television News
LFS	Labour Force Survey
MORI	Market and Opinion Research International
MOSAIC	name of a type of geodemographic system
MRS	Market Research Society
NOP	formerly National Opinion Polls, now known as NOP
NRS	National Readership Survey

OED	*Oxford English Dictionary*
ONS	Office of National Surveys
OPCS	Office of Population Censuses and Surveys (now ONS)
ORC	Opinion Research Centre
PAF	Postcode Address File
PSU	Primary Sampling Unit
RDD	random-digit dialling
RSL	Research Services Ltd
SCA	Shadow Communications Agency
SDP	Social Democratic Party
SEG	Socio-Economic Groups
SOC	Standard Occupational Classification

Introduction – a question
of definition

Because something is happening here.
But you don't know what it is

Public opinion polls are nowadays such a major part of everyday life, and especially of journalistic life, that they seem, for good or ill, inextricably wedded to the democratic process. During the British general election of May 1997, 59 nationally representative opinion polls were conducted by mainstream polling companies for the national press or national television,[1] plus uncounted numbers of local polls conducted by a wide variety of organisations of widely differing abilities. For an election campaign lasting 45 days, this represents an average of 1.3 national polls published on every day of the campaign. In 1992, with a shorter campaign, the average per day was 1.7. In 1992 Butler and Kavanagh calculated that 18% of all newspaper front-page lead stories were given over to coverage of the polls.[2]

For every column inch given over to polls there were several journalists or politicians who complained, particularly after the failure of the polls in 1992 to predict the winner of the election, that the polls were a pernicious parasite on the body politic, and that they had somehow worked themselves into a position where they could corrupt democracy itself, by reducing an election to the level of a horse race. Later chapters look at the possible causes of the error of the polls in 1992, and at the way they work within the electoral system, but it is first worth looking at where they came from, and how they got to where they are now.

To do this, we need to establish some form of definition to fit the term 'public opinion poll'. Taken literally, its meaning is far too broad for our purpose. The (domestic) British market research industry was estimated by the Association of Market Survey Organisations (AMSO) to be worth £750 million in 1997. Public opinion polling, as the term would be understood by most people, almost certainly accounted for less than half a per cent of that, and yet most of the rest involved people being polled about their opinion, If someone is stopped in the street and asked whether they think the new Daz washes whiter than the old one, or asked what they think are the most attractive and unattractive features of the Ford Mondeo, they are being polled and expressing an opinion, but it is not one which comes within the ambit of this book.

Here, then, is the first narrowing-down of the definition: when people talk about opinion polls, they are usually talking about political opinion. There are probably many people who, faced with the term 'public opinion poll', think only of polls that set out to predict the result of the next election, but this is too restrictive for two reasons. The first is that one could only thus describe polls that were carried out during the course of an election campaign, or more exactly, only the last polls conducted on election eve. Polls being published in newspapers three years before an election is due cannot possibly by predictive of the result, and yet they are undoubtedly public opinion polls. Also, public opinion polls concern more than just voting intention. If they did not, they would be better referred to as public behaviour polls, which does not have the same ring. In the terms of this book, the definition of an opinion poll is more broad than voting intention, and less broad than opinion on any topic under the sun.

The word 'political' is often used in place of 'public', and 'political opinion poll' conveys a lot of the sense of what this book is about, but it is still too restrictive. A newspaper commissioning a poll asking people for their opinions about the most recent budget certainly qualifies, but then how different is a newspaper commissioning a poll about divorce, or the ethics of reproductive technology? To encompass this range of topic matter, my definition is that the opinion in public opinion polls must be about political or social topics. To make the definition circular, they must be about matters that are in the general public interest.

Having defined 'opinion', albeit in a rather vague way, what of 'public' and 'poll'? Here again we cannot escape some circularity, for the origins of the word 'poll' are tied up with elections. The *Chambers Dictionary* gives the opinion-poll meaning of the word only as its fifth definition of 'poll': 'a taking of the public opinion by means of questioning'. *The Complete Oxford Dictionary* gives no such definition, even in the *Supplement*. To the *OED*, the eighth definition given for the verb is the closest to our purposes: 'to take the votes of, register the suffrage of'. It is this definition that is alive today in the form of 'polling station', 'polling card' and so on. The immediately preceding definition in the *OED* shows how poll came to mean election: 'to count heads; to enumerate'. It is the still earlier meaning of a poll as a head that led to polls about the poll tax being conducted in the 1980s.

To all intents and purposes, the election connection in the modern definition of 'poll' is spurious, or as the lexicographers would have it, *obs*. What originally meant measuring votes has come to mean measuring opinion, but in doing so is has taken on a connotation of scientific method. A journalist going into a pub and asking a dozen locals whom they intend to vote for in the forthcoming by-election is unlikely to write up his findings as a public opinion poll. However, he or she may describe it as a 'straw poll', which has come to mean almost any small-scale measuring of opinion which lacks the basis in sampling and question design present in a public opinion poll, but which in its original form, 'straw vote', was the precursor of modern polls, discussed in detail below. For the purposes of the definition for this book, to count as a opinion poll rather than a random collection of anecdotal information, there must be some form of scientific approach. What that scientific approach may be is discussed in Chapters 2 to 4.

For the final leg of the tripodal definition, 'public', there is today no doubt what is meant by the general public, although there are methodological questions about the relative merits of surveys of the whole adult population and surveys of the electorate, or to go a stage further, surveys of those people who actually go and vote. This has become a slightly abstruse point of polling technique, as Chapter 8 shows, but there is a philosophical point here which again has resonance in the early history of opinion polling. The argument, very briefly, is that if one is trying to predict the result of an election, a good sample of voters will be more reliable than a good sample of the population at large. The opinions of those who will not vote may be interesting, but they will not affect the result. It was the same attitude over a hundred years ago which meant that the history of opinion polls began in America rather than in Britain or elsewhere in Europe.

There is little point in polling the population at large if the majority of them are not enfranchised. While political power was in the hands of a small elite of voters drawn from a narrow social spectrum, all the aspiring politician needed to know was the views of that elite, and since he was from the same social spectrum this was unlikely to be a problem. It was the introduction of universal suffrage, or at least of universal male suffrage, that made knowledge of opinion among a broader public vitally important. This is not to say that there was no polling of any kind before then, merely that there was no need for it to be all sophisticated. Indeed, before the use of the ballot papers and polling booths that are an essential part of modern elections, voting in Britain was often by means of poll books, in which people recorded their votes. These were often open for several days, so someone wanting to predict the outcome would not need to question voters; he could simply add up the actual votes cast so far.

With much wider suffrage, America provided more fertile territory for the development of polling, and it was in the Atlantic states that most writers place the first opinion polls. Many, such as Teer and Spence[3] and Bradburn and Sudman[4], refer to the presidential election of 1824 as a definite starting point, and quote particular straw polls in the newspapers, though more recently Tom Smith has queried this.[5] He claims that the reference to 1824 was originally made by George Gallup, and that other writers have simply followed this, without much in the way of corroborative investigation.

It is quite likely that some form of straw poll did indeed take place slightly earlier, or simultaneously elsewhere, without making its mark on posterity, but in a sense the exact details do not matter. What can safely be assumed is that the first systematic attempts to measure in advance electors' behaviour at a future election took the form of straw polls, conducted in America, in the 1820s. (As a lexicographic aside, despite the common modern usage of the term 'straw poll', the *OED* gave no meaning for such a phrase, but instead listed 'straw vote', meaning the same thing, and gave as sources an American diction-ary of 1891 and the *Daily Chronicle* in 1906.)

Smith accepts the strength of the case for 1824 as the first opinion-poll elec-tion: 'While the roots of polls and surveys have been traced back to censuses, administrative records, and other collections of information in ancient times there is no current contender for earlier preelection polls.'

He also enters the caveat: 'Still, it is likely that similar tallies were collected at least occasionally before 1824 – both militia musters and conventions had been going on for 20 years.'

Since there is a wealth of documentary evidence about the straw votes of 1824, and since it has at least as good a claim as any other, it seems acceptable to treat that election as seeing the birth of polling. One reason for this is simply that there was little need of them before, since the 1824 election was the first one to be decided largely by the popular vote.

The election of 1824 also marked the beginning of a major period of politi-cal transition. As well as the effective collapse of the old congressional caucus system, and the attempt to develop a new nomination process, there was the formation of new party groupings, and therefore heightened interest in the process. Any period of significant structural change in the system of political parties sparks off an increased demand for information on these new groupings. This is as true today as it was in the 1820s, as demonstrated by the flurry of published opinion polls at the time of the launch of the Social Democratic Party (SDP), and the subsequent creation of the Liberal/SDP Alliance.

For the purposes of this book, I continue to date the birth of opinion polling as 1824. In the rest of the book I trace the history of polling from then until the present day, and explain the changes in methodology which have occurred along the way. The main emphasis is on pre-election polls for publication, but the special topics of exit polling and private polling are also covered as separate topics. Given its importance in the history of opinion polling, considerable attention is given to the 1992 general election, in particular the possible reasons for the failure of the polls, and changes that have been made since then. As Chapter 7 shows, opinion research is still in a period of transition, which means that from a polling perspective, the next election is likely to be as inter-esting and important as 1997.

Notes

1 This is a slight exaggeration, because Gallup conducted a daily 'rolling poll'. Each day the *Telegraph* reported on an aggregate of three days of fieldwork, so each day was reported on three times. If we follow most users and treat each discrete three days as a separate poll, the total number of polls is reduced to 42.
2 D. Butler and D. Kavanagh, *The British General Election of 1992* (Macmillan, 1992).
3 F. Teer and J. Spence, *Public Opinion Polls* (Hutchinson, 1973).
4 N. Bradburn and S. Sudman, *Polls and Surveys* (Jossey-Bass, 1988).
5 T. W. Smith, 'The first straw? A study of the origins of election polls', *Public Opinion Quarterly*, 54:1 (1990).

1

The early history

Lookin' into the lost forgotten years

Most histories of opinion polls do not merely agree that 1824 was the first election in which polls were used, but they even agree on the newspaper in which the first-ever poll appeared. This was the *Harrisburg Pennsylvanian*, which published the result of a straw vote in July 1824, showing Andrew Jackson leading John Quincy Adams by 335 votes to 169. Later that same summer, the *Raleigh Star* published the result of a poll of over four thousand voters at political meetings, and again showed Jackson well ahead. It seems, however, just as likely that these are the only ones to have survived, as that these were indeed the first-ever polls. There were certainly others conducted and published during that election campaign.

Smith cites a number of different ways in which straw votes were taken, and draws a subtle distinction between nominations, which he says were seen as the official position of the meeting or group, while straw votes represented members' sentiments.[1] Also, nominations tended to come from established groups holding a meeting specifically to make a nomination, while straw votes were often taken at meetings organised for an entirely different purpose, such as military musters or grand juries. Harking back to English practice, poll books were sometimes left out for people to record their preference over a period of days. Not surprisingly, these soundings were often taken in a very haphazard way, with little understanding of the principles of sampling, but there was some informed criticism of them. Since Andrew Jackson was a military man, some writers pointed out that straw votes taken at militia musters would inevitably be biased in his favour. Others complained that the straw votes included the views of those not entitled to vote. In terms of methodology, the early straw votes had little if anything in common with modern polling techniques, and Teer and Spence concluded that 'These first attempts to quantify electors' opinions were an unscientific extension of normal journalistic soundings. No attempt was made to ensure that a representative sample was taken, but they provoked interest and caught the eye of politicians.'[2]

In respect of the last two effects, the early straw votes were very similar to modern polls, though the coverage they received, and the importance attached to them, varied greatly from one newspaper to another. Some newspapers gave them great coverage, while others preferred to concentrate on the views of elites and local leaders. Smith also points out that while the newspapers reported these straw votes, they did not themselves commission them or carry them out, they merely reported their findings.

Although most commentators agree that the origins of modern opinion polls can be traced in these straw votes, it must be noted that they represented only a slight extension of the soundings traditionally – and still – taken by journalists. It was effectively only the number of people canvassed that set them apart, for there was no real scientific basis to them, no attempt to ensure that the sample of people polled was a representative one. Indeed, in the absence of any tradition of sample-based survey research there was no reason why there should be.

Straw votes were used in similar ways at succeeding elections, more at some than at others, but with little development of technique. Teer and Spence credit the *Columbus Despatch* with moving the methodology along the first step at the end of the century, by recognising the importance of the representativeness of the sample. The *Despatch* used trained interviewers, sending them each into designated areas of the city, and the sample was controlled to be representative in terms of age and occupation. If Teer and Spence are correct, the *Despatch* was a long way ahead of its time, as events described later in this chapter will show.

Bradburn and Sudman are much more dismissive of the newspaper straw polls throughout the nineteenth century and into the twentieth. In a technique that will seem familiar to many current readers of local newspapers or the tabloid press, many newspapers simply published ballot forms as part of the newspaper, and invited readers to fill them in. There were, indeed there could be, no controls on the sorts of people who filled them in as opposed to those who did not, and little to prevent organised mass returns. Even where straw votes were taken by supposedly independent canvassers at election meetings, votes from different locations were simply added up without any real concern for potential biases in the sample. Where there undoubtedly was progress in these early polls was in the sample size, which grew inexorably until the bubble finally burst in an election that can in some ways make a greater claim than 1824 to be the genesis of modern polling.

By 1904 sample size had risen to the 30,000 electors polled by the *New York Herald*, but it was to grow much higher still, as interest began to switch from measuring local opinion to trying to forecast the election result across the whole country. Interest spread beyond just newspapers, and in 1912 the somewhat unlikely *Farm Journal* became the first US magazine to join in the fun.

While the *Farm Journal* is doomed to the role of minor footnote in the history of polling, the next presidential election in 1916 saw the entry into the fray of the first major player in polling history, the *Literary Digest*. Beginning in 1916, the *Literary Digest* produced a number of correct predictions, and acquired a reputation as market leader as a result. As well as trying to predict the election winner, the *Literary Digest* surveys, like those of today, also included questions to measure public opinion on topics of the day.

The *Literary Digest* polls were based entirely on postal ballots, but rather than the *ad hoc*, interview-anyone approach of the early straw votes, the *Literary Digest* had at least grasped the basic principles of the sample. People were selected from available frames to be sent postal ballots, the most frequently used frames being lists of telephone subscribers and records of car registrations. Because the postal technique is cheap per response compared with the expense of sending out interviewers, the *Literary Digest* was able to work with some very large samples indeed. By the presidential election of 1936 the number of postal ballots sent out had risen to around ten million, and the number completed and returned to well over two million. As Chapter 2 shows, size is not everything, but the sheer scale of such an exercise lent it a great degree of credibility. It is tempting to mock the audience of the *Literary Digest* poll for their lack of sophistication, but if a newspaper were to publish an opinion poll today based on over two million responses most people would believe it.

The *Literary Digest* polls had earned respect not just because of their size, but because they were successful in predicting the winner of the presidential races. Fuelled by this success, they diversified slightly and conducted large-scale postal surveys on attitudes to Prohibition in 1922, 1930 and 1932. But while there was this one successful strand of research methodology, whose authority lay mainly in vast numbers of respondents, and to a lesser extent in the idea of a sample systematically drawn from available lists, a separate strand of research was developing, based on smaller numbers but a greater level of sophistication in design.

Political straw votes were not the only forms of systematic opinion-gathering to have developed during the later nineteenth century. One strand was social surveys, which grew out of the censuses of population which governments the world over have been conducting as long as there have been governments. Joseph and Mary went to Bethlehem because of a census, Britain has a well-known one, recorded in the Domesday Book of 1086, and there is evidence of censuses being taken in Venice and Florence during the Renaissance in fifteenth-century Europe. The current sequence of censuses began in Britain in 1801 and in America in 1790.

One of the key figures in the development of social statistics was Owen Chadwick, the founder of the Registrar General's office, and instigator of the continuous recording of births and deaths. Also in Britain, another key step was taken by Charles Booth, one of the first people to use the interview survey as a means of collecting data about prevailing social conditions. Booth wrote his survey up in his classic 1890s work, *The Life and Labour of the People of London*, while slightly earlier Henry Mayhew had taken steps in the same direction with his *London Labour and the London Poor* in the 1860s. While one might take issue with the reliability of their methodology, the basis of these works was similar to that of organised polling. Most importantly, they drew attention to the importance of systematic and objective collection of data.

The main methodological failings in these early social investigations lay mainly with the sampling, which was often haphazard at best and inherently biased at worst. Rowntree avoided these problems by interviewing every wage-earning household in the town, but this was a luxury permitted only for local studies, and even then the cost and effort involved were enormous. As society became more complex, the need grew for a more scientific approach, if sample surveys were to provide accurate measures of behaviour or opinion. One of the key figures in the development of systematic samples was Arthur Bowley, an economist at the London School of Economics. He too was a specialist in studies of poverty in particular towns, beginning with Reading. Because he did not have the resources to interview every household in the town, he proposed the use of a sample of households instead of the more typical enumeration. It was his subsequent work on probability sampling which was to lead to the development of sampling methods that then formed the basis of almost all social surveys until the latter half of the twentieth century.

Though the initial work on the development of techniques for social surveys was carried out in Britain, these techniques soon crossed the Atlantic, where they merged with a separate strand of development which was later to make the move in the opposite direction. This was commercial market research. Lockley attributes the origins of market research to an American advertising agency named N. W. Ayer & Son, which contacted state officials in 1879 to gain estimates of that year's grain production, and similar exercises were carried out by other firms for the rest of the century, although the important thing to note is that these were carried out by firms whose main line of business was in fields other than research itself.[3] The first specialist market-research firms appeared in 1911. The Business Bourse was the first firm to have its own team of interviewers, while in the same year the Curtis Publishing Company set up a commercial research department, which was to grow to be one of America's largest research organisations, employing over a thousand interviewers. Also in 1911 the Harvard Business School set up a Bureau of Business Research. Despite the field forces of the Business Bourse and Curtis, this market research was not conducted entirely by personal interview. Using techniques similar to those of the *Literary Digest*'s election polls, the Kellogg Company conducted the first readership survey in 1911, using a questionnaire postcard mailed to various types of people.

By the 1920s there were a number of specialist market-research companies, and a number of market-research divisions within major corporations and advertising agencies. They followed the lead of Arthur Bowley in Britain, referred to above, in that they generally used quite small sample sizes, knowing that these would still be reliable enough for the necessary action to be taken as a result of their findings with a reasonable chance of success. Attempts were made to set demographic quotas, though these were far from perfect, and there was also a recognition that question wording could have a considerable impact on the answer obtained. These organisations were the forerunners of today's market-research companies, but their development of methodology was also to provide a stimulus to the progress of opinion-polling organisations, and indeed it proved to be an issue of methodology which ended the initial phase of opinion polling – typified by the *Literary Digest* – and led to the success of the opinion-polling companies, of which George Gallup was the pioneer.

The *Literary Digest* had been successful in predicting the results of the 1920, 1924, 1928 and 1932 elections, using its technique of mailing huge numbers of questionnaires to households listed in telephone subscriber lists or state records of car registrations. In 1936 the *Literary Digest* mailed no fewer than ten million questionnaires, and was confident of another success, but it did not have the field to itself. In 1935 George Gallup set up the American Institute of Public Opinion, and he was soon followed by the Crossley Poll and the Fortune survey. This latter was run in part by Elmo Roper, founder of the Roper Centre.

The distinguishing feature of all these companies, which set them apart from the *Literary Digest* school of polling, was that they relied on relatively small numbers of respondents, selected systematically and interviewed personally by trained interviewers. Using these methods, Gallup, Roper and Crossley all predicted a Roosevelt victory, while the *Literary Digest* poll showed Republican candidate Alfred Landon was headed for a comfortable victory. Unabashed by this discrepancy with the market leader, Gallup in particular stuck vociferously to his forecasts, and claimed that the *Literary Digest* would get the result wrong because of its outdated methods. He even infuriated the *Digest* by predicting publicly, some six weeks before it was even carried out, that its poll would show around 56% for Landon and only 44% for Roosevelt. *Digest* editor Wilfred J. Funk was outraged at this cheek, and warned George Gallup ('our fine statistical friend') in print that the *Digest* would continue 'with those old fashioned methods that have produced correct forecasts exactly one hundred percent of the time'.

In the event Roosevelt did of course win, with Landon getting only 38.5% of the votes cast, and this proved a major stimulus to the development of the more scientific opinion polls as opposed to the large-scale, postal approach. There are several examples on both sides of the Atlantic of new polling techniques producing a prediction that was unexpected enough to lead to them being scorned, and then proved right enough for the subsequent praise for them to be magnified severalfold. It is easy to see why the *Literary Digest* poll was so wrong, without relying on hindsight. The problems were recognised at the time by George Gallup. Funk's unhappiness at calling the result wrong must have been made even worse by the fact the *Literary Digest* poll showed almost exactly what Gallup had predicted: 57% for Landon and 43% for Roosevelt.

So how did Gallup, Crossley and Roper all manage to be much more accurate with much smaller sample sizes than the *Digest*, and how was Gallup able to predict the result of the *Digest* poll weeks before it happened? The principles of polling methodology are covered in more detail in Chapters 2 and 3, but the key flaw in the *Digest* poll lay in its approach to sampling. The *Digest* had learned the importance of a systematic sample, rather than just sending questionnaires haphazardly, and in drawing names at random from its sampling frames it would seem to have followed the basic rules of probability sampling, in partic-ular that everyone in the frame has an equal and known chance of selection.

The problem was that its sampling frames were not representative of the electorate as a whole. By using only lists of telephone subscribers and car owners, the *Digest* restricted its polling to the better-off portions of the American public. There were many Americans who had neither a telephone nor a car, and they effectively brought about the demise of the *Literary Digest*, which, already in financial difficulties, never really recovered from the disaster of 1936 and soon after ceased publication. The same sampling flaws had been present in the *Digest* polls of the four previous elections, and yet the *Digest* had correctly predicted the result, so why did those methods suddenly fail in 1936? In those previous elections there had been little class- or income-based compo-nent of voting: the poor were not particularly more likely to vote for either party than were the rich. What changed things was principally Roosevelt's espousal of the New Deal. This radical programme of social reform opened up new fault-lines between Democrats and Republicans, particularly in their bases of support. Measures such as the National Recovery Administration, the Labour Relations Act and the setting-up of bodies such as the Tennessee Valley Authority were all more likely to be attractive to the poor and underprivileged. Any measures that appear socially redistributive, however mildly, are likely to repel the better-off, and so the Republicans in 1936 were much more likely to be supported by the wealthy.

A sampling design that leads to an over-representation of the wealthy and an under-representation of the less well-off was doomed to overestimate support for the Republicans. With his knowledge of the principles of represen-tative sampling, it was relatively easy for Gallup to predict that the *Literary Digest* would overscore Landon's vote, and not very difficult for him to guess how wrong they were likely to be. Where he did have to go slightly out on a limb was in estimating what the true picture was, so he could apply the *Digest* bias and predict what the *Digest* poll would say. One can only assume that he had enough faith in his own polls to assume that they would be right, and to extrap-olate the *Digest*'s figures from that.

In just the same way that the *Literary Digest* had followed its own first successful election poll with a series of correct calls at subsequent elections, the American opinion-polling agencies followed up their success in 1936 by correctly predicting the winners of the 1940 and 1944 elections, before they too came badly unstuck in 1948. The 1936 election marked the end of one style of polling, and though the 1948 election was not similarly terminal for Gallup's or Roper's styles, it was still a major waypoint in the development of polling.

The main pollsters were the same three as in 1936 – Gallup, Roper and Crossley – and all three agreed in showing Republican Thomas Dewey ahead of Democrat incumbent Harry Truman, although there were differences in the predicted scale of victory. Roper showed Dewey ahead by a comfortable 15%, while the other two showed leads of 5%. Following their success in 1936, the pollsters had become an accepted part of the political landscape, with more and more newspapers and politicians making use of them. That people were prepared to rely on the polls to a great extent can be dramatically seen in the famous photograph showing a victorious Truman holding up an early edition of a newspaper, whose headline is proclaiming a Dewey victory in huge print.

Given that people had come to rely on increasingly on the polls, and to trust their predictions, the wrong call in 1948 had a massive public impact. The pollsters themselves were forced to re-examine their methods, and there was an independent enquiry conducted by the US Social Science Research Council. While it had been possible for Gallup to spot in advance the flaws in the *Literary Digest* poll, the pollsters' errors in 1948 were equally clear, but this time only with hindsight.

Before looking at what these errors were, it is important to enter an important caveat about 1948. Because the polls called the wrong winner, the election is usually described in such terms as 'a disaster for the polls', but in fact the actual error of the polls – the gap between the predicted and actual share of the vote for each candidate – was less than it had been in 1936, the year of the pollsters' first great triumph. This was an important lesson for the polls, for it showed that published opinion polls are required to work to different criteria from most other surveys. It is almost inevitable that any survey will have error, for the reasons discussed in Chapter 2, and in most cases the basis for judgement of a survey that can be validated at all is the gap between the percentage found by the survey for whatever variable is being investigated, and the actual percentage for that variable in the whole population.

Depending on the purposes of the survey, the size of gap permitted before the survey can no longer be judged a success will vary from only 1% or 2% where accuracy is vital, to as much as 10% or more if the purpose is merely to give a broad indication of preference. Whatever the permitted error level, surveys are usually judged by whether they fall within that range. With opinion polls the situation is subtly but crucially different, for the overwhelming criterion for judging their success is not the magnitude of error, but getting the parties or candidates in the right order – predicting the actual winner. Crossley and Gallup came within 5% of the actual figure for both Dewey and Truman, which, while less good than one would desire, is by no means dreadful, but they attracted attention and opprobrium because they failed to fulfil their main role – predicting the winner.

In 1936 they had been out by more than 5%, but they got the winner right, and so in the public eye 1948 was a worse performance by the polls than 1936. In view of the purpose of opinion polls, at least those carried out on the eve of the election, it is inevitable that polls will be judged thus. Pollsters will judge themselves more by how close they came to the actual scores for each party, but the media and the general public will not. If an election is very close, with both parties within the range of survey error, then pollsters will say the election is too close to call, but in a situation where a poll predicts Labour winning by 43% to 41%, and in the end the Conservatives win by 42% to 40%, the polls will be judged by most people to have failed. This topic is returned to later in this chapter.

In objective terms, then, the American polls performed better in 1948 than they had in 1936, but this is not to disguise the fact that they performed less well in 1948 than they should have done. The Social Science Research Council enquiry identified four main sources of error, some of which were easier to correct than others. The one regarded by many commentators as the most important was that the pollsters stopped interviewing too soon, and thus were not able to detect a strong switch towards Truman in the last few days. Had the final polls continued until the day or two before the election, they would probably have called the right winner. The pollsters then compounded this error by combining results from early and more recent polls, thus missing out even more on the later movements in opinion. These mistakes at least were easy to correct, and American pollsters now interview right up until the evening before an election.

Another of the sources of error in 1948 identified by the enquiry was, ironically in view of the 1936 election, that the sampling methods used were biased towards those on middle and higher incomes, and thus biased towards the Republicans. The third main source of error was that the questionnaire did not establish whether respondents would actually vote, and the fourth was that undecided voters were not allocated between the candidates in any consistent or even objective fashion. Those who believe that one of the signs of intelligence is the ability to learn from the past should read Chapters 5 and 6 at this point.

As well as their failings of technique, Gallup and Crossley have been criticised for not expressing enough caution about the relatively small leads their polls showed. A gap of 5% between the candidates would be wiped out if the polls were wrong by 3% on each candidate, and being more accurate than plus or minus 3% is quite an achievement. Media clients would stop buying if pollsters described every election short of a walkover as too close to call, but it is important for pollsters to try to stop newspapers talking up a lead at the margins of statistical significance. One result of this criticism was that in 1952 the American pollsters were over-cautious, and talked down a much larger lead for Dwight Eisenhower when they in fact proved to be fairly accurate.

At this point the historical narrative switches from the USA to Great Britain, not because further developments in the USA are of little interest, but because this book is primarily about opinion polling in Britain, and the US experience discussed above has been included because the development of polling in Britain follows on from its earlier development in the USA. Taking this brief to extremes, the US strand should have ceased after 1936, the point at which polling began in Britain, but it was extended in order to cover the critical election of 1948.

Opinion polling in Britain can be clearly dated to the founding of the British Institute of Public Opinion (BIPO) in 1937. This was the British arm of Gallup, followed in 1938 by a sister organisation in France; the first two of many around the world. For convenience, the Institute is referred to in this book simply as Gallup, which indeed it later became. Henry Durant, newly graduated from the London School of Economics, was recruited as the first head of British Gallup, working part-time from home. His initial work was in postal surveys, until he received a major boost when the *News Chronicle* commissioned BIPO to conduct a survey during the West Fulham by-election in 1938. Apart from a one-year period when Labour won the seat in 1929 before losing it again in a by-election, West Fulham had been Conservative since 1918. BIPO's prediction was that the Labour candidate, Dr Edith Summerskill, would win the by-election, while most experts had expected the Conservatives to hold on. In the end Dr Summerskill did win, and BIPO's predictions proved to be within 1% for each party. Gallup thus began in Britain as it had in the USA, by producing an unexpected finding and being proved right.

As had also happened in the USA, this led to an immediate increase in status, and the *News Chronicle* continued to publish Gallup polls, including their prediction for the 1945 general election. Here again Gallup proved to be almost alone in forecasting a Labour victory, and proved to be accurate within 2% on each of the two main parties, as is shown in Table 1.

Fuelled by this success, the nascent British polling industry grew rapidly. While Gallup had been the only poll in 1945, there were three in the 1950 general election, Gallup being joined by in-house polls from the *Daily Mail* and the *Daily Express*. The *Daily Mail* poll was a precursor of the founding of National Opinion Polls (now NOP), while the *Express* poll was to continue as a separate entity until 1966. Two of the main features of the *Daily Express* were the almost total lack of technical details supplied about how the polls were carried out, and the disarming public distrust the paper showed of its own work. Its poll in 1959 (which proved to be very accurate) was accompanied by a disclaimer: 'the *Daily Express* for its part acknowledges that it has no confidence in its own poll, although it is conducted with complete integrity and all possible efficiency'.

Table 1 *Actual and predicted results, 1945 general election (%)*

Pollster	Gallup	
Newspaper	News Chronicle	**Actual result**
Fieldwork	24–27 June	5 July
Conservative	41.0	39.3
Labour	47.0	48.8
Liberal	10.5	9.2
Other	1.5	2.7
Labour lead	6.0	9.5
Error on lead	−3.5	–
Average error on share (±)	1.5	–

As Table 2 shows, all three polls in 1950 were in close agreement, with a range of only 2% on the estimates of the Conservative vote, and of 2.5% on the Labour vote. In the event the polls proved on average to overscore the Conservatives by 1.5%, and to underscore Labour by 3%. While this would seem to suggest a successful performance, in fact two of the three called the wrong winner, because of the closeness of the race. Because the shares of the vote were close, the polls largely escaped criticism, and most commentators saw it as a distinct improvement on the performance of the American polls in 1948. It is also probably true to say that as polling was still very new in Britain, the polls attracted less attention than they had in America two years previously.

Table 2 *Actual and predicted results, 1950 general election (%)*

Pollster	Own	Own	Gallup	
Newspaper	Daily Mail	Daily Express	News Chronicle	**Actual result**
Fieldwork	5–11 Feb.	17–21 Feb.	17–20 Feb.	23 Feb.
Conservative	45.5	45.0	43.5	43.0
Labour	42.5	44.0	45.0	46.8
Liberal (+ others)	12.0	10.0	10.5	9.3
Others	n/a	1.0	1.0	0.9
Labour lead	−3.0	−1.0	+1.5	+3.8
Error on lead	−6.8	−4.8	−2.3	–
Average error on share (±)	2.9	1.4	0.9	–

As a footnote to Table 2 and the tables for subsequent elections, the figures for the actual election result are given to the nearest decimal place, since they are real figures. The poll results, on the other hand, are expressed only as whole percentages. This is because they are estimates, subject to sampling error of at least 3%, and while it is possible to express the poll results to any number of decimal places, it is implying a spurious level of accuracy to quote a figure of 34.3%, when it is really 34.3% plus or minus 3%. The exception to this presentation of poll figures is the Gallup results, which are always presented by Gallup rounded not to the nearest per cent, but to the nearest half a per cent. Without access to the raw data, it is impossible to recalculate these in a comparable form to the other polls. The same is true of some of the newspapers' own polls.

A new company joined the polling ranks in time for the 1951 general election. Research Services Ltd (RSL), like many of its later competitor research agencies, grew out of an in-house research department, in its case an advertising agency, the London Press Exchange. RSL was founded as a separate company in 1946, and began polling in 1951, although this was never more than a small part of its business, and RSL has only been an occasional pollster since then. Its early political work was under the guidance of Dr Mark Abrams, one of the key figures in British market and social research.

Table 3 *Actual and predicted results, 1951 general election (%)*

Pollster	RSL	Own	Gallup	
Newspaper	Daily Graphic	Daily Express	News Chronicle	**Actual result**
Fieldwork	n/a	19–23 Oct.	22 Oct.	25 Oct.
Conservative	50.0	50.0	49.5	48.0
Labour	43.0	46.0	47.0	48.8
Liberal	7.0	3.5	3.5	2.5
Others		0.5	0.5	0.7
Labour lead	−7.0	−4.0	−2.5	+0.8
Error on lead	−7.8	−4.8	−3.3	−
Average error on share (±)	3.9	1.5	1.1	−

As Table 3 shows, RSL's experience in 1951 was an unhappy one, as they predicted a clear Conservative victory, showing them 7% ahead. Although the Conservatives did form a government, they were able to do so only because of a skewed seats distribution, despite polling 1% fewer votes than Labour. Because of variations in constituency sizes which favoured the Conservatives, fewer votes were required to win a Conservative seat than a Labour one, and so the distribution of seats differed significantly from the distribution of votes.

While they did have the ultimate winner in front, by the standards against which polls can reasonably be judged the RSL poll was poor. In the Butler and Kavanagh book on the election, David Butler identified a number of probable causes of RSL's error.[4] As well as the repeat of the 1948 US error of stopping polling too soon (in this case some two weeks before election day), Butler also pointed to an implausibly high figure for the Liberals and the minor parties, because RSL failed to make sufficient allowance for the fact that although there may have been Liberal supporters across the whole country, the Liberals were not contesting all the seats, and their share of the ultimate vote was thus artificially limited.

The *Daily Mail*'s in-house poll in 1950 proved to be a one-off, but the *Daily Express* returned in 1951, as did Gallup. They both showed the Conservatives ahead, but by much less than RSL, and both again stopped polling two or three days before the election. However, their error on the Conservative share was only 2%, and on the Labour share 3% and 2% respectively; well within the expected margins of error.

Table 4 *Actual and predicted results, 1955 general election (%)*

Pollster	Own	Gallup	
Newspaper	Daily Express	News Chronicle	**Actual result**
Fieldwork	n/a	21/24 May	26 May
Conservative	50.0	51.0	49.7
Labour	47.0	47.5	46.4
Liberal	2.0	1.5	2.7
Others	*	0.0	1.2
Conservative lead	3.0	3.5	3.3
Error on lead	−0.3	0.2	–
Average error on share (±)	0.6	1.2	–

Note: *=less than 0.5%.

No new companies had emerged before the 1955 general election, and RSL did not poll in that year, leaving the field for just the *Daily Express* and Gallup. It is obviously easier to get a low average error the fewer observations there are, but even so the results, shown in Table 4, were a great vindication of the polls' techniques. The *Express* figure for the Conservatives was exactly right, and that for Labour within 1%; while Gallup were within 1% on each party. It should be noted that small though the errors were, they were in the same direction (a pro-Conservative bias) in both polls, just as they had been in the same direction in all three polls in 1951. This is a pattern that can be seen in many subsequent British elections, as shown below. The implications of this, and in particular the differences between error and bias, are discussed in Chapter 2.

The next polling company to join the fray was NOP. Like RSL it grew out of an in-house research department, in this case that of the *Daily Mail*. It was set up as a wholly owned subsidiary company of Associated Newspapers, owners of the *Daily Mail*, under the energetic leadership of Mick Shields, who was to remain an active chairman until his death in 1988, even while he was group managing director of the whole Associated Newspapers empire. Like Gallup, and unlike RSL, NOP has been constantly involved in opinion polling since its foundation.

Much of NOP's early published work was in by-elections rather than general elections, and in particular it had a coup at the Orpington by-election in 1962. This was the first great modern Liberal by-election triumph, in a seat they were certainly not expected to win, and was important for two reasons within the history of polling. NOP were widely criticised when their poll showed the Liberal candidate slightly ahead, and yet he went on to win the seat with a huge majority. As NOP's own later experience with exit polls showed (see Chapter 7), one of the best ways to build up a reputation is to produce a result which is universally disbelieved but then proved to be right, and NOP certainly benefited from this phenomenon in Orpington.

More importantly within the history of polling in general, Orpington is one of the first examples where it can reasonably be suggested that a poll influenced the result of an election. Post-election work by NOP supported the hypothesis that many Labour supporters were persuaded to vote Liberal in order to keep the Conservatives out. Key in this persuasion was the emphasis that the Liberals placed on the poll. They argued that it proved that a vote for the Liberals would not on this occasion be a wasted vote, and that they had a real chance of winning. Much the same phenomenon was seen two decades later in the Bermondsey by-election, where polls gave a clear pointer as to which of the non-Labour candidates had the best chance of winning.

NOP published its first general election poll in 1959, which proved extremely accurate, as indeed were all the polls in that election. Four are shown in Table 4: NOP, the *Daily Express*, and two effectively from Gallup, although one was published under the name of Forecasting Statistics, a sister company. All four polls were within 1% of the actual vote for the Conservatives, and within 2% for Labour. Because they were so accurate for the Conservatives there was little chance of a consistent underestimate or overestimate, but three of the four overestimated Labour's share, thus reversing the trend of the previous three elections.

There were again four polls in the 1964 general election, the return of RSL making up for the disappearance of Forecasting Statistics. While less good than the exceptional performance of 1959, the results, as shown in Table 5, were again better than sampling error would lead one to expect. All were within 2% on both the two main parties. Also, all overestimated the Conservatives' share of the vote, confounding the pattern of 1959 and returning to that of 1950–55.

The same four polls appeared in 1966, again with considerable success. The average error shown in Table 6 is inflated by the poor performance of NOP, which at the end of the campaign re-interviewed a sample of people interviewed earlier during the same campaign, but ended up heavily biased towards Labour. The other three polls were yet again within 2% on both parties. Once again the direction of error was consistent, with all four overestimating the Labour share.

Table 5 *Actual and predicted results, 1959 general election (%)*

Pollster	NOP	Forecasting statistics	Own	Gallup	
Newspaper	Daily Mail	Daily Telegraph	Daily Express	News Chronicle	**Actual result**
Fieldwork	2–5 Oct	1–4 Oct.	n/a	3–6 Oct.	8 Oct.
Conservative	48.0	49.0	49.0	48.5	48.8
Labour	44.0	46.0	45.0	46.5	44.6
Liberal ⎫	8.0	5.0	5.0	4.5	6.1
Others ⎭		1.0	0.5	0.5	0.6
Conservative lead	4.0	3.0	4.0	2.0	4.2
Error on lead	−0.2	−1.2	−0.2	−2.2	–
Average error on share (±)	0.8	0.6	0.6	1.0	

Table 6 *Actual and predicted results, 1964 general election (%)*

Pollster	RSL	NOP	Gallup	Own	
Newspaper	Observer	Daily Mail	Daily Telegraph	Daily Express	**Actual result**
Fieldwork	n/a	9–13 Oct.	8–13 Oct.	n/a	15 Oct.
Sample size	n/a	1,179	3,829	n/a	–
Conservative	45.0	44.0	44.5	44.0	42.9
Labour	46.0	47.0	46.5	43.0	44.8
Liberal ⎫	9.0	8.0	8.5	11.0	11.4
Others ⎭		*	0.5	1.0	0.9
Labour lead	+1	+3.1	+2	−0.8	+1.9
Error on lead	−0.9	1.2	0.1	1.1	–
Average error on share (±)	1.65	2.0	1.6	0.8	–

Note: *=less than 0.5%.

By now opinion polls were a major part of the electoral process, and were accorded widespread credibility. Indeed, the fact that the polls showed Labour clearly ahead throughout the 1966 campaign was felt by some to have pre-empted the result and to have removed the element of uncertainty and surprise from the election (see Table 7). There were calls for polls to be banned for this reason, but Prime Minister Harold Wilson rejected such calls, as his successor Ted Heath was also later to do.

Table 7 *Actual and predicted results, 1966 general election (%)*

Pollster	RSL	NOP	Own	Gallup	
Newspaper	Observer	Daily Mail	Daily Telegraph	Daily Express	**Actual result**
Fieldwork	n/a	27–29 Mar.	n/a	24–28 Mar.	31 Mar.
Sample size	n/a	1,693	n/a	3,596	–
Conservative	42.0	37.0	42.0	40.0	41.4
Labour	50.0	54.0	51.0	51.0	48.7
Liberal ⎤	9.0	8.0	8.0	8.0	8.8
Others ⎦		1.0		1.0	1.1
Labour lead	+8.0	+17.0	+9.0	+11.0	+7.3
Error on lead	+0.7	+9.7	+1.7	+3.7	–
Average error on share (±)	0.8	2.7	1.4	1.2	–

The later 1960s saw four more companies starting to publish polls, three of which are still polling today. The first was the Opinion Research Centre (ORC), set up in 1965 by T. F. Thompson, previously political editor of the *Daily Mail* and former NOP director Humphrey Taylor, with encouragement from Conservative Central Office, for whom Taylor had been working while with NOP at the 1964 election. ORC polled for the Tories from 1966 to 1979, and published polls in media outlets in 1970 and both elections of 1974. They also had a major hand in the founding of the third of the new pollsters of the late 1960s – Harris. Louis Harris Research Ltd was established in 1969 as a joint venture between ORC, the American pollster Louis Harris Associates, and Beaverbrook Newspapers, publishers of the *Daily Express* and *Sunday Express*. It too made its public debut at the 1970 general election, and renamed as the Harris Research Centre, is still actively involved in political polling, both for media clients and until recently for the Conservative Party.

Sandwiched between the somewhat incestuous creation of ORC and Harris was Marplan, which carried out its first public opinion poll in 1968, although it had been in existence since 1959. Like RSL and NOP, Marplan emerged from the research department of a larger company, in this case advertising agency

McCann Erickson. It became independent of McCann in 1959, but remained a subsidiary of the McCann parent company, Interpublic. The first Marplan polls appeared in *The Times* in 1968, and, like the other two new firms, Marplan published its first general-election poll in 1970. After a complex series of changes of ownership in the 1970s, Marplan finally effectively ceased trading after three of its directors left in 1989 to set up ICM, which is still a major player in the field.

Last of the 1960s pollsters, and the third to be still polling, was Market and Opinion Research International (MORI). Under the leadership of expatriate American Robert Worcester, this was originally a joint venture between NOP and the Opinion Research Corporation of Princeton, New Jersey, but is now an independent company.

Three of these four new companies, the exception being MORI, published polls in the 1970 general election, along with NOP and Gallup. The election of 1970 proved to be one that played the same role in the demonology of British polling as 1948 does in the USA.

Between the 1966 and 1970 elections, public opinion proved to be unusually volatile. In May 1966, two months after its election victory, Labour enjoyed a 20% lead in the polls, but within two years had fallen to 20% behind. When the election was finally called in May 1970 Labour was once more in the lead, although not by much. During the campaign itself the polls seemed to be at odds with each other, with one showing a rise for Labour over the same period that another showed a fall. When it came to the end of the campaign, however, their final predictions were within sampling error of each other, with the Conservatives shown at 44% ± 3% in all five, and Labour shown at 47.5% ± 3% in all five.

As Table 8 shows, being within sampling error of each other in a close election was not enough for the polls to be able to tell the same story. Marplan showed Labour with a lead of almost 9%, with Gallup showing only a slightly smaller Labour lead. NOP and Harris both had much smaller leads but the outlier – the one most distant from the cluster of others – was ORC, published in the *London Evening Standard* on polling day itself. The only poll to predict a Labour defeat, even ORC underestimated the scale of the Tory win.

Although a detailed discussion of methodology, in theory and in practice, is the subject of the next three chapters, the failures of the polls in 1970 were so tied up in a particular aspect of methodology that it needs to be discussed here. The observant reader of Table 8 will notice that although the election was held on 18 June, the final Marplan poll began seven days earlier and finished four days before the election. Similarly, Gallup's fieldwork began four days before the election and NOP's six days before. In each case fieldwork stopped two days before polling day. The exception was the ORC poll, whose fieldwork ran up until the day before the election. More important than the simple dates was the fact that the ORC poll was conducted in two parts – a main wave of interviews conducted from 13 to 15 June, and a subsequent recall on a small sub-sample of these respondents on the two days before the election.

Table 8 *Actual and predicted results, 1970 general election (%)*

Pollster	ORC	Harris	NOP	Gallup	Marplan	
Newspaper	London E. Standard	Daily Express	Daily Mail	Daily Telegraph	The Times	**Actual result**
Fieldwork	13–17 June	n/a	12–16 June	14–16 June	11–14 June	18 June
Sample size	1,583	2,661	1,562	2,190	2,267	–
Conservative	46.5	46.0	44.0	42.0	42.0	46.2
Labour	45.5	48.0	48.0	49.0	50.0	43.8
Liberal	6.5	5.0	6.0	7.5	7.0	7.6
Others	1.5	1.0	1.0	1.5	1.0	2.4
Conservative lead	1.0	−2.0	−4.0	−7.0	−8.0	−2.4
Error on lead	−1.4	−4.4	−6.4	−9.4	−10.4	–
Average error on share (±)	1.0	2.1	2.2	2.6	3.2	–

The original poll showed results similar to those of the other pollsters, with a Labour lead of 4.5%, but the later re-interviews suggested a swing to the Tories. The even more observant reader of Table 8 will notice that even the follow-up interviews did not give a Tory lead – they showed the two parties neck and neck. However, ORC bravely made a further allowance for differential turnout, and for an extension of the trend they had observed in the last two days, to produce their final figure of a small Tory lead, and gathered the plaudits as a result.

The clear conclusion reached by most observers on the basis of these data was that there was a late swing to the Tories which the polls failed to detect by stopping interviewing too early. Although the evidence for the late-swing hypothesis is very limited, based as it is on a recall sample of only 257, and there were undoubtedly some problems with the setting of the quotas (see Chapter 2 for an explanation of quotas), the main lesson the pollsters drew from their experience in 1970 was the need to continue polling as late as possible, and, equally importantly, the need to condense fieldwork into as short a time as possible. There is little to be gained by polling up until election eve, if fieldwork for the final poll started a week earlier. A last-minute swing might be picked up by the later interviews, but its effect would be diminished by the volume of interviews conducted before that change began.

This pressure on timing itself led to some modifications in technique, as some techniques could not feasibly be used in the context of a short, late field-period. As a result of this the elections after 1970 can be said to belong to another era, and they are thus discussed in a later chapter. The same year also raised some important questions of survey practice, and the next three chapters deal with the theory and practice of survey methodology.

Notes

1 T. W. Smith, 'The first straw? A study of the origins of election, p. 9 polls', *Public Opinion Quarterly*, 54:1 (1990).
2 F. Teer and J. Spence, *Political Opinion Polls* (Hutchinson, 1973).
3 L. C. Lockley, 'Notes on the history of marketing research', *Journal of Marketing*, 14 (1950).
4 D. Butler, *The British General Election of 1951* (Macmillan, 1951).

Polling methodology:
the theory

Do I understand your question, man, is it hopeless and forlorn?

At bottom, opinion polls are surveys just like any other, and with some particular exceptions discussed later, there is little methodological difference between a survey designed to measure support for political parties and one designed to elicit attitudes to different brands of cat food. They are broadly the same in execution, and the theory underpinning each of them is also broadly the same. This chapter looks at the theory which underlies the opinion poll and the cat-food survey, and indeed almost all surveys based on samples of the population. Those ways in which opinion polls differ from other surveys in practical application of this theory are discussed in Chapter 3.

While there are many different aspects to sample survey design, and thus many opportunities to get it wrong, there are two elements which above all others are crucial to the success of a sample survey. These are the design of the sample and the wording of the questions. Coding of verbatim replies, data entry, interviewer error and reaction to it, weighting of the data, and analysis, are all possible sources of error, but none have the same potential to make a survey disastrously wrong. Also, many of these errors can be corrected once discovered, but it is virtually impossible to take later corrective action if there is a fundamental flaw in the sample or the wrong questions have been asked.

In the context of opinion polls, the discussion of question wording is more a matter of practical application than pure theory, and so the topic is covered mainly in Chapter 3, with a brief description of the basic principles in this chapter, which concentrates mainly on sampling.

The principle of samples

One of the things which those who are opposed to opinion polls, and those who simply cannot understand them, are wont to say is that it is impossible for a mere 1,000 people to represent the views of an electorate of 40 million. (US sceptics think it is even more impossible, as their electorate is so much larger.) At first sight the aim of an opinion poll does seem an impossible task, as it is based on the views of only one in 40,000 people. How can pollsters be sure that they have picked one person who can represent all the other 39,999? In fact the sampling fraction (i.e. one in 40,000) is pretty much a red herring, for the accuracy of a survey is dependent on the absolute number of people interviewed, not the proportion they represent of the population being sampled. This is something which even those broadly sympathetic to, and understanding of, opinion polls have difficulty with. It seems illogical that a sample of 1,000 is just as reliable whether one is trying to measure the entire population of Great Britain or the views of people in a town of only 30,000 people, and yet sampling theory shows us that this is true.

Sampling theory is a branch of mathematics of considerable antiquity, although this chapter will try to avoid mathematical formulae as much as possible. It is common to describe sampling in terms of analogies, and two in particular are particularly well worn. Like all good, simple explanations they are frequently used, but stand just on the right side of cliché.

The soup analogy is the less scientific, but best explains the 'sample size is more important than sampling fraction' conundrum. If someone places a bowl of soup in front of me, and asks me what kind of soup it is, I do not need to eat the whole bowl before I can answer the question. Unless it is an unfamiliar soup, the first mouthful will identify the flavour. I have thus drawn a sample of the total volume of soup, and used that to determine the flavour of the whole bowl. I need to have quite a good mouthful to have a reasonable chance of picking up the nuances of flavour: if I only had a tiny sip I might fail to spot that the mainly oxtail soup also had a few mushrooms in it. However, assuming I have a standard-size soup spoon available draw my sample of soup with which to (and provided the soup has been reasonably well stirred), then I will be equipped to judge the flavour regardless of the total volume of soup. Put a bowl in front of me, and my spoonful will tell me the flavour. If you put the whole industrial-sized saucepan, whence the soup had been served, in front of me, I would not need to taste 100 spoonfuls just because the saucepan contained 100 bowlfuls. It is the size of the sample of soup that matters, not the proportion it represents of the whole saucepan. What is true of sampling soup is also true of sampling human populations.

The soup analogy is descriptive rather than mathematical, but there is another common analogy which introduces the mathematical concepts involved. It comes in two standard variants, the socks variant and the ping-pong balls variant, but they are broadly the same. Their main purpose is to introduce the basic principles of sampling theory in a lay fashion. Let us suppose you have a drawer full of jumbled-up socks, or a large bag full of ping-pong balls, which you know to be a mixture of black ones and white ones, but you don't know the exact proportions of black and white. Do you need to examine every single sock/ping-pong ball to determine these proportions? If you want to be sure exactly how many of each there are, then you must indeed examine every single ping-pong ball. However, if you just want to know whether the proportions are roughly 50:50, or 75:25 in favour of white, or 67:33 in favour of black, you can find this out reasonably reliably without having to examine every one.

If there are 1,000 ping-pong balls in this (rather large) bag, split equally between white and black, and you draw out 100 at random, then you probably won't get 50 white and 50 black, but you will probably get something close to it. And if you put those 100 back, and draw another 100 at random, then those too will be approximately half white and half black, and so on with another sample. It is this principle of repeated samplings from the same population that allows number theory to explain how sampling works in practice.

When you draw the first ball out of the bag, there is a one in two chance of it being black, and the same of it being white. If that first one is black, the chances are fractionally higher that the next one will be white (because there are now 500 white but only 499 black available for selection), but to all intents and purposes the chances are again one in two. If 100 balls are drawn, they could be all black ones, all white ones, or any combination in between, from 99 black and 1 white, to 99 white and 1 black. Out of all these possible combinations, some are much more likely than others. Combined probabilities are multiplicative, as any gambler knows. If the chance of drawing a white ball first is one in two, then the chance of drawing two white balls first is one in two squared, i.e. one in four. The chance of the third ball also being white is one in two to the power of three, i.e. one in eight, and so on. The chances of drawing 100 white balls out of our bag is one in two to the power of 99, or one in six hundred million trillion trillion. (This is of course using the now standard American definition of billion and trillion; in the old English system the odds would be a mere one in six hundred million trillion.) The chance of drawing 99 white and 1 black is fractionally higher, but the chance of drawing 50 of each is far higher, at approximately 1 in 1.25.

We can use these probabilities to see what would happen if we drew a whole series of samples of 100 balls, one after the other. To keep the numbers easy, we will draw 100 samples, each of 100 balls. We can plot the number of white balls in each sample on a frequency distribution, where the horizontal axis represents the number of white balls, and the vertical axis the number of times that particular combination of white and black balls came up in the 100 separate samples. The resulting frequency distribution will inevitably look like the one in Figure 1. Very few samples will have tiny numbers of white balls, or of black ones, but there will be quite a few around the two to one mark, and even more around the 50:50 mark. The pattern of this frequency distribution is what provides a theoretical basis to sampling theory. The mid-point of the curve, labelled 0, is the true population mean (in this case 50% black), and the curve shows

Figure 1 *Normal distribution curve*

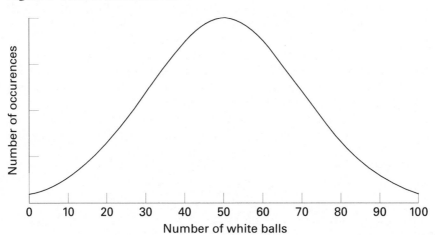

how close each of the samples drawn was to getting the right answer. Most are fairly close to the true answer, and as the error gets bigger in either direction, the number of samples with that particular finding decreases.

The shape of the curve is referred to as a bell curve, and the distribution it marks is called a normal distribution. Any series of samples drawn randomly from a population will exhibit a normal distribution, provided the samples are big enough and there are enough of them. This exercise proves that a sample can represent the make-up of a whole population, and it has the advantage that it is easy, if somewhat tedious, for anyone who does not believe the theory to try it out in practice. It is also possible to use this experiment to prove that it is the absolute size of the sample which determines reliability, not the proportion it represents of the total population. The exercise discussed above involved samples of 100 drawn from 1,000 balls in the drawer. If we increase the total number of balls to 10,000, and again draw 100 samples, each again of 100 balls, we will get exactly the same distribution as in Figure 1. If there were 100,000, or 1,000,000 balls in the (now improbably large) bag, we would still get the same pattern.

Sampling error

This simple exercise thus proves that even quite a small sample can be representative, and that sample size is more important than the sampling fraction, but it can also be used to explain the principle of sampling error, and the role of sample size in determining sampling error. The shape of the distribution shown in Figure 1 will always be broadly the same, but it will vary with the size of the samples drawn. The higher the size of each sample, the narrower and higher will be the bell curve, meaning that more samples are very close to the true figure, and fewer are wrong by a large amount. There is a mathematical way of expressing this change, and this involves the standard error and the standard deviation.

Standard deviation is a measure of the dispersion of values around the mean in a population or sample. When it comes to presenting results, it is the measures of central tendency which are of most immediate interest, but measures of dispersion are also important. Although there are several ways of measuring central tendency, the arithmetic mean is the most commonly used. This is the measure which is usually referred to as the average: it is the sum of all the values divided by the number of observations.

Let us suppose we interview ten people, ask them the number of pints of beer they drink a week, and get the answers shown in Table 9.

Table 9 *Measurement of central tendency by arithmetic mean*

	Beer drunk per week (pints)
Person 1	4
Person 2	2
Person 3	2
Person 4	3
Person 5	5
Person 6	1
Person 7	2
Person 8	6
Person 9	2
Person 10	3

The total number of pints drunk a week by the sample is 30, and so the mean or average number of pints drunk per week is three. This tells us something about the population, and is likely to be the top-line figure presented in any report on that data: 'Average beer drinker drinks three pints a week, says new survey'. However, it only tells us a little about the population. Consider a survey with 100 interviews, 50 with men aged under 25, and 50 with men aged 25 and over. Figure 2 shows the distribution of the answers in the two sub-samples. The horizontal axis shows the number of pints of beer drunk per week, and the vertical axis shows the number of respondents giving that answer.

The mean answer for both groups is five pints a week, but there is a considerable difference in the two distributions. For men aged under twenty-five the answers cluster very closely around the mean, while for those aged twenty-five and over they were much more widely dispersed. The simplest measure of this dispersal is the range. Among the under-twenty-fives the range of answers given was only from three to seven pints a week, while for older respondents answers ranged from one to ten. This figure alone gives an idea of the different

Figure 2 *Measurement of distribution*

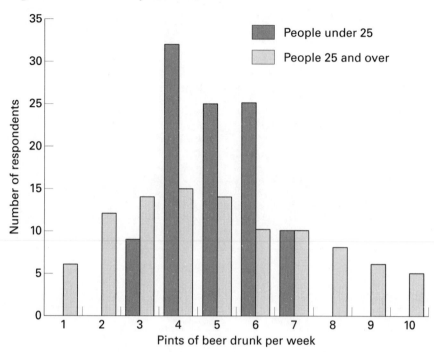

distributions in the two samples, but range is not generally very useful. It is firstly very susceptible to untypical values at the extremes, and more importantly gives no idea of the way the population is spread across the range.

If we modify the answers from the under-twenty-fives by adding in two more respondents, one of whom drinks only one pint a week, and one of whom drinks nine, the range is now exactly the same as for the older group, but, as Figure 3 shows, the answers from the under-twenty-fives were still overall more clustered.

We therefore need a calculation which will better reflect the overall pattern, and the two most important measures used for this are the variance and the standard deviation, the latter simply being the square root of the variance. The formula for calculating variance is

$$V = \frac{\Sigma(x - \bar{x})^2}{n}$$

In this formula x is the answer from each respondent, and $\bar{x}$ is the population mean. What we are doing is calculating how different each person is from the mean, then taking the sum (Σ) of all those differences. By then dividing that figure by the sample size, we get an *average* of differences from the overall average.

Figure 3 *Revised measurement of distribution*

Table 10 *Calculation of average of differences*

	Pints (x)	$x - \bar{x}$	$(x - \bar{x})^2$
Person 1	4	1	1
Person 2	2	−1	1
Person 3	2	−1	1
Person 4	3	0	0
Person 5	5	2	4
Person 6	1	−2	4
Person 7	2	−1	1
Person 8	6	3	9
Person 9	2	−1	1
Person 10	3	0	0
Σ	30	0	22
Average ($\bar{x}$)	3		

To illustrate this in practice, Table 10 takes the data from Table 9 and shows the necessary calculations.

Thus the variance in the sample on that measure is 22 divided by 10, or 2.2, and the standard deviation is the square root of that, which is 1.48.

A high standard deviation (or variance) shows that the population is widely dispersed around the mean, while a low one indicates that the population is quite tightly clustered around it. There are many further ramifications beyond this, involving the calculation of further measures such as the coefficient of variation, all of which will be covered in any book on survey statistics, but what concerns us here is the role of standard deviation in measuring sampling error. To calculate this we need to go one step further than standard deviation, and calculate the standard error. This is simply the standard deviation divided by the square root of the sample size.

To return to the distribution shown in Figure 1, the shape of the curve tells us that provided we have drawn a large number of samples, we can be sure that in 95% of them the answer found will lie within ± 1.96 standard errors of the true figure, and that in 99% of them the observed figure will be within ± 2.58 standard errors of the true one. Of itself this is no more than mildly interesting, although it is something else which can easily be put to empirical test with the bag of ping-pong balls. What makes it more important is the fact that generally we do not draw 100 separate samples and then compare the results of all of them: in most surveys we can only afford one sample. However, we can use the normal distribution, and the figures on dispersal and standard error, by turning them on their head. If 95 out of 100 samples will have an answer within ± 1.96 standard errors of the true figure, then if we draw just one sample there is a 95% chance that the figure found in it will be within 1.96 standard errors of the truth, and there is a 99% chance that the survey figure will be within 2.58 standard errors of the truth.

Once we have calculated the standard error on a survey, we can thus calculate the range within which we can be 95% certain the real answer lies. This range is known as the 95% confidence interval. We can calculate a 99% confidence as well, simply by using 2.58 standard errors rather than 1.96, but it is the 95% confidence limit which is most widely used. When a poll story in a newspaper says the sampling error on the poll is ± 3%, it is almost certainly the 95% confidence limit it is referring to, rather than a 99% limit or any other possibility.

It should be noted that despite all the mathematics involved in the calculation, one can never be certain that the true answer lies within a given range. If the 95% confidence limit on a survey estimate is ± 3%, there is still a 5% chance that the real answer will be more than 1.96 standard errors different from the truth. By widening the range we can increase the chance that the survey is within the range, but we can never be absolutely sure. Using a 99% confidence limit, there is only a one in 100 chance that the survey finding is wrong by more than 2.58 standard errors, but the chance still remains.

The formulae given above for calculating variance, standard deviation and standard error are based on data where for each member of the population we have a numerical finding, e.g. the number of pints of beer drunk each week. In many surveys, especially opinion polls, the data collected are not numerical findings like this, from which means can be calculated, but classification of respondents into categories – car-owner or not, type of housing tenure, political party supported, etc. – which are not expressed as means but as percentages falling into each category. If we have data from a question on whether people will vote Labour in a forthcoming by-election, we cannot calculate a mean, and thus cannot measure differences from the mean, and so the formula given above simply will not apply. Instead, for such data a different formula gives the standard error. If we have a sample of size n, and $p\%$ of that sample say they will vote Labour, then the formula for the standard error is

$$\sqrt{\frac{(p*(100-p))}{n}}$$

The expression $(100 - p)$ is often referred to as 'q', and so many people refer to the formula as

$$\sqrt{\frac{pq}{n}}$$

Two important points arise from this formula. The first is that, as one would expect, the error varies depending on the size of the sample. However, because the formula involves not

$$\frac{pq}{n}$$

but

$$\sqrt{\frac{pq}{n}}$$

then the standard error is a function not of the sample size, but of the square root of the sample size. This means that if the sample size on a survey is doubled, the standard error will decrease by only root 2, or 1.414. In order to halve the standard error we need to quadruple the sample size, which will cause the cost of the survey to increase dramatically.

The other point about the formula is that the survey finding itself (p) has an impact on the standard error. Because the nominator is found by multiplying the survey percentage by 100 minus that percentage, the value of pq, and thus the standard error, will be much higher for survey findings around 50% than for findings around 10%. Where $p = 50\%$, $q = 50\%$ also, and $pq = 2500$. Where $p = 90\%$, $q = 10\%$, and $pq = 900$. Allowing for the impact of the square-root function, then for any given sample the standard error on a finding of 10% (or 90%) will be only three-fifths of the error on a finding of 50%.

It is easy to see why this should be the case in the real world rather than just in formulae. To take the extreme, if only 1% of the population have a certain characteristic it is hard for a survey to get that percentage wrong by much. Even if no such people are found in the survey at all, the survey has only underestimated the true position by 1%. Conversely, even if the survey found four times as many such people as it should have, it is only wrong by 3%. This is another piece of number theory which can be put to the test with our large bag of ping-pong balls. If there are 500 black and 500 white ones, it will be found that the variability across 20 samples each of 100 drawn from the bag will be much greater than if there are 50 black ones and 950 white ones.

Before moving on from sampling error, two important misconceptions need to be corrected. The first stems from the way survey findings are often presented. A survey figure of 40% is often accompanied by a bald statement that it is subject to a sampling error of ± 3%. To many readers this implies that the real answer *definitely* lies somewhere between 37% and 43% – the concept of a 95% confidence limit is hard to grasp, and many people wonder what is the point of giving a range if there is still a chance of the answer being outside that range. More importantly, people also tend to assume that not only is the real answer in the range 37%–43%, but it is equally likely to be at any point on that range: the real answer is just as likely to be 37% as it is to be 40%. In fact reference to the bell curve shown in Figure 1 shows that if a survey finding is 40%, the chances are very strong that the real answer is 40%; that the chance of the real answer being 39% or 41% is lower; and that the chance of it being 37% or 40% is much lower. While a survey may well be in error, it is much more likely to be right than it is to be significantly wrong.

The second common misconception is the assumption that sampling error is all that can go wrong with surveys, and that all differences between the observed and actual figures are due to sampling error. In fact sampling error is just one of four basic components of survey error, but it is the easiest to measure (because it is based simply on number theory) and thus is the one most often quoted.

Sample bias

Survey error can be classified in two ways. One split is between sampling error and response error. The former is caused by the fact that we are interviewing a sample rather than the whole population, while the latter occurs during the interview itself. It may result from errors by the interviewer, or failures of memory by the respondent. The second split is between simple error and correlated error. Simple error is random in its operation – it is just as likely to give results out in one direction as another, and the scale of the error will vary from survey to survey. Correlated error operates in the same direction, and often to the same extent, in any survey.

The conjunction of these two factors gives us the four types of error:

	Simple	**Correlated**
Sample	Simple sample Variance	Correlated sample Variance
Response	Simple response Variance	Correlated response Variance

Simple sample variance is what has been described as sampling error in the section above. Simple response variance is a chance tendency for interviewers to make random mistakes, or respondents to give the wrong answer by accident. Correlated sample variance is the result of a fault in the sampling process, which causes some types of people to be systematically oversampled at the expense of others. Correlated response variance can be caused by an interviewer making the same mistake on all her interviews, and thus causing one whole cluster of respondents to have wrong data recorded, or it can be caused by some types of respondents giving the wrong answer, whether unwittingly or deliberately.

The two simple variances are examples of error, and they are just as likely to be wrong in one direction as another, and therefore likely to be mainly self-cancelling. The correlated variances will always cause an error in one direction throughout a survey, and they are thus example of bias rather than error. Bias is more pernicious than error, because it cannot be self-cancelling, although two different biases in the same survey can cancel each other out.

As Chapter 5 shows, in most of the general elections since 1970, the opinion polls have tended all to overestimate one party in any one election. This overestimate or underestimate has usually been within the scale of sampling error stated, and people have thus assumed that the difference between polls and reality is caused by survey error. In fact if the polls all overestimate one party, they are exhibiting bias. If they were merely subject to error, then some would overestimate that party and some would underestimate it.

Response bias in opinion polls is mainly a function of question wording, and is thus discussed later. Sampling bias can be introduced in a number of ways. As most of these are dependent on the detail of sampling practice, they are discussed mainly in Chapter 3, but to illustrate the principles of bias we can return again to our bag of ping-pong balls. All the formulae and tables above are based on the assumption that balls are being drawn in a way which gives each ball an equal chance of being picked up. In this case, any variation in the samples from a 50:50 spilt between white and black is simply a result of sampling error. Let us suppose, however, that the balls are being selected not by hand but by a machine which swirls them around and then ejects them one at a time through a hole just big enough for one ball to pass through. Let us further suppose that due to a fault in manufacture, the black balls are fractionally smaller than the white ones. This will make it easier for a black ball to pass through the opening than for a white one, and no matter how many times a sample is drawn, it will always tend to contain more black balls than white ones, and this will be the result of sampling bias rather than sampling error. Those whose numbers have still not come up on the National Lottery may feel some resonance with this example.

To recap what we have learned so far about sampling, number theory, as tested by our bag of ping-pong balls, tells us the following:

- a small sample can accurately reflect a large population
- the size of the sample matters much more than the fraction it represents of the total population
- we can be 95% sure that the true figure will be within the range of ± 1.96 standard errors from the survey finding
- the standard error is in proportion to the square root of the sample size
- the standard error is higher for percentages around 50% than for percentages around 10% or 90%
- the true figure is more likely to be close to the sample finding than it is to be at the extremes of sampling error
- sampling error will cause sample findings to fluctuate either side of the true figure, while bias will cause all samples to be wrong in the same direction.

Drawing samples

Ignoring for the moment the ball-selecting machine, and returning to the idea of selecting balls from the bag by hand, all the formulae for variance, sampling error and so on are dependent on us drawing the ping-pong balls from the bag in a completely unsystematic manner – like the august gentlemen who used to make the FA Cup draw, we put our hand into the bag and take balls out without being able to see them. This is known as simple random sampling, a crucial element of which is that every member of the population to be sampled has an equal chance of being selected. When we put a hand into the bag, no one ball has a greater chance of being selected than another, provided we give the bag a good shake. This is all very well when we are drawing balls from a bag, but in the case of human populations simple random sampling is rarely practical.

If we are trying to sample people working in a factory, or members of an organisation, it would be feasible to obtain a list of all of them, put them on separate pieces of paper, screw up the pieces of paper, put them in a bag, and draw the required number out at random like a raffle. In fact we can still achieve the same simple random sample slightly more easily. Let us suppose we need to sample 100 people from a company workforce of 4,000. We could number every person on the list from 1 to 4,000, and then use random-number tables, or a random-number generator on a computer, to draw 100 random numbers between 1 and 4,000.

However, if we are trying to sample a large population, the task of numbering every single person on the list (the question of where the list comes from is addressed in Chapter 3) would be tedious. In cases such as this, we can use instead of simple random sampling an alternative technique known as systematic random sampling. Provided we know the total size of the population being sampled, we can just divide the total by the size of the sample we wish to draw. Thus if we wish to sample 100 people from a population of 4,000, we need to sample every fortieth person on the list, reading down the list in order. To start off, we choose a random number between 1 and 40, which identifies the first person to be selected, and then keep adding 40 to that number until 100 people have been chosen. This technique is also, and more properly, known as systematic probability sampling, rather than random sampling. The word 'random' has connotations of haphazardness which is fine for drawing balls out of a bag, but does not fit the more scientific approach. Because we are sampling every fortieth person on the list, we know that everyone has the same probability of being selected.

As well as being easier to administer than a simple random sample, a systematic sample has the advantage of guaranteeing an even spread across the whole population. There is a chance that a simple random sample would draw all its members from the first half of the list, and in fact there is a (very small) chance that it would just draw the first 100 people on the list. If the list is organised in a particular way, such as in increasing order of age, or men first and then women, a sample which did not cover the whole list evenly could be seriously biased.

Systematic probability sampling is thus superior to simple random sampling, but in many cases it too can be improved further by the use of stratified sampling. If the list of the population also includes extra information about each person which is likely to correlate with the variables being measured in the survey, this information can be used in the sample. Suppose the list of 4,000 staff also gives their age and sex, and the survey is mainly about maternity provision and pensions. It would thus be important to include men and women in the sample in the same proportion that they are in the whole workforce, and similarly, to reflect the age balance. A systematic probability sample may well do this, but it cannot be guaranteed. If men and women are listed alternately on the list, then an even-numbered sampling interval would lead to the sample being either all women or all men. If the list of staff is reordered so that all the women come first, and then all the men, and within each sex the staff are listed in increasing order of age, then a systematic sample drawn down that list will guarantee to get the correct proportions of men and women, young and old.

While this stratified systematic probability sample is ideal for a survey of a workforce, or of members of an organisation, it is impractical as it stands for a survey of the whole UK population. If interviewing is being conducted face to face, then the cost of a sample scattered across the whole country would be prohibitive. Each interviewer would have to travel great distances to get from one interview to the next. Even if the survey were being conducted by telephone, when geographical scatter would not be important, the cost of stratifying a list of all telephone numbers in the country and then selecting every 2,000th number from it would also be prohibitive.

The solution is to use multi-stage, clustered samples. Instead of drawing 1,000 names from a single list of 40 million people, we can split the list up into a number of large units, known as primary sampling units or psus, and start off by drawing a sample of them. In the case of a national sample, parliamentary constituencies would be the natural choice for psus. Before being selected, they are stratified in just the same way as the stratification of the list of individuals discussed above. Region of the country is an obvious stratification variable, and constituencies could also be stratified into urban versus rural, or upmarket versus downmarket. If 50 constituencies are chosen for a sample of 1,000, it will much cheaper to have 50 interviewers, each of whose set of 20 respondents will be contained within a single constituency, than having the 1,000 spread across the whole country.

In interviewing terms, the sample can be made even more efficient by adding further stages of sampling. Even contained within a constituency, the distance between respondents could still be quite high. It would be cheaper still if all respondents were in a smaller area within the constituency. This can be achieved by taking a second-stage sampling unit, typically an electoral ward. All the wards within the constituency are listed, possibly again stratified in some way, and one (or perhaps two) is then chosen. The process can be taken one stage further, by selecting a single polling district within the selected ward, and sampling individuals only from that polling district. The final stage in the whole process of reducing the interviewer's travel time is not to sample across the whole polling district. If a polling district has 3,000 electors, and 20 are to be selected, then the systematic probability method described above would involve sampling every 150th elector from a random start point. Even after several stages of sampling unit selection, the distance between each 150th person can still be high. The final way the interviewer's travel time can be reduced is not to sample every 150th, but to draw a random start point and then select every 10th, or very 15th name thereafter. In this way the 20 sampled people will be drawn from a group of only 200 electors, rather than the whole polling district.

This whole process is known as clustering the sample. One result is that it is no longer true, as it is with single-stage samples, that every member of the population has an equal chance of selection. Once the fifty constituencies have been chosen, people not living in those constituencies have no chance of selection, and the same is true of people not living in the chosen ward, and so on. However, although not everyone has an equal chance of selection, they all have a *known* chance of selection, and that is sufficient.

What is more of a problem is that the act of clustering itself makes the sample less reliable. If a constituency contains a number of mostly Conservative wards, and a number of mostly Labour ones, then if all the interviewing is clustered in only one ward it will not represent the whole constituency properly. In practice, for every constituency where a more Labour ward is chosen, there will be another one somewhere else where a more Conservative one is chosen, and overall it will balance out. However, this is not the only problem caused by clustering. By and large, people who live near each other are like each other in many ways, particularly in terms of wealth and social status. In statistical terms, this is known as intra-cluster homogeneity. In an extreme case, it could mean that all 300 people within a polling district covered by the sample are exactly alike. If this is so, there is nothing to be gained by interviewing 20 of them – interviewing only one would be just as effective. Thus although there are 1,000 interviews, there are effectively far fewer because of all the cases where people in clusters are alike.

This has an effect on sampling error and the reliability of the survey. The formula given above for standard error was based on a simple random sample. Stratifying the sample can actually decrease sampling error, but clustering will almost inevitably increase it. This is something which is very often ignored by people commenting on surveys, who calculate sampling errors as if it were an unclustered sample, and underestimate the real error. The amount by which sampling error is increased by clustering depends on the size and number of clusters, and on the levels of intra-cluster homogeneity and inter-cluster heterogeneity – in simple terms, the extent to which people in a cluster are like each other, but unlike the people in other clusters. The level of increase of error is known as the design effect. Calculation of design effects is complex, and outside the scope of this book, but in a typical political survey the design effect might be 1.3. This means that if the sampling error calculated for a simple random sample is ± 4%, then for the clustered sample it should be ± 5%.

Quota samples

All the discussion above about sampling theory is based on random, or probability samples. The reason for this is that the number theory on which it all based only works for probability samples, but there is another form of sampling which is far more often used, in this country at least, than probability sampling, and that is quota sampling. Ironically, although probability sampling is the method which has a scientific theoretical base developed long before the idea of survey interviewing, it was quota sampling which was first used in surveys. The straw votes referred to in the Introduction had more in common with modern quota samples than they did with probability samples.

The key principle of a random sample is that once someone has been selected to form part of the sample, by whichever of the possible means outlined above, he or she cannot be replaced by any other person. The accuracy of a random sample depends on getting interviews with as high a proportion as possible of the sampled names, and this can involve making several trips to those who are not in when the interviewer first calls. It can also involve second trips to attempt to convert those who initially were reluctant to take part. The higher the response rate achieved, the less opportunity there is for bias, but repeated interviewer visits can make the survey both costly and time-consuming.

The key principle of quota sampling is that if one theoretical member of the sample is unavailable, or does not wish to take part, then a replacement can be selected instead, provided that the replacement is sufficiently like the original. Thus instead of being given a list of people to try to interview, the interviewer is given instructions to interview so many people of one type (e.g. full-time working men), so many of another, and so on. Provided the people interviewed fit these profiles, the interviewer has a completely free choice over whom to interview. If a house is empty, the interviewer need not to return to it later, but can simply go next door, or further down the street, to find someone who fits one of the categories being sought.

The basis for this supposition is that people who are alike do tend to behave in similar ways. Men working full-time in professional jobs will generally read broadsheet newspapers, while the unemployed and those in unskilled manual work tend to read tabloids. This argument does not go so far as to say that *all* people of a certain type behave in exactly the same way, just that enough of them do so to make it reasonably likely that a replacement would give the same answer as the originally selected person. The trick lies in knowing how alike two people have to be before they are likely to answer a survey question the same way.

Clearly people are not so segmented that all women would give the same answer, so it is not enough just to replace one woman with another. But if the women are of the same age, that will make it a little more likely; if they are both working part-time that may make it more likely still; and if they are both married to skilled manual workers that will make it even more likely. It is therefore very important to choose the right variables on which to set the controls for the interviewer. Two factors come into play here. The most important is to choose variables which correlate with whatever the survey is mainly about. If the survey is about use of public transport, it is important to make sure the achieved sample includes the correct balance of people with and without cars. If it is about use of medical services it would be important to cover the whole age range. Thus the variables used to set quotas may vary from survey to survey.

On top of this is a consideration which applies to all surveys, and that is that some types of people will be easier for interviewers to find than others, and so will predominate in quota samples unless controls are imposed to prevent it. Given that many quota sample surveys are carried out in the street, and during the daytime, an interviewer sent out to interview with no controls would interview far more women than men, far more non-working people than working ones.

In the case of opinion polls, neither age nor sex correlate particularly strongly with voting intention, but quotas are set for these nevertheless, simply to achieve a sample which appears representative to the lay reader (reflected on page 58).

As well as the problem of choosing variables on which to set quotas, there is also the problem of knowing what targets to set for each cell. It is no good telling interviewers to get a certain number of men aged 18–35 if we don't know how many men aged 18–35 there are in the whole country. For some of the variables likely to be set in a typical survey there will be comparable data available from the Census, but as the Census only happens every ten years this soon gets out of date. Also for some variables, such as the social class classification used in market research surveys, there are no data in the Census. The only alternative here is to use other surveys, but there is obviously a risk that if the survey used for quota-setting was inaccurate, the resulting quota sample will also be.

There is an ongoing argument within the research community about the relative merits of quota and random sampling. As it does not have the same basis in number theory, one cannot make the same assumptions about sampling errors for a quota survey as for a random one. In fact, strictly speaking one should not talk about sampling error at all on quota surveys, as the basic principles are so different. However, if one looks at quota surveys over the years they tend to come up with answers well within the levels of sampling error one would expect for random samples of comparable size.

There are certainly more ways of getting a quota sample wrong. One can choose the wrong variables on which to set quotas, or one can set the wrong targets for the quota cells. As well as this, there is a wider potential problem inherent in all quota surveys, that the people who are not interviewed are somehow different from those who are interviewed in their stead. A quota sample will inevitably be biased towards those who are more easily available: someone who hardly ever goes out is far more likely to be in if a quota interviewer calls, than someone who is almost always out. In many cases this will not matter – this is the whole point of quota sampling – but if the survey were about how often people go out it is easy to see how the quota sample could lead to a biased sample. This is particularly important, because while random samples may well be subject to error, they are much less likely to be subject to bias.

Question wording

As stated at the start of this chapter, question wording in opinion polls is more important as a point of practical application rather than one of theory, and so the topic is covered mainly in Chapter Four. The theory of questionnaire design is also so wide a topic that it deserves a book to itself, and there are indeed several excellent ones available. The key texts are Sudman and Bradburn,[1] Converse and Presser,[2] Schuman and Presser,[3] Oppenheim[4] and Belson.[5] There are, however, some general points that are worth making here.

The general rules for the design of survey questions are that they must be simple, be capable of only one interpretation, not lead the respondent, and be possible to answer. A former NOP field director used to rebuke executives who wrote questions that were complicated, or that used many long words, by reminding them that half the population was of below average intelligence. People writing survey questions are usually better educated than the majority of respondents, and this is a very easy fact to forget.

Several writers have laid down rules for good question practice, and these are useful, but the search for the simple question can be carried to extremes, and one should avoid being overly constrained by hard and fast rules on word usage in questions. Stanley Payne, for example, in his generally useful book *The Art of Asking Questions*[6] says that words should not be used if they have more than two definitions in *Chambers' Dictionary*, and that words should only be used if they are found in the lists that were produced at that time of the most commonly used words in newspapers and magazines. As general principles these are fine, but if followed slavishly would lead to a ban on words like 'book' or 'train', and would prevent the use of specialist terms which are sometimes essential, and which may be common parlance among respondents to particular surveys.

It is also very easy to ask leading questions, whether consciously in the case of unethical researchers or unconsciously in the case of ethical ones. There is again a large literature on the subject of questions which themselves influence the answers,[7] and it is too wide a topic for this book. The main general rule is that a question must be balanced – if it asks respondents to choose between two options, and presents the benefits of one option, it must present the benefits of the other as well. For example, rather than asking 'Do you think the government should do X, or not?', it is better to give a substantive alternative: 'Do you think the government should do X, or should it do Y?'

A crucial point about questionnaire design is that errors or deficiencies in question wording are a primary cause of correlated response variance – response bias. If a question is phrased in such a complex way that only those with a degree-level education are likely to understand it, while everyone else is likely to misinterpret it, then those two groups are effectively answering different questions, and the results may well be biased. Similarly, if a question is asking about something which people may feel embarrassed about admitting to, a proportion will answer untruthfully in the negative, and the result will be that the survey underestimates the incidence of this socially unacceptable variable.

A prime example of this tendency is research on alcohol consumption. Social researchers have devised many ways of trying to get accurate information about consumption from survey respondents, prompting those who might have forgotten some drinking occasions, and coaxing the reluctant into admitting to drinking as much as they actually have, by trying to avoid giving any impression in the interview that drinking is something people should feel too ashamed to admit to. But even after all these efforts, if a high-quality sample is quizzed in detail about its drinking, and the results then grossed up to reflect the whole country, the volumes of alcohol fall hugely short of the volumes which we know – from Customs and Excise figures – are actually drunk.

On a more simple level, every survey which asks people whether they intend to vote in a forthcoming election, or whether they have voted in a recent one, finds a higher proportion of people who claim to be voters than the turnout figures show actually to be the case. This is because in a democracy many people feel that citizens have a *duty* to vote as well as the *right* to. Those who do not vote may feel guilty about admitting to a failure in their democratic duty, so they claim in an opinion poll that they are voters.

It must be remembered that although respondents can be promised confidentiality in a survey, and given guarantees that no one outside the research company will know the answers that they as an individual have the fact remains that the respondent is still talking to an interviewer. If the question is about something respondents would not admit to an acquaintance that they had done, they will not admit it to an interviewer.

It must therefore be recognised that there are some topics which cannot successfully be asked about, and others which can only be asked about with great care, but provided the researcher is aware of the potential pitfalls, and of the basic rules, then questionnaire design should not be too daunting a task.

This chapter has set out to explain the theory behind the ways surveys in general are conducted. The next looks at how this theory is applied in practice in the case of opinion polls.

Notes

1 S. Sudman and N. Bradburn, *Asking Questions: A Practical Guide to Questionnaire Design* (Jossey-Bass, 1982).
2 J. Converse and S. Presser, *Survey Questions: Handcrafting the Standardized Questionnaire* (John Wiley, 1991).
3 H. Schuman and S. Presser, *Questions and Answers in Attitude Surveys: Experiments on Question Form, Wording and Content* (Academic Press, 1981).
4 A. N. Oppenheim, *Questionnaire Design and Attitude Measurement* (Heinemann, 1966).
5 W. A. Belson, *The Design and Understanding of Survey Questions* (Gower, 1982).
6 S. L. Payne, *The Art of Asking Questions* (Princeton University Press, 1951).
7 Most of the books referred to notes 1–6 above contain discussions of leading questions.

3

Methodology in practice: sampling

Half of the people can be part right all of the time,
Some of the people can be all right part of the time

Election polls versus between-election polls

The preceding chapters have, I hope, made it clear that there are a number of different ways in which surveys can be carried out, and that over the life of opinion polling in the UK most, if not all, of them have been used at some time or other. There is a time-series element to this, with the broad pattern being one of early polls using random samples, a middle period with some pollsters using random and others quota, a modern period in which quota became the norm for all but academic polling, then finally an unclear present when, as is discussed in Chapter 9, there is a plurality of methodology among the pollsters.

Rather than go through the methodology prevalent at each election in turn, this chapter mainly describes the methodology in use from the general elections of 1974 to that of 1992. The reason for this is that it was a period which became one of broad stability in polling methodology, with a certain amount of tinkering from time to time, but no fundamental change in underlying approach. The Market Research Society (MRS) enquiry into the polls after the 1992 general election revealed that there were many differences in approach between the various polling agencies, but that all were following the same basic system. The fact that, despite these differences, all the polls had roughly the same figures all the way through the campaign, underlines the stability and robustness of their basic approach.

The choice of 1974 and 1992 is more than a coincidence, for the period is bounded by the most recent polling disaster, 1992, and the previous disaster in 1970 which followed on from a run of successful predictions. Although the problems in 1970, discussed in Chapter 1, were mainly to do with the timing of fieldwork, issues of methodology were raised which led to the emergence of a common approach.

Since the 1992 debacle, discussed in more detail in Chapter Six, all the polling companies have been experimenting with alternative methodologies, but at the time of writing no new consensus has emerged. ICM, after flirting with a secret-ballot approach, have now placed their faith in telephone surveys, and Gallup have also made the switch to the telephone, though for different reasons. Harris, MORI and NOP are still using face-to-face quota samples, so in describing what was common in the period up to 1992, this chapter also describes what is still (just) the majority method today.

The common approach to methodology was not adopted wholesale immediately after the 1970 election, and in the two elections of 1974 there was a mixture of random and quota sampling. However the trend was unmistakably towards quota sampling, with the 1974 random samplers using it for re-interviewing rather than initial interviews, and this chapter is therefore mainly about quota-sampling techniques. The separate issues involved in sampling for telephone surveys are discussed separately in Chapter 9.

The chapter also concentrates on one particular type of opinion poll, but it should not be thought that all published polls use a similar methodology. Because of its greater relevance and, arguably, importance, it is the election-campaign poll which is the apotheosis of the opinion poll. There are now five mainstream opinion polling companies in Britain – Gallup, Harris, ICM, MORI and NOP – and all five used broadly the same technique for their election polling until 1997. However, polling in between elections is a very different matter, and it is worth discussing this briefly before considering the methodology of the election poll in more depth.

The principal reason for the differences in methodology in non-election periods is financial. Between elections less importance is attached to opinion polls, and even before 1992, those who expected the polls to provide an accurate prediction of the election result a few days before it took place did not see polls conducted three years before an election as anything even approximating a prediction. Since they were less interesting, newspapers understandably preferred to use cheaper techniques for their polls than they did during elections, and were also likely to give them less space. The smaller space meant that there was room to write up fewer questions, which meant that polls became shorter, and thus cheaper still.

In the period between the 1992 and 1997 elections, and also since 1997, only three of the five main pollsters polled regularly and continuously for publication. By far the most significant is Gallup, which asks a large number of questions each month, as well as simple voting intention, on behalf of the *Daily Telegraph*, a relationship which has continued unbroken for over thirty years. ICM and MORI both poll each month, for the *Guardian* and *The Times* respectively, but both frequently contain little apart from voting intention. NOP polled monthly, and on a scale comparable to Gallup, for the *Sunday Times*, but did so only from July 1995 until the 1997 election. This pattern was broadly the same in the period between the 1987 and 1992 elections, except that in that time when NOP again joined in later on, it was working for the *Independent* and for BBC *Newsnight* instead of for the *Sunday Times*.

NOP was not only unusual in that it had only sporadic periods of regular published polling. Its polling also differed from the others in that it is the only one which used throughout the inter-election period a methodology which was basically the same as election polling. All the others usually put their questions on what is known as omnibus survey, which is a far more cost-effective means of asking a small number of questions, but which is quite different from an election poll. (Since their switch to telephone polling, discussed in Chapter 9, ICM now also use the same methodology for their monthly polls as for their election polls.)

The basic principle of an omnibus survey is that the survey company providing it contracts to carry out the fieldwork, and effectively sells space on the questionnaire to all comers. The beauty of it from the clients' point of view is that the cost of finding each respondent – a significant element of the fieldwork on any survey – is spread amongst all the clients. The same is true for the cost of the demographic questions – age, sex, social class and so on – which only need to be asked once but can then be used for analysis by all the clients. For clients who want to ask only a small number of questions, omnibus surveys represent a far more cost-effective method than conducting their own survey. The cost per question ranges between around £500 and £800, with discounts on offer for those prepared to commit themselves to questions on a series of surveys rather than just one.

Some of the pollsters run their own omnibus surveys (at the time of writing, Gallup, MORI and NOP do so), while others buy space on someone else's omnibus. Whether they use their own omnibus or subcontract, an omnibus represents the ideal vehicle for a regular monthly political survey involving only two or three questions a month. Also, for those who run their own omnibus, the cost of putting on extra questions – for methodological experimentation, for example – is virtually nil.

Because of its portmanteau nature, an omnibus interview is usually far longer than an *ad hoc* political opinion poll. Depending on the level of demand, an omnibus interview can easily run to half an hour or even more. This immediately means that it is impossible to conduct omnibus interviews in the street, and this factor, combined with the interview length, means that fieldwork for an omnibus survey will inevitably run over several days, and up to almost a week in the case of NOP.

This in turn means that the methodology of an omnibus poll may well be quite different from that used for *ad hoc* polls of the type conducted during an election campaign. Whilst NOP's omnibus is the only one conducted using random sampling, the omnibus surveys based on quota sampling are sufficiently different from election polls to be considered a separate species. This chapter therefore does not consider omnibus methodology, but concentrates on *ad hoc* quota polls.

Random versus quota polls

The last face-to-face random sample polls conducted in a British general election, apart from the post-election surveys that have formed part of the academic British Election Study (BES) at each election, were during the October 1974 election, but even by then they were in the minority, and this chapter deals only with the quota polls. The switch to random sampling by Gallup, and to semi-random by ICM, in 1997 was inextricably tied to their move to telephone, and is discussed in Chapter 9. The main reason why all face-to-face polling since 1974 has been based on quota samples is primarily to do with timing.

Chapter 1 concluded with a discussion of the problems faced by the polls in the 1970 election, and in particular the implications of fieldwork periods, which meant that many respondents in the prediction polls had been interviewed nearly a week before election day. As the lessons of 1970 were absorbed, the trend has been towards shorter and shorter fieldwork periods, with interviewing for the final prediction polls now typically being conducted on the Tuesday evening and Wednesday before election day on Thursday. This is not just a reaction to 1970, and the pollsters' concern to try to catch any last-minute swing, but also reflects demands from newspaper clients to have information as up to date as possible.

Secondary coverage of their polls in other broadcast and published media is increasingly important for the polls' clients. Newspapers commission polls for a number of reasons. One of these is simply the desire to give readers information that is relevant, in the same way that papers commission economic analyses of the budget. Another is that polls are something that readers expect and want to read, in the same way that newspapers pay for horoscopes. There are also considerations which go beyond merely keeping the existing readers happy, however, and these are more overtly commercial. Having a poll may itself get more readers for that day's issue, as people try to get first-hand details of a new 'POLL SHOCK', but there is also the free publicity to be obtained by having *News at Ten* refer to 'an NOP poll for the *Sunday Times*', or by having the rival *Guardian* refer to 'a MORI poll for *The Times*'.

The editor of the *Daily Mail* decided against commissioning any polls in the 1992 election on the grounds that he could find no evidence that polls sold any more copies. Even if he was right, he was at least acknowledging the commercial purposes of a newspaper when it buys polls. He is far from alone in this, for when NOP polled for the *Observer* in the early 1980s, the money for polls came entirely from the marketing budget rather than the editorial budget.

This expectation of secondary reporting of polls has its own effect on the way polls are conducted. A newspaper editor knows that if two polls are published on the same day, one of which was actually conducted the day before and the other two days earlier, the television bulletins and other newspapers will concentrate on the most recent one at the expense of the older one.

The pollsters thus find themselves under commercial pressure from their clients to produce information that is as up to date as possible, and face methodological pressures to avoid missing out on any late swing. This was a prime reason for the eventual abandonment of random sampling in favour of quota sampling in the 1970s, and was cited frequently after the 1992 election as a reason why it would be impossible for the polls to adopt the random techniques beloved of academic researchers, who are used to deadlines of months rather than days.

There is little or no point in conducting a random survey unless a good response rate is obtained. The chances of response bias are bad enough if a response rate of 70% is achieved (which is an extremely good response rate for a non-government survey); they will be unacceptably high for election prediction purposes if a response rate of only 50% is achieved. Response rate is affected by a number of factors, such as the subject matter, and the sponsor of research, but all other things being equal, response rates are determined by the performance of the interviewers.

The only way to get interviews with those who are rarely at home is to make a lot of calls spread out over a long period. One of the best ways of dealing with a potential refusal to be interviewed is for the interviewer to tell the respondent that it is clearly not a good time now, and to arrange to call back later. This is obviously the case if there are children running amok, babies crying or pans boiling over, but even if there is no evidence that the interviewer has indeed called at a bad time, the technique can be effective. Once respondents have actually said 'no', the interviewer has to try to persuade them to change their minds, and this is harder than merely withdrawing immediately and making a second attempt later.

Both of these interview techniques require a long period of fieldwork to have full effect, and it is very difficult to get a response rate approaching 70% (a widely accepted figure for a good-quality survey) with a fieldwork period of less than a month, and on large-scale surveys field periods are often longer still. There is simply no possibility of conducting a random sample within the time required by the polls' media clients, and so for the last four elections up to 1992 all election polling has been by means of quota samples.

Sample design

The actual sample design used has varied from one polling company to another, but until the advent of telephone interviewing by ICM and Gallup, they tended to be broadly the same. Sample sizes, quota controls and number of sampling points all differ little across the main pollsters. There has been a recent trend towards an increase in sample size, and this has been followed by all the pollsters. In the 1983 general election the final Gallup poll had a sample size of 2,000, but none of the other prediction polls had samples bigger than 1,000. Just four years later, the smallest sample size for the final polls in the 1987 general election was over 1,500, and two polls had samples in excess of 2,000. These increases have been achieved by doing the same thing but on a larger scale, rather than by any change in basic approach.

The first stage of any sample design is the selection of primary sampling units – the places where interviewing takes place. In other surveys these could be local authority districts, or postal districts, but for a political poll the only logical choice for first-stage sampling units is parliamentary constituencies. Numbers of sampling points have risen as the sample size has risen, and the typical number now is between 75 and 100. The choice of the number of sampling points is not a primary part of the design process, for it is basically a function of the total number of interviews required and the number of interviews an interviewer can reasonably conduct in a day.

The most cost-effective way for a polling organisation to manage its fieldwork on a political poll is to give each interviewer a quota equivalent to a standard day's work. While it is ideal to have as many sampling points as possible, in order to minimise the design factor (see Chapter 2), it is not cost-effective to double the number of sampling points and give each interviewer only half a day's work. Interviewers are effectively self-employed freelances, who choose to accept or refuse work on an assignment by assignment basis. Many work for more than one agency (there are, of course, far more market research agencies than there are polling agencies), and would be unlikely to accept an assignment offering only a half-day's pay, since there is little possibility of finding another assignment for the other half-day, and they will thus be more likely to accept an alternative assignment covering the entire day.

Most political-poll interviews are fairly short. For the reasons stated above, media clients want results quickly, and this is more easily achieved with a short questionnaire. Also, there are limits to the amount of space a newspaper will give to a poll, and there is no point in asking more questions than could be fitted in the space available. This limit is even more tight for broadcast media, where it is very unlikely that a television item on a poll could include details from more than four or five questions. Because of these pressures, a typical political opinion poll has around ten to fifteen questions.

As well as interview length, the number of interviews an interviewer can carry out in a day also depends on the nature of the quota controls, and any other factors such as whether interviewing takes place in home or in the street. In a typical design, an interviewer can conduct between 15 and 20 interviews in a day. Thus in the early 1980s the norm for an *ad hoc* political poll was 1,000 interviews in 50 constituencies. With increasing concern about the need for greater reliability, this has now become more like 1,500 in 75 or 100 constituencies, or even 2,000 in 100 constituencies.

Because each interviewer carries out the same number of interviews, it is important that constituencies are selected with a probability proportional to size. As outlined in Chapter 2, the two approaches to multi-stage sampling are either to give each sampling point an equal chance of selection, and then to conduct more interviews in larger sampling points than smaller ones; or else to give larger sampling points a larger chance of selection in the first place and then to conduct the same number of interviews in each. The latter approach is far more practical, since it is a lot easier to give each interviewer the same assignment, and this is the one that is universally used.

Given that the same number of interviews is conducted in each constituency, if constituencies were selected with an equal probability this would lead to a bias towards smaller constituencies at the expense of larger ones. If there were no differences other than size between larger and smaller constituencies this would not be a major problem. However the nature of political geography in Britain, and in particular the impact of the decisions of successive boundary reorganisations, is such that smaller constituencies are more likely to be Labour-held than larger ones. In 1992 the average Conservative-held seat contained around 70,000 electors, but the average Labour-held one contained only around 59,000. The redistribution of seats by the Boundary Commission between 1992 and 1997 alleviated this, but in time population movements mean that imbalances will reappear.

Thus if constituencies were selected with equal probability, the resulting sample would in 1992 have been considerably biased towards Labour, and in the future may be biased in an unknown way. This is why it is crucial that seats are selected with a probability proportional to size. The selection of constituencies themselves is usually carried out from a stratified list of all constituencies. Northern Ireland is omitted, because the main parties do not contest the seats there and voting behaviour there can have no *direct* effect on the election result, and on grounds of practicality some seats in Scotland are also omitted. Orkney and Shetland, and the Western Isles, are invariably omitted, and some polling agencies also omit all seats north of the Caledonian Canal.

The remaining seats are typically arranged first into Registrar General's Standard Region, and within region are then sorted by various other factors. Some agencies use an urban/rural variable in their stratification. For example, each constituency may be allocated to one of four strata: metropolitan (usually defined as those constituencies within the former metropolitan counties of Greater London, the West Midlands, South Yorkshire, West Yorkshire, Merseyside, Greater Manchester and Tyne and Wear), urban, mixed urban/rural and rural. The allocation of constituencies into the last three categories is dependent on population density.

In any multi-level stratified sampling scheme it is also usual to have a further level of stratification based on a class-related variable. This could take the form of ranking all the constituencies within each cell of the region and urban/rural stratification matrix by the proportion in Registrar General's social class I, or within Socio-Economic Groups 1–5 or 13. Given that the primary purpose of opinion polls concerns voting behaviour, an alternative form of stratification is to rank constituencies in each cell by the percentage who voted Conservative at the last general election.

Table 11 shows an example of part of a stratified listing of constituencies, while Table 12 shows how the constituencies are sampled. Alongside each constituency is listed the electorate, and the second number alongside is the cumulative electorate working down the list. This is the number which is used in the actual selection of constituencies. The selection is made by repeatedly applying a constant sampling interval, which is calculated by dividing the total population by the number of constituencies required. Thus if the total electorate is 44,456,987 and the number of constituencies required is 75, the sampling interval would be 592,760. A random number is selected between 1 and the sampling interval, and this defines the first sampling point: the constituency which contains the elector whose number down the cumulative list matches the chosen random number. The sampling interval is then added to the random start point, which in turn identifies the next constituency, and then the sampling interval is added again, and so on until the bottom of the list is reached, by which point the target number of constituencies will have been selected.

In the example shown in Table 12, the interval is 262,735 and the start point is 136,355, which falls in the third constituency on the list. Adding the interval to the start point gives 399,090, which lies in the sixth constituency, and this is also selected. Adding the interval again gives 661,825, which selects the tenth constituency, and so on.

This approach is a standard one used for the selection of primary sampling units for any survey, and works equally well for surveys based on random samples and on quota samples. Normally once the selection had been made it would not be subjected to any further inspection, as it is a random sample of all sampling points in the universe. However, the fact that it is a random sample means that, even with careful stratification of the kind described above, it may be skewed in some way.

It is possible to check the sample against the universe by looking at the demographic make-up of all the constituencies in the sample, and comparing them with the demographic make-up of the country as a whole, but this is only likely to be done on a very major survey, where it is worth putting in a lot of extra effort to check against a very unlikely circumstance.

Because it is so important that the sample for an opinion poll is a true reflection of the country as a whole, the sample of constituencies for an opinion poll is checked for political balance. This is done in much the same way, by cal-

Table 11 *Stratified list of constituencies*

Region	Urban type	Constituency	% AB
North	Metropolitan	Newcastle upon Tyne Central	45.0
		Tynemouth	37.5
		Newcastle upon Tyne North	29.7
		Blaydon	28.5
		Sunderland South	28.2
		Gateshead East & Washington West	25.7
		Jarrow	25.7
		Newcastle upon Tyne East & Wallsend	25.1
		South Shields	24.4
		Houghton & Washington East	22.1
		Tyneside North	22.0
		Sunderland North	22.0
		Tyne Bridge	19.6
	Other 100% urban	Stockton South	34.2
		Darlington	27.2
		Blyth Valley	26.0
		Durham North	25.7
		Hartlepool	24.8
		Stockton North	24.5
		Middlesbrough	24.4
		Carlisle	24.0
		Redcar	23.0
		Easington	19.7
	Mixed urban/ rural	Durham, City Of	35.9
		Middlesbrough South & Cleveland East	33.2
		Sedgefield	29.0
		Wansbeck	28.4
		Barrow-in-Furness	24.6
	Rural	Hexham	43.5
		Penrith & The Border	35.4
		Westmorland & Lonsdale	34.4
		Durham North West	29.6
		Berwick-upon-Tweed	29.6
		Workington	27.8
		Copeland	26.7
		Bishop Auckland	25.5
Yorkshire & Humber	Metropolitan	Sheffield Hallam	59.3
		Leeds North-East	44.6
		Leeds North-West	44.1
		Shipley	39.2
		Sheffield Central	35.4

Table 12 *Sampling from a stratified list*

Constituency	Electorate	Cumulative	Selected
Rochdale	69,226	69,226	–
Salford	58,961	128,187	–
Stockport	65,755	193,942	136,355
Leigh	70,386	264,328	–
Warrington North	73,394	337,722	–
Southport	70,724	408,446	399,090
Halton	65,656	474,102	–
Congleton	69,714	543,816	–
Manchester Withington	66,639	610,455	–
Stalybridge & Hyde	66,146	676,601	661,825
Ribble South	72,510	749,111	–
Worsley	69,488	818,599	–
Manchester Blackley	62,879	881,478	–
Bootle	57,760	939,238	924,560
Hyndburn	67,395	1,006,633	–
Altrincham & Sale West	71,371	1,078,004	–
Ashton under Lyne	72,801	1,150,805	–
Oldham East & Saddleworth	73,740	1,224,545	1,187,295
Oldham West & Royton	69,742	1,294,287	–
Wythenshawe & Sale East	72,695	1,366,982	–
Knowsley South	71,096	1,438,078	–
Blackpool South	76,395	1,514,473	1,450,030
Preston	73,492	1,587,965	–

culating the share of the votes at the last general election just in those constituencies sampled, and comparing it with the national result. If the result in the sample does not match the actual result to within, say, 0.5%, the sample can be modified. Theoretically it would be better in that case to draw a fresh sample, and then test that against the overall result, but it is easier and in practice not significantly less reliable to drop one or more constituencies and replace them with those which take the sample nearer the actual result. Thus if the result across all the sampled constituencies were slightly too Conservative, a constituency with a fairly high Conservative vote is dropped from the sample and replaced by one with a slightly lower one. If necessary this process can be repeated several times. Each time a constituency is dropped, it must be replaced by another from the same stratum in the stratification matrix.

The same process is often carried out to ensure that the sample is also politically representative at the regional level – that the result in the sampled seats in the North-West matches the overall result in the North-West, for example. At this greater level of detail it is not reasonable to expect any random sample to match exactly, so changes would only be made in any given region if the sample result differed from the overall result by more than 2% or so.

The next question to be addressed in the sample design is whether to stop the process there and use constituencies as the primary sampling units, or whether there should be a further selection process to select a smaller unit, such as an electoral ward or even a polling district, within each constituency for the interviewer to work in. The advantage of doing so is that it imposes greater control over what the interviewer can do, and thus makes the process more scientific.

One of the key complaints about quota sampling made by random sampling advocates is that it allows too much freedom for the interviewer, and thus lacks scientific rigour. Because the interviewer has responsibility for choosing respondents, rather than being given a list of pre-selected people to interview, he or she can exert a certain amount of influence over the selection process, and thus introduce bias. One of the ways in which this can be done is by choosing where to conduct the interviews, and the larger the primary sampling unit, the more freedom the interviewer has to interview where he or she chooses.

To some extent this freedom is curtailed by the quota controls. An interviewer cannot simply choose to conduct an entire assignment in a pleasant upmarket area, because the quota controls require some interviews to be with people from lower social-class groups, who are unlikely to be found in such an area. However, within each class-quota group the interviewer will have a range of choices of places to interview, and experience will suggest some areas rather than others. Since people who live in any one area are likely to be different from people living in different areas, this is what the opponents of quota sampling worry about. However, there are two separate, contradictory arguments put forward about what interviewers do, and since each seems very plausible, it may indeed be that any resulting biases are self-cancelling.

On the one hand it is argued that in order to maximise the efficiency of their search, interviewers go to the most stereotypical areas. Thus when looking for working-class households, interviewers will, it is said, go only to council housing estates, because they know that most people there will fit the quota. Similarly, when looking for white-collar households they will go to executive housing developments, or an area with big houses. By doing this they miss out altogether on more mixed areas, and also they miss out on better-off, working-class households living in upmarket areas, or worse-off, white-collar households living in working-class areas.

The alternative argument is that interviewers avoid the extremes of the social-class scale because they know that interviewing is more difficult in those areas. In very upmarket areas there will probably be porter-controlled access in blocks of flats, which may well mean that there will be many refusals, or very long drives in the case of detached houses, which may well mean much wasted time walking up drives, only to be met by a refusal to be interviewed. At the other end of the scale, the very poorest areas are often also areas with high crime rates, where interviewers will not choose to go, for obvious reasons. Also, high-rise blocks in areas with high crime rates are increasingly being fitted with extensive security devices, including entryphones, which again are likely to lead to higher refusal rates.

It is easy to see how consistently avoiding the most upmarket areas would lead to a bias against the Tories, while avoiding the worst-off areas will not necessarily lead to an anti-Labour bias to the same extent, because registration and turnout are both lower in those areas. However, if there are other interviewers concentrating on the most stereotypical areas at the expense of the middle ground, the effects may cancel each other out.

It is possible to limit the ability of the interviewers to choose the kinds of areas in which to work, by allocating them specific areas. The problem traditionally has been in choosing a geographical unit which has some meaning, and which can easily be explained to the interviewers. The next step down from a constituency is an electoral ward, but this then means that the interviewers need detailed maps showing them the ward boundaries, since they are unlikely to know these themselves. Wards are still quite large units, and if one were wanting more geographical control the next alternative would be the polling district – the building-blocks from which wards are made. However, while it is usually possible to acquire ward maps by going to the relevant town hall, many local authorities do not publish maps showing polling districts. It is possible to compile lists of streets in each polling district, but this is a cumbersome process, and may not be of much use to an interviewer unfamiliar with the area.

There is a further problem affecting polling districts but not wards, and this concerns the quotas (which themselves will be discussed in more detail below). It is possible to design nationally representative quotas and then set the same quotas in every sampling point, but this will make the interviewers' life much more difficult. A nationally representative quota would require an interviewer to get around nine white-collar respondents and five unskilled working class respondents in a quota of twenty, but finding five unskilled working-class respondents in an upmarket constituency like Hazel Grove could be very time-consuming, as could finding white-collar respondents in a downmarket constituency like Bethnal Green and Bow. The solution is to make the quotas reflect the population of the sampling point – to require the interviewer to get perhaps fourteen white-collar respondents in Hazel Grove, but only four in Bethnal Green.

Setting locally based quotas at the constituency level is fairly easy, because census figures are published broken down by parliamentary constituency. Setting them at the ward level has always been possible, since the figures are available at ward level, though it usually involved a trip to inspect the microfiche at the library of the Office of National Surveys (ONS). However, the figures are not published anywhere by polling district, since it is an administrative unit used only for voting purposes. This means setting quotas based at best on the ward, but requiring the interviewer to apply them to a much smaller unit, when there is a reasonable chance that any one polling district will not be a perfect microcosm of the ward.

Class-related variables are very highly clustered geographically. In almost every constituency, if not every ward, it would be possible to find a small area of relatively upmarket housing in a predominantly downmarket area, or vice versa. If the quotas are set on the basis of the downmarket whole, and the interviewer is assigned to work in the one upmarket part, meeting the quota will be very difficult. This problem of specificity gets more pronounced the smaller the areas that are used as the primary sampling units, but the more control that is wanted over where the interviewer works, the smaller the units have to be.

Fortunately, recent developments in computing have resolved this conundrum, by allowing research companies to set very small areas for the interviewers to work in, and at the same time to set quotas based only on the population of that small area. It is the relatively recently created geodemographics industry which has made this possible.

Geodemographics rests on the principle of class homogeneity referred to above. By and large, people tend to be quite like their next-door neighbours in a lot of ways. If someone lives in a council flat, it is almost inevitable that their next-door neighbours will also live in a council flat (right to buy notwithstanding), and very probable that they will be alike in other ways as well – social class, disposable income, choice of newspaper, and so on. The process of gentrification has much the same effect. A few pioneers move into a run-down area and start doing it up, and as the number of renovated houses grows, more people think it is a desirable place to move to, and soon the whole area is full of yuppies.

Such obvious similarities can be seen by the naked eye, but the geodemographic industry is far more complex. Put simply, the technique involves collecting data on forty or so key census variables for every single enumeration district in the country, enumeration districts, or eds, being the smallest unit of census geography, typically containing 100 households. Cluster analysis is then used to find groups of eds which most resemble each other. A number of cluster groups, or families, are created, and the competing geodemographic systems – ACORN, MOSAIC and others – then allocate descriptive names to each family – well-off retirement areas, mainly terraced inner-city areas with a high ethnic-minority population, better-off rural areas, and so on. The key stage is the next one, of allocating postcodes to enumeration districts, and thus to these families or groups. In this way, once you know someone's postcode, you also know what geodemographic type area she lives in, and can as a result predict a lot of things about her behaviour.

The main purpose behind the process is to enable mailshots to be targeted much more effectively – rather than send out two million mailshots at random across a region, a marketing company can send out just 200,000, but only to areas where they are most likely to be successful. But in order to keep the whole system running, geodemographic companies have to have the whole census data on an ed-by-ed basis, plus a list of addresses matched to those eds, and this is where the benefit to survey samplers comes from.

Within each of the sampled constituencies for a political poll, a geodemographic company can select an enumeration district on the basis of a stratification process similar to that described above for selecting constituencies. Quotas can then be set which match the census data just for that ed, and a list supplied for the interviewer of all the addresses which fall within the ed. If a larger than usual number of interviews is required, an enumeration district may not be a big enough area for the interviewer to be able to fill the quota. In that case a second ed can be chosen – either elsewhere in the constituency, selected in the same way, or (more efficiently from the interviewer's point of view) pairs of contiguous eds can be selected at the start.

Sampling such as this is often described as random-location interviewing, because small areas have been randomly selected for the interviewers to work in, and it has become very widely used over the last ten years or so. It should remove all the biases that are likely to be caused by allowing the interviewers too much freedom, and lead to more reliable figures. In fact, as far as opinion polls are concerned, setting tighter controls seems to make very little difference. In the 1992 general election the different polling companies used different degrees of geographical controls, and yet there were no systematic differences between them. In the 1987 election NOP used tighter geographical controls than the other companies, including the use of two different wards within each constituency, but did no better than the others as a result. In 1992 there were again differences between the pollsters which seem to have had little effect on the answers achieved.

Thus while it may seem that setting closer geographical controls ought to be more reliable, it does not seem that this is the case. More important is the setting of the quotas themselves, to which we now turn.

Setting the quotas

In any quota survey there are two initial questions to be resolved – the quota controls which are to be applied, and the data which are to be used to set those quotas.

The quotas which are usually set for opinion polls are some or all of age, sex, working status and social class. Many who argue against quota sampling *per se* also argue that the matter is made worse because these are not the right controls to set, but this is somewhat to miss the purpose of quota-control setting. As discussed in Chapter 2, there are in fact two considerations underlying the setting of quotas. One, and the one which the academic critics think is most important, is to set quotas on variables which correlate strongly with the key dependent variable – in this case, voting intention.

Any sample is bound to be unrepresentative in terms of some characteristics, and the trick in successful sampling is to ensure that these don't have any effect on the results. Thus if a sample has twice as many left-handed people as it should have, or not nearly enough people who keep gerbils, these problems are not likely to have any impact on the voting intention figures. If, on the other hand, there are twice as many self-employed people, or not nearly enough people who earn over £30,000 a year, then this would almost certainly affect the answers, the former overestimating the Conservative vote, and the latter underestimating it.

The criticism of the academics is that only one of the four variables frequently used correlates strongly with voting intention, and this is social class. Psephologists may, and indeed do, disagree fiercely about the extent to which Britain has a class-based voting system, but none would disagree that class-related variables correlate strongly with voting intention. There is also generally a gender effect, with men more likely to vote Labour and women more likely to vote Conservative, but these differences are small, and not consistent. There is often also an age effect, with older voters less likely to vote Labour, but this too is relatively small and inconsistent.

If the aim was just to pick variables which correlate with voting behaviour, then quotas would be set for social class, car-ownership, housing tenure, and perhaps the number of foreign holidays taken in the previous year. There would be no quotas set for sex, age, or working status. However, this is to ignore the other reason for setting quotas, which is to ensure that the types of people interviewers are most likely to under-represent are interviewed in their correct proportions.

It would in theory be possible to increase the number of quota controls to include both variables which correlate strongly with voting behaviour, and variables which control for the imbalances which are likely to crop up if interviewers are left to their own devices. However, the interviewers' task has to remain manageable, and the more controls there are the harder it is for the interviewers to find people who meet them. The last person to be interviewed is the hardest to find, since the interviewers have no flexibility over whom to choose. If there are a lot of controls, an interviewer would be left looking for someone as specific as a 35–54-year-old non-working man from a working-class household who has two or more cars and owns his own home. Not an easy person to find!

With a lot of opinion-poll interviewing taking place on street, any inspection of a shopping centre on any weekday will show that it is far easier to find women to interview than it is to find men. With no sex controls, an interviewer would probably end up with three-quarters of the assignment as women respondents. Similarly, with much interviewing taking place during the day, it is obvious that it is much harder to find people who are working full-time than it is to find those who are not. In either case, the voting-intention figures are unlikely to be much affected, but there are two other reasons why such a sample would be undesirable.

The first is that although academic psephologists may be able to prove that a sample composed almost entirely of women would not vote significantly differently from one that was representative by gender, the lay person is unlikely to be convinced by this. Neither a newspaper editor, nor the newspaper readers, will place much store on a survey of this kind. The second drawback is that, while voting intention may not correlate with age or sex, other variables used in an opinion poll may well do. There is no cost difference between a questionnaire with one question, and one with eight or nine (because so much of the interviewers' time goes in finding respondents in the first place), and commissioners of opinion polls will get their money's worth by including a number of questions on topical issues. If the issue of the time is divorce, or education, or the National Health Service, a sample consisting mainly of women will have very different answers from a representative one, while questions on environmental issues will get very different answers if the age distribution of the sample is biased.

It is thus in part to keep the sample in balance in terms of basic demographics that the quota controls are chosen. Underlining this point is the fact that twenty years or so ago, it was rare to see quotas set for working status, but the advent of widespread unemployment meant that on-street interviewing started to have too many unemployed men, and controls were introduced.

One other way in which quota controls have adapted over the last twenty or so years is the introduction of interlocked instead of simple quotas. With simple quotas, separate controls are set for age, for sex, for social class, and so on. Thus an interviewer might have to find nine men and eleven women, and also have to find six 18–35-year-olds, seven 35–54-year-olds, and seven over 55, but have freedom to allocate the different age groups between the sexes in any way. There is nothing to stop an interviewer choosing only men for the 18–35-year-olds, and only women for the over-55s. Also, if the quota requires nine people working full-time and eleven not, there is again nothing to stop the interviewer interviewing only working women and non-working men.

To avoid extreme outcomes of this sort, the quotas can be interlocked, so that they are set in greater detail. Thus a quota might require three men aged 18–35, three aged 35–54, and three over 55, or require five working men and four non-working men. The quotas can be interlocked still further, by combining three different controls. A quota may require an interviewer to find two middle-class men aged 18–34, one skilled working-class man of the same age, and one unskilled working-class man of that age, and so on.

This was in fact the form of interlocking of quotas widely used in the 1970s: age interlocked with sex and class. The introduction of a fourth quota control, working status, made full interlocking unwieldy, and in the 1980s it was more usual to have two separate interlocked quotas: age interlocked with social class, and sex interlocked with working status. There is a logic to interlocking the controls in this way, one of which is probably obvious to anyone on reflection, while the other may be less obvious. The obvious one is the interlocking of sex with working status. Because far more men work than do women, if the controls were not interlocked an interviewer would be likely to end up with nearly all the men working, and nearly all the women non-working.

The less obvious interlock is of class with age, and to understand this it is necessary to look at how the market-research social-class categories work. There are technically six class categories, although it is very rare to see them all used, either in quotas or in analysis. It is far more usual to group two or more of them, to form larger groups. The groups, with a very rough description of the types of people found in each one, are shown below. Coding used to be based on the occupation of the head of the household, with the man automatically being the head of the household in the case of couples, but in these more enlightened times it is based on the occupation of the chief income-earner in the household. It is a household variable, so all people in the same household are assigned the same social class.

A   Senior professionals – barristers, professors, bishops, managers in very large companies
B   Other professionals, executives, managers of other companies
C1   Junior executives and clerical staff
C2   Skilled and semi-skilled manual workers
D   Unskilled manual workers
E   Those entirely dependent on state benefits

The normal groupings are to put As and Bs together as ABs. (It is very doubtful whether a team even of experienced interviewers would come up with a consistent set of codings of managerial and professional staff into A as opposed to B.) Because even this combined group is still only a small proportion of the population – currently around 17% – it is also quite common to combine them further with C1s, to produce the overall white-collar category, ABC1s.

The other frequent grouping – that of Ds with Es to form the DE group – is less defensible on grounds of the difficulty of distinguishing between them. The reasons for it lie in the purpose for which the classes were originally drawn up by the advertising industry: to discriminate between groups with different degrees of spending power, and different ways of spending it. The least skilled workers are likely to be the lowest paid, and state benefits are not set at a level to allow any more than essential expenditure, if that. As an aside, people who are unemployed are coded according to their previous job until they have been unemployed for either three or six months (depending on the research agency), and only become Es after that time, while those who have any occupational pension are coded according to the main job they retired from.

In spending terms, Ds and Es may be very similar, but in political terms they are often quite different. The great majority of Es are people relying entirely on a state pension, with women over-represented because of their greater life-spans. Older people tend to be somewhat more Conservative, women tend to be somewhat more Conservative, and older women tend to be a lot more Conservative. Low-paid, unskilled workers, on the other hand, are among the groups most likely to vote Labour – historically they have been Labour's natural constituency.

Combining Ds and Es thus mixes together people of very different political beliefs, and if the poll is to represent this divergence it is important that it gets the Ds and Es at least roughly in the right proportions. With non-interlocked quota controls, this is very likely not to happen. One of the easiest groups to find is pensioners, who are both quite numerous and tend to be available, having no paid work and generally few family commitments. An interviewer will thus tend to fill up the DE quota with pensioners, which in turn means that the over-55 age group tends to be mainly over 65. This then means that the younger respondents will all have to be ABC1s and C2s to maintain the quotas. Thus the DE group, instead of being split between Labour unskilled workers and Conservative pensioners, will tend to be all Conservative pensioners, with an obvious resulting bias in the overall results.

By interlocking the age and sex quotas, around two-thirds of the DEs will have to be under 55, and so the interviewers must find some unskilled workers. Similarly, with the need to find older ABC1s and C2s, the interviewers will tend to split the over-55 quota between working 55–64-year-olds and pensioners, and a better-balanced sample will result. A typical quota sheet is shown in Figure 4.

Assuming that we are not drawing an ed-based sample, with quotas ready-supplied as described above, but are instead working on a constituency-based sample, then having decided which quota controls to use, and how to interlock them, the next problem is to decide what values to set on each of the cells. This effectively means deciding on a source of data to show what proportion of the population falls into each of the quota cells. If the poll is being carried out within a few years of the most recent Census being published, then this is the most obvious source, but even then it cannot be used as a source of information for setting the social-class quotas. The social-class system described above is used only by the market research and advertising business, and government surveys and the Census all use alternative grading schemes. While the market-

Figure 4 *Sample quota sheet*

Please interview 20 people according to the following controls.		
	Quota set	***Quota achieved***
Male working full-time	6	
Male not working full-time	3	
Female working full- or part-time	4	
Female not working	7	
18–34 ABC1	3	
18–34 C2	2	
18–34 DE	2	
35–54 ABC1	3	
35–54 C2	2	
35–54 DE	1	
55+ ABC1	2	
55+ C2	2	
55+ DE	3	

research social-class system has remained pretty much constant in design for many years, the government coding schemes have undergone frequent change.

There are in fact several 'official' coding schemata, each serving a slightly different purpose, but capable of being linked to each other. The three most significant for the purposes of comparison with the market-research system are SOC, SEG and Registrar General's Social Class. The Standard Occupational Classification (SOC), is a means of coding people according to the job they do, and is enormously detailed. It is a hierarchical system, with ten major groups, each covering a broad employment type, and each broken into a number of minor groups, breaking the detail down slightly more. Finally each minor group is broken down into one or individual codes. At the individual-code level it is far too detailed for use in all but the most large-scale surveys, while at minor-group and certainly at major-group level it is unable to distinguish between different levels of seniority or skill.

The seventeen Socio-Economic Groups (SEGs) are more manageable, and have a strong class-related element. It is possible to make a reasonable approximation between SEG and the market-research system at least at the top level. Very broadly, ABs can be compared to SEG codes 1, 2, 3, 4 and 13. Lower down the scale, however, the comparisons become much more difficult, and although many cross-industry working parties have looked into it, no good match can be made between the two scales for the whole population. The most recent examination of the whole issue of matching the various schemata was by an Economic and Social Research Council (ESRC) Working Group headed by Professor David Rose.[1] Whilst a useful work, this admits that the problem of matching government classifications to market-research ones has not been solved, and work is continuing in this area.

The Registrar General's Social Class categories seem at first sight much more promising for cross-matching. Firstly, it is a household-based coding system, while technically SOC and SEG only give a classification for one person, and in the case of non-workers are automatically based on the last main job, however long ago that may have been. Secondly, the Registrar General's schema has exactly the same number of codes as the market-research one, and even breaks the middle category down into white- and blue-collar. Thus the market research schema has C1s and C2s, while the Registrar General's has III Non-manual and III Manual.

However, the differences between the two scales, particularly in the treatment of non-workers, are sufficient to prevent any reliable cross-matching between the two. No matter how up to date the Census may be, the pollsters have to look elsewhere for quota-setting information on social class, and for much of the time they have to look elsewhere for other variables as well. The Census is only conducted every ten years, with the 1966 10% mid-point Census now a faded memory, despite occasional attempts to resurrect one. Over the ten years between successive censuses there is usually considerable change, which means that the census data start becoming out of date after a while. Indeed, because it takes so long to produce the results (which is not altogether surprising given the vast scale of the undertaking), it can be argued that the Census is out of date before the results are even published. One of the ironies of the 1992 general election is that had the data from the 1991 Census been available by the time of the election, the pollsters would have been more accurate than they actually were, as is discussed in more detail in Chapter 6.

The Census is so authoritative (the problems of underenumeration in 1991 notwithstanding) that there is no comparable source of data in the intervening years. The most reliable alternatives are the other large government surveys, such as the General Household Survey (GHS), conducted quarterly, and the Labour Force Survey (LFS), conducted continuously throughout the year. These are based on multi-stage random samples, are relatively unclustered, and achieve high response rates, so should provide a very accurate picture of the population. They too tend to take some time to be published, but not enough to be a serious problem, and they remain the best source of data on variables such as housing tenure and working status. Up-to-date information on the sex and age breakdown of the population can be easily obtained from the monthly figures published by the Office of National Statistics (ONS), produced by using the previous Census as a baseline and then amending the figures on the basis of birth and death certificates.

This leaves the question of social class, which is the hardest variable about which to glean reliable information. Because it is used only by market-research agencies, the only source of data is surveys by these agencies, and there are few which have large enough sample of sufficiently high quality to be totally reliable. The two most significant are the National Readership Survey (NRS), conducted by RSL, and the Broadcasters' Audience Research Board (BARB) establishment survey – the survey conducted by Taylor Nelson/AGB which is used to recruit and calibrate the sample of homes used to measure television viewing.

Both are based on random samples, conducted to high standards, and have reasonably long field periods, but even so the response rates are much lower than for the GHS or LFS. More problematic than this, though possibly resulting from it, is the fact that the social class profiles are often quite different between the two samples. BARB is different because only housewives are interviewed, but since social class is a household variable this should not matter greatly.

At the time of writing, BARB showed 19% in social class AB, while the NRS showed 22%. Conversely, the NRS showed 12% in class E while BARB showed 16%. With figures as variant as this, there is not much to be done except pay your money and take your choice, although some cross-checking can be undertaken by comparing the values in each survey of other variables, such as car-ownership and housing tenure, with the values for the same variables in the GHS or the Census.

One other important point about using government survey data to calibrate opinion polls is that both housing tenure and car-ownership – the two variables most likely to be used – are always presented in the Census, GHS and so on as household variables, percentaged on all households, whereas opinion polls are trying to be representative of the adult population. This means that the government data must be repercentaged based on all adults rather than all households. Because many single pensioner households live in council flats, the proportion of *people* living in council accommodation is lower than the proportion of *households* who do so.

Having decided which quota controls are to be used, and found reliable data to show what proportion should be in each cell, the final stage is to translate all this into individual quotas to give to each interviewer. Since it is unlikely that every percentage will be such as to produce a whole number when multiplied by the number of interviews being conducted in each point, it will not be possible to set a single quota and then apply it to all constituencies. If for, example, 34% of the population are men working full-time, that would mean 6.8 out of every twenty interviews. Since an interviewer cannot interview 0.8 of a person, this means that some of the interviewers must have quota sheets which tell them to interview six working men, and some must have quota sheets which tell them to interview seven.

This requires there to be a number of different variants of the quota sheet, which fact can then be used to make the interviewer's life easier. As discussed in the previous section of this chapter, it is preferable to set quotas which reflect the actual make-up of each sampling point. Rather than calculating fifty separate sets of quotas, one for each constituency, the much simpler approach of a national quota just discussed is much easier to calculate. For most variables this is perfectly acceptable, for the sex, age and working-status distributions do not vary hugely from one constituency to another. Social class does, however, vary considerably from one constituency to another. The percentage of households in the social class ABC1 varied in 1992 from 15% in West Bromwich West to 63% in Chelsea. Rather than set quotas which all have around nine ABC1s, it is much easier for the interviewers if some variants of the quota have as many as fourteen or fifteen ABC1s, with correspondingly fewer in the other groups, while other variants have only four or five ABC1s, and more C2s and DEs. A reasonable compromise for our hypothetical example would be to have five variants of the quota, each allocated to ten constituencies. The constituencies are ranked in order according to the proportion of ABC1s in each one, and variant 1 is allocated to the first ten constituencies on the list, variant 2 to the next ten, and so on.

In this way the sample is nationally representative, and each interviewer has a task which is reasonably easy to carry out. Making quotas easy to fill is more than a matter of just keeping the interviewers happy. If the quotas are too difficult to fill, the interviewers will have no choice but to go out of quota in order to complete their twenty interviews. Once they start having to go out of quota the rigidity of the rules collapses, and interviewers will be tempted to relax the quotas still further if they have no respect for the original quotas. Under the pressure of time on a typical opinion poll the interviewer's task is hard enough without it being made unnecessarily worse.

Notes

1 D. Rose and K. O'Reilly, *Constructing Classes: Towards a New Social Classification for the UK* (ESRC Research Centre for Micro-Social Change, University of Essex, 1997).

4

Methodology in practice: interviewing

I'm on the pavement,
Thinking about the government

The questionnaire

As I have explained previously, the main constraint on the questionnaire is the limited amount of material that can be used in the media presentation of the poll, so opinion-poll interviews rarely consist of more than around a dozen or so questions. Many books have been written about questionnaire design, and it is far too big a topic to go into in detail here, but there are a number of cardinal rules worth mentioning briefly, and some considerations which apply particularly to political polls, which are covered in more detail.

There are three vital attributes which every question must possess, and getting this part right is by far the most important part of most questionnaire design. These state that for any question in any questionnaire, the respondent must be:

- able to understand the question
- capable of answering the question
- willing to answer the question.

The first of these conditions requires that the question is simple, and capable of only one interpretation. The words used need to be those in common usage, and complex constructions should be avoided. Payne has produced a list of rules for the suitability of words in questionnaires, and while the rules are over-prescriptive if taken literally, they provide very useful guidelines.[1]

In order to achieve the goal of simplicity, it is important that the question includes only one construct. One of the commonest problems in question design, particularly in opinion polls, is the question which requires respondents to answer a question which is really two questions in one. The following example, intercepted before it reached an actual questionnaire, would be impossible for many respondents to answer.

> Q. Which of these best fits your own opinion of Tony Blair? He would be a good Prime Minister because he is strong and has firm policies, or he would be a bad Prime Minister because he would be weak and dominated by the unions.

The problem is that a respondent who thinks Tony Blair would be a good Prime Minister because he would be consensual, and prepared to be flexible about policy, would not be able to choose either option. If a draft question does contain two different questions in one, it should be broken down into two separate questions. The respondent's ability to answer the question is most likely to be threatened in two ways: by asking questions about matters outside the respondent's competence, and by putting an unrealistic strain on respondent's memory. Examples of the first include asking a single respondent in a large organisation about both production and personnel issues, or asking detailed questions about grocery shopping of someone who is not the main household shopper.

As for memory, there are no hard and fast rules about how far back it is reasonable to ask someone to remember, though common sense is, as so often, a good guide. Broadly speaking, the more significant the event, the further back it is reasonable to expect respondents to remember. The British Household Panel Study has successfully asked questions about changes in employment going back through the respondents' entire lifetimes, but it is difficult to collect accurate information about television viewing on the night before the interview.[2]

The respondent's willingness to answer the question will depend on how sensitive the subject matter is, and how sensitively the question is phrased. There are various ways of making sensitive questions seem less intrusive, exemplified by Alan H. Barton, but context is also critical.[3] A question on a fairly sensitive topic may be refused if it seems out of place or arbitrary, whereas another much more sensitive may be answered if it seems justified within the overall questionnaire. NOP recently asked young people detailed questions about their sexual behaviour, and had virtually no refusals.[4] In many surveys these questions would have seemed intrusive, and would not have been answered, but in the context of a questionnaire about awareness and use of condoms, and exposure to risks of HIV, the questions seemed reasonable to respondents, and were answered.

While the three golden rules of comprehension, ability to answer and willingness to answer apply to all questionnaires, the questionnaire design issue which most often affects opinion polls is that of leading questions. The good question does not lead the respondent in any way, but this rule is often broken when political opinion polls are conducted by organisations without experience in this area, though the sin is usually one of omission rather than commission. Pressure groups involved in a wide variety of issues often commission opinion polls which they hope to use to show popular support for their cause. Either intentionally, to try to maximise support, or unintentionally because they are merely reflecting the way they usually think, pressure groups often put forward leading questions, and it is the job of the research agency to rephrase them into more balanced ones. For this reason, question wording requires great care.

Question wording

The reason why question wording is so important is that it is very easy for the exact wording used in a question to affect the answers given, even if no conscious attempt is being made to influence the respondent. When two polls dealing with the same issue are published close together, but which have quite different answers, detailed examination of the questions asked often reveals small but significant differences between the two, which explain the different answers. Even matters such as whether the question was asked using a showcard (a visual prompt shown to the respondent with the possible answer categories on it), or with a list read out by the interviewer, or with the respondent allowed an unprompted choice, can have a considerable effect.

Although it is now very dated, one of the best examples of the effect of question wording on the answers received comes from the time of the 1975 referendum on Britain's membership of the Common Market. As the first-ever British referendum it provoked a great deal of methodological discussion, in particular about the ability of Prime Minister Harold Wilson to influence the outcome by his choice of the question to appear on the ballot. The *Daily Mail* commissioned NOP to conduct an experiment using different wordings. The starting point was the belief that almost any form of wording would contain some form of value loading, and would thus make one option more attractive than another. The only totally neutral option was to have just two words on the ballot:

In

Out

but this was felt to be too terse to be practical. However, as soon as any extra words were added, some form of steer was inevitable. Once this was accepted, the aim was to find two options which were a matching pair on either side of the simple In/Out option. One was slightly biased in favour of the Common Market, and one slightly biased against. These two options were:

Should Britain stay in the Common Market?

and

Should Britain leave the Common Market?

each with a 'Yes' and 'No' option. These would seem to be perfect mirror images of each other, with everyone who said 'yes' to one being expected to say 'no' to the other. However, because of a tendency for respondents, all other things being equal, to agree with an offered proposition rather than disagree with it – known variously as 'yea-saying', or the acquiescence response set – the first would be expected to produce a better result in favour of continued entry than the second.

In an attempt to quantify the effect of the bias being introduced, a scoring system was used, with each option being given a score to indicate its level of perceived bias. With the very simple option being scored 0 to indicate a complete absence of bias, the next two options were scored as +1, meaning a small amount of bias in favour of the Common Market; and −1, meaning a small amount of bias against it, respectively.

No one could have complained at either of these wordings being used, and most people would not see them as biased, but the theory being tested was that they were. The experiment then went on to test slightly stronger levels of expected bias, by introducing the government's own views into the question. In this next pair, the wordings were

The government recommends that Great Britain should stay in the Common Market

and

The government recommends that Great Britain leave the Common Market,

each being followed by the question 'Do you accept the government's recommendation?' with 'yes' and 'no' boxes. Again, since the government was calling the referendum to ask for support for its preferred policy, it would be hard for anyone to object to the use of questions like these, but again the hypothesis was that these would have a greater bias than the previous two. It may be hard to imagine in the current wave of cynicism about politicians, but many people, all other things again being equal, will tend to accept that the government knows what it is doing, on the grounds that they are experts and the public are not. Adding the government's imprimatur meant that the bias scores were higher, meaning a greater level of bias, and these options were scored at +2 and −2 respectively.[5]

Two other statements were included in the experiment, but these were extreme examples which most lay people would consider biased. They were therefore not options seriously likely to be considered, and the obvious bias seemed to confuse respondents, so they are not discussed here.

The central, no-bias question was asked twice, and the other versions were all asked once each, using split samples of around 1,000 per version from NOP's Random Omnibus Survey over a four-week period.[6] The ultimate result of the referendum – conducted some months after the experiment – was a victory for the stay in lobby by roughly two to one. Bearing this in mind, it is unsurprising that none of the versions produced a majority against the Common Market.

Figure 5 *Effect of bias in wording on 1975 European referendum results (%)*

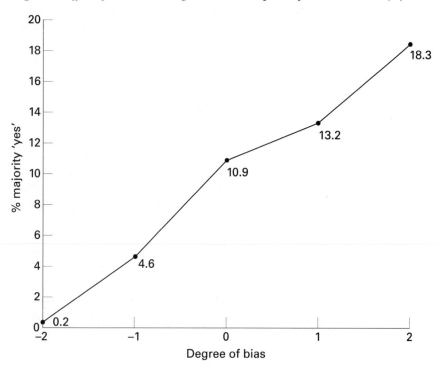

There was, however, a very wide range in the level of support, from a majority of less than 1% for the version scored as −2, through to a majority of 18% on the version scored as +2. In fact, although the scoring of the versions had been somewhat arbitrary – one could not, for example, be sure that the addition of the government to the question gave twice as much bias as the version which did not mention the government – the answers lay on an almost perfect straight line from −2 through −1 through 0 to +1 and finally to −2, as Figure 5 demonstrates.

As Figure 5 shows, by the use of words which most people would consider unexceptional, the overall result could vary by as much as 18% – a 9% swing. This is a somewhat specialist, and extreme, example, but it serves to show how easily voters can be swayed by a particular choice of words in a question.

Most of the important rules for good questionnaires do not deal with anything as dramatic as this example, and are largely based on common sense.

In the typical opinion poll, the two questions which require special treatment are the voting-intention question itself, and the question on likelihood of voting.

Any survey which asks people if they intend to vote or not, especially if it concerns a 'minor' election such as local or EC elections, will overestimate the proportion who actually do. In the last European elections in 1994, the turnout in Great Britain was 36%. An ICM poll which, after corrective weighting, proved an accurate predictor of the election result found over 50% said they had voted. (The survey was conducted after the Thursday election but before the results were published on the Sunday.) The picture is less extreme in general elections and significant by-elections, but there is still always some overclaiming.[7]

The reason for this is probably connected with social acceptability, often a factor in the interaction between interviewer and respondent. In Britain, voting in elections is very much seen as the norm – it is what good citizens do. Someone who does not intend to vote may well feel inhibited about admitting as much to an interviewer. On the surface, this would not seem to matter much, because the main aim of opinion polls is not to predict the turnout. However, at most elections, supporters of one main party are more likely to vote than supporters of the other. It is likely that those most likely to say in an opinion poll that they will vote and then not actually do so are those who are the least determined about voting and, in this case, the party they support will appear stronger in the poll than it does in practice. Inaccurate measures of likely turnout are thus a significant source of potential bias.

To try to minimise this overclaiming, the pollsters have developed a questioning technique which, while not having solved the problem, has gone some way towards reducing it. There are two elements to it, both of which depend on introducing deliberate bias, which in any other circumstance would see the question criticised for being leading.

The first is to tell respondents that one form of behaviour – not voting – is perfectly acceptable. A standard turnout question begins by explaining that non-voting is quite normal – 'As you may know, many people do not manage to vote in elections.' By letting respondents know that a lot of people fail to vote, the hope is that they will feel it is less embarrassing to admit that they are unlikely to vote, and so the question makes it less likely that respondents will overclaim. (The 'many people' approach is one of those identified by Barton as a way of encouraging people to answer sensitive questions.[8]) The use of the word 'manage' in the question is also important, as it implies that non-voting is not a conscious decision, but the result of good intentions being thwarted by circumstance. This almost subliminal point is further emphasised by repeating the word 'manage' in the question itself – 'How likely is it that you will manage to get along to vote?'

The underlying message here is that voting is such a major effort that it should be hardly any surprise if something occurs to prevent it. This makes it very definitely a leading question, but experience has shown that in this case a leading question produces more reliable answers. Even so the proportion who say they are 'likely' to vote is still usually far higher than the proportion that actually does.

The other way in which pollsters attempt to minimise overclaiming of turnout is to offer a list of options which emphasises not voting. As with many questions which involve respondents choosing from a number of options, a card with the various options on it is shown to respondents. Research has shown that items on the top of the list are more likely to be chosen than those at the bottom of the list. To counteract this it is common, when using show-cards, to have two versions, with the options in opposite orders on each. Thus one option might start with 'Very Satisfied' and finish with 'Very Dissatisfied', while the other would start with 'Very Dissatisfied'. In this way it is hoped that any respondent bias caused by order effect will be self-cancelling.

With the likelihood-of-voting question, only one version of the card is used, so that the first item each respondent sees is 'Certain not to vote'. As with explaining that lots of people don't vote, the aim is to make it as easy as possible for respondents to choose the not-voting option.

The options on the list are also carefully chosen, again to encourage respondents to choose the 'honest' option. There are two very similar items at the beginning of the list (mirrored at the end) – 'Certain not to vote' and 'Very unlikely to vote'. (Some pollsters even add another one – 'Extremely unlikely to vote' – in between those two.) The idea behind this is that again research has shown that many people are reluctant to choose the extreme ends of a list. If the second item is very strong, and similar in meaning to the first item, the two can validly be combined. The overall effect is to maximise the number who say they are very unlikely to vote or certain not to.

Sometimes there may not be a great deal of difference in voting behaviour between those giving different answers to the likelihood-of-voting question, but at times when support for one party is much more solid than that for another, there can be great differences between the overall voting-intention figures and those for people who are certain to vote. If an election is not imminent, this may be merely commented on in passing, or even kept as internal information and not actually published, but as an election looms, and people are likely to have thought more about whether or not they will vote, pollsters pay increasing attention to these figures.

During an election campaign, any differences in party support based on likelihood of voting would feature strongly in any analysis of the poll. This would usually be in the form of fine-tuning the election prediction, and both the results based on all respondents and the results based on those certain to vote would be presented alongside each other. By the time of the final poll before the election, normal pollster behaviour is to take only those who say they are certain to vote, or possibly those certain or very likely, and treat this group as the actual voters. The final polls on election eve are normally published with figures based only on those certain or very likely to vote, and not on the voting intention of the entire sample.

Having weeded out at least some of those who are more likely to say they will vote than actually do so, the pollsters' other standard questionnaire trick is the voting-intention question itself. The first thing to note is that, except during an election campaign, pollsters always ask respondents to imagine that there will be an election tomorrow. The wording is always something very similar to 'If there were a general election tomorrow, how would you vote?' Those more concerned with usage than grammar say 'If there was a general election tomorrow', and some ask 'Which party would you vote for?', on the grounds that in every poll asking 'How would you vote?', at least one wag can be relied upon to say 'by putting a cross against my preferred candidate'; but the basic wording of the question is always the same.

This is done to ensure that respondents are all responding in the same way. If, two years before a general election, people were asked 'How do you intend to vote in the next election?', they could interpret the question in many different ways. Some, especially those who always vote the same way, would know beyond any doubt, while others would just assume that their current intention would be the same as their election-day one. Others, however, would seek to hedge their answers with conditionals, either known or vague. 'I'll vote Conservative so long as William Hague is (isn't) still leader', or 'unless mortgage rates come down I'm not voting Labour next time' are both examples of known conditionals. Other people will just say they will vote for a particular party 'if they get their act in order', or 'unless they muck up the economy'.

Asking people to guess what the economy, or their personal circumstances, will be like in two or three years' time is to set them an impossible task. By always asking about a hypothetical next-day election, pollsters seek to collect every respondent's *current* voting intention. While this ensures comparability between polls conducted at around the same time, it does lead to a temptation among commentators to regard all polls as predictive, regardless of how far off the election is. Thus a poll showing Labour 20% ahead, two years before the likely date of the next election, may be headlined 'POLL PREDICTS LANDSLIDE LABOUR VICTORY', when all the poll is actually doing is indicating who is ahead at that moment. The doyen of British polling, MORI Chairman Bob Worcester, is fond of describing the election process as a horse race, with an opinion poll merely a photograph showing who is ahead at any one moment. As an any gambler will tell you, the horse that leads by several lengths coming up to the last fence is not guaranteed victory.

This problem is mainly one of the interpretation of polls rather than anything to do with their actual conduct, but a different problem which may have arisen more recently concerns respondent reaction to the whole idea of polling. It has long been apparent that voters use by-elections as a means of expressing a protest against the government of the day, and it seems that this trend may be strengthening. Between 1987 and 1992 the Conservative government lost seven by-elections in seats that they had won at the 1987 general election, and yet in the 1992 general election they recaptured all seven of them – an unprecedented feat. It now appears that voters may be using opinion polls in the same way – to send a message to an unpopular government without running the risk of actually changing it – and this compounds the difficulty of treating at face value question wording which posits an election tomorrow. This point is further discussed in Chapter 6.

The other standard question approach common to all the pollsters is the follow-up or 'squeeze' question. Anyone who says that they are not sure how they would vote, or who refuses to answer, at the initial voting question is asked a supplementary question. This is 'Which party are you most inclined to support?', or possibly 'Which party is it most likely that you will vote for?'

The reason for the inclusion of this second question is purely pragmatic – history has shown, and the present has continued to show, that pollsters get better results by having it than by not having it. When the extra question was first introduced, it was found to increase the Labour vote, and make it closer to the actual figure, but currently it is the Conservatives who have tended to gain from the squeeze question. The theory behind the question is that some people are hesitant to reveal their voting intention, and thus refuse to answer, or say they are not sure, but when pressed will give a party name. Also, there will be those who are genuinely undecided, but if they can be pressed to give the party to which they lean more than the others, the chances are that the majority of them will go on and actually vote for that party.

As long as successive elections continue to show that the figures including the squeeze question turn out to be more accurate than the simple question alone, the squeeze question will continue to be used. In analysing the results, the answers from the two questions are treated equally. Someone who answers 'Conservative' at the first question is given no more weight in the final results than someone who is undecided at the first question, but who answers 'Conservative' at the squeeze question. *A priori* one might expect to have to give Conservatives from the squeeze question a score of only half a vote, or three-quarters of one, but no algorithm has been found which works better than equal treatment.

Question order

For the most part, the order in which questions appear in a survey does not have a major impact on the results. Schuman and Presser concluded after a number of experiments that 'order effects are not pervasive in a typical attitude survey', but while certainly not pervasive, order effects can be significant in certain types of question.[9]

The main way in which question order has been said to have an effect on the results of opinion polls concerns the difference between what are referred to as warm-start and cold-start questionnaires. The cold-start approach involves asking respondents how they would vote if there were a general election tomorrow as the very first question in the interview. In the warm-start approach, on

Figure 6 *Sample warm-start questionnaire*

Q1 SHOWCARD A How good or bad a job do you think the government is doing at running the country? CODE BELOW

Q2 SHOWCARD A How good or bad a job do you think the Prime Minister, Tony Blair, is doing? CODE BELOW

Q3 SHOWCARD A How good or bad a job do you think the Leader of the Opposition, William Hague, is doing? CODE BELOW

Q4 SHOWCARD A How good or bad a job do you think the Leader of the Liberal Democrats, Paddy Ashdown, is doing? CODE BELOW

	Govt	Blair	Hague	Ashdown
Very good	1	2	3	4
Fairly good	1	2	3	4
Neither good nor bad	1	2	3	4
Fairly bad	1	2	3	4
Very bad	1	2	3	4
Don't know	1	2	3	4

Q5 Which party would you vote for if there was a general election tomorrow?

IF UNDECIDED OR REFUSED ASK Q6

Q6 Which party are you most inclined to support?

	Q5	Q6
Conservative	1	1
Labour	2	2
Liberal Democrat	3	3
Scottish National Party	4	4
Plaid Cymru	5	5
Other party	6	6
Would not vote	7	7
Undecided	8	8
Refused	9	9

the other hand, the voting-intention question is preceded by a small number of other political opinion questions. Typically these would concern satisfaction with the party leaders and with the government as a whole. A typical warm-start questionnaire is shown in Figure 6.

With a cold-start questionnaire the same questions may well be asked, but voting intention would be at the very beginning of the questionnaire and would then be followed by the satisfaction questions. Historically, Gallup have tended to be in the warm-start camp while the other main pollsters tended to be in the cold-start camp. However, somewhat confusingly, Gallup themselves switched to the cold-start approach at the beginning of each election campaign.

The theory behind the warm-start approach was that it made for more accurate measurement of support for the different parties, particularly for minor parties such as the Liberals. By making respondents think about each of the parties in turn, and in particular by reminding them about the existence of the

Liberal Party, this approach forced respondents to consider more carefully their answers to the voting question. Common belief had it that Liberal support would always be higher in a warm-start than in a cold-start questionnaire.

While there were these differences between the pollsters during the 1970s, no one, including the pollsters, paid a great deal of attention to the issue of warm start versus cold start until the fissures in the Labour Party led to the foundation of the Social Democrat Party in 1981, and then the subsequent combining of the Social Democrat Party with the Liberals into the Alliance in the 1983 general election.

With an entirely new party coming on to the scene, considerations as to whether voters who may actually vote for that party in an election some months or years later would even be aware of it at the time of the poll, led to a sudden increase of interest in the relative merits of cold- and warm-start questionnaires. The Social Democrats themselves believed very strongly that it was important that questions should be asked about their own party leader as well as about the Conservative, Labour and Liberal party leaders, and that this should be done before the voting questions. Their leader, Roy Jenkins, was a popular man with higher approval ratings than the other party leaders, and the feeling was that if voters were asked about Roy Jenkins first of all this would serve not merely to remind them about the existence of the SDP, but also to make voters feel more favourable towards it because of their approval of Mr Jenkins.

In the early 1980s, therefore, NOP set out to test whether it should switch from its traditional cold-start approach to a warm-start approach in order to reflect better the standing of the SDP. Rather than switch over straight to the alternative method, some split-sample tests were carried out. These were done using NOP's Random Omnibus Survey, a weekly survey with a sample of around 1,800 adults of voting age. For a number of weeks half the sample were given the warm-start approach, and the other half of the sample were given the cold-start approach. If the generally held theories about warm start were true, we would expect consistently to find a higher score for the Social Democrats, by perhaps 2% or 3%, in each of the warm-start versions as opposed to the cold-start versions.

However, while this was indeed sometimes the case, there were other occasions where there was no difference between the two methods, and others still where the SDP scored higher under the cold-start approach than under the warm-start approach. Even with relatively large sample sizes of over nine hundred, analysis of these experiments was made more difficult by the fact that there were often measurable political differences between the two halves, where in one week the cold-start version containing a disproportionately high number of people who voted Conservative at the previous election, whereas in the following week's experiment the cold-start version may contain relatively too many who had voted Labour at the last general election.

All in all, over several months of experimentation carried out initially at the time of the founding of the SDP, and then at the time of the formation of the Alliance, NOP failed to find any consistent effect caused by use of warm start rather than cold start. On the whole, warm-start versions were more likely to lead to higher figures for the minor parties, but the differences between warm and cold start were at the very margins of significance. Because of this NOP chose not to amend their methods and continue to use the cold-start approach.

The question re-emerged in earnest, however, following the 1992 election. The reasons for the polls' failure to predict the result are discussed in more detail in Chapter 6, but some evidence suggests that question order may have been a factor.

During the election NOP carried out a large-scale survey on behalf of the Independent Television Commission, or ITC (the body charged with regulating the independent broadcasters in Britain). At each election the ITC carries out a survey among the general public asking them about their media usage during the election campaign and their views of the way the media portrayed the election. The ITC's purpose in doing this is to investigate whether the broadcast media are fulfilling their obligations during an election campaign.

The design of the poll was a large-scale, face-to-face survey conducted in the week of the election itself, followed by a much shorter telephone follow-up of a sub-sample of respondents, conducted some while after the election. One of the principal aims of the research was to see how opinion varied before and after the election, and for this reason the data from the original survey were not processed at all until after the election. With so many other surveys going on it was a relief to have one client who was not in a hurry for its data. It should be stressed that although the survey was on a larger scale, to the extent that the questionnaire was much longer than in a normal opinion poll, the basic design of the survey was exactly the same at that used for all the opinion polls.

The extra length meant that all interviews had to be carried out in respondents' homes, whereas for the opinion polls some interviews were carried out in the street and some in the home; but in terms of the basic sample design – use of quota rather than random sampling, and the actual application of the quota themselves – the ITC poll was carried out in just the same way as NOP's and all the other pollsters' opinion polls. Given the similarity of method, my colleagues and I were stunned to discover, when we eventually got round to processing the data a week or so later, that the voting-intention question from the ITC poll was completely out of line with the prediction polls discussed in Chapter 6. A simple average of the six polls conducted over the last three days of the campaign showed Labour ahead by 1.5%. The actual result showed the Conservatives ahead by 7.6%. The ITC first-stage survey, conducted on 6 and 7 April, showed the Conservatives ahead by 9% (see Table 13).

The ITC poll was clearly very different from all the other pre-election polls, but why should this be the case? One possible explanation lay in a key difference between the ITC survey and the prediction polls in the design of the question-naire. It has been mentioned that the ITC questionnaire was much longer than the usual opinion poll, being typically between 20 and 30 minutes long. Perhaps more importantly, the voting-intention question came at the very end of the interview, along with all the standard demographics.

Table 13 *1992 general election ITC poll (%)*

	Conservative	Labour	Liberal Democrats
Average of published polls	38.0	39.5	19.2
Actual result	42.8	35.2	18.3
ITC media poll	42.0	33.0	22.0

Because the ITC's aim was not to predict the election results, but merely to understand how the supporters of different parties felt the various media had performed, the voting-intention question was an analysis variable only, and thus tucked away with all the other analysis variables. This then gave a clue to a possible reason for the difference in results.

One of the purposes of the ITC survey was to discover the extent to which television had succeeded in explaining the issues of the election, by analysing whether those who had watched a lot of television were more familiar with the policies of the main parties than those who had not. To attempt to measure this (though this does not resolve the question of the direction of causality) the ITC questionnaire asked respondents how much they knew about each party's policy on different areas. Thus respondents were asked how much they knew about Labour's taxation plans, about the Conservatives' plans for public trans-port, about the Liberal Democrats' plans for education, and so on. This would then have had the effect of making them think much more about the different policies being put forward by each party than would normally be the case for a respondent stopped in the street and asked straight away which party were they going to vote for.

In particular, one of the reasons cited for the polls' failure to measure the Conservative win was that many people told the pollsters that they intended to vote Labour (which indeed they did at the time), but they then subsequently went on either not to vote at all or to vote for the Conservatives in the general election. Labour were certainly seen as the popular option and there was almost certainly some reluctance among Conservative voters to profess their support publicly. The idea that people might be unwilling to admit to support for a party seen as unpopular was first put forward by Noelle-Neumann,[10] in what she describes as a 'spiral of silence'. (This whole issue is discussed in more detail in Chapter 6.) If some form of spiral of silence was operating against the Conservatives in 1992, then Labour was likely to be the first answer to come into many, basically undecided, respondent's minds.

Labour's weakness throughout the election was certainly its economic and particularly taxation policies, and one of the criticisms levelled (with the benefit of hindsight) at the pollsters after 1992 was that they had relied too much on a simple voting-intention question, and had not looked enough at the answers to questions on the economy and taxation which showed Labour to be lagging well behind the Conservatives.

We at NOP thus speculated that by forcing respondents in the ITC survey to consider the taxation implications of a Labour government, many who would otherwise have said that they intended to vote Labour went through a process during the interview similar to the process that many others went through during the last few days of the campaign: a process of looking at the real possibility of a Labour government and then recoiling from it.

If this were true, then we had succeeded in measuring party support more accurately, simply by taking the warm-start approach to very considerable extremes. This then raised the question of whether this was a repeatable effect, and then whether it is possible to make practical use of the effect. One problem that would need to be overcome was that if it was only this extreme version of warm start which had had the required effect, then the impact of any warm start was likely to be altered, depending on the exact questions used. Our theory was that it was the concentration of questions on Labour's tax policy that had frightened off their less committed supporters. Had the questionnaire concentrated on some of the more unpopular aspects of the Conservatives' policy, and asked respondents only about Labour's policies on social issues such as health, welfare and education (where they enjoy almost permanent large leads over the Conservatives), one might expect any effect to be in the opposite direction.

This raises the serious question about comparison between the polls if this approach were widely used. Let us suppose that during a general election campaign there are a number of pollsters, each polling weekly for different Sunday newspapers. It has been common recently for British media clients of the polls to have a particular topic each week on which the poll concentrates, as well as the obvious questions on voting, economic competence, and so on. But one week a Sunday paper may commission a poll concentrating on the state of the National Health Service, and the next week look in detail at people's willingness to spend more on taxes to fund welfare programmes, and then in the third week look at the strengths and weaknesses of a series of individual politicians.

If the approach of putting the voting question at the very end of the questionnaire were followed, one might reasonably expect that within the first week Labour would do relatively well, in the second week relatively badly, and the third week the popularity of the parties would depend on the different popularity of various politicians. This would then lead to swings from one poll to another which would appear to be far greater than was actually the case, and the problem would then be significantly compounded if the various Sunday newspapers did not follow a consistent pattern of concentrating first on topic A and next on topic

B. If during week one the *Sunday Times* decided to concentrate its poll on the National Health Service while the *Sunday Telegraph* concentrated on taxation, and then the following week the two reversed, one would expect the *Sunday Times* poll to show a considerable decrease in the Labour vote from week one to week two, while the *Sunday Telegraph* would be expected to show a considerable increase. The secondary analysis of published opinion polls, by television news programmes in particular, is an important part of the opinion-polling process, and chaos would ensue if the trendlines of support recorded by the different poll-sters for any one party seemed to swap back and forth over each other.

One possible way round this would be to agree on a standard set of questions which would always precede the voting-intention question: a sort of super-warm start. However, it is likely that there would need to be several such ques-tions for the whole process to work consistently, and it is very unlikely that clients would be prepared to spend most of their valuable questionnaire space on a series of questions which are not necessarily of interest to them and which are identical to those used by their competitors. Any possible impact of this 'very warm' start could thus be damaging to the pollsters. It was therefore important to discover whether the ITC poll was part of the consistent trend of order effects, or whether it was merely a fluke.

The problem with putting this theory to the test is that most opinion polls are so short that they do not provide a comparison with the much longer interview used by the ITC survey, and just adding voting intention at the very end of an opinion-poll questionnaire would not be a fair test of the whole process. Fortunately, soon after the election NOP had the opportunity to carry out a much more reliable test. We were commissioned to carry out a series of surveys as part of a political tracking study, each on a much larger scale than typical opinion polls.

The surveys were carried out using random rather than quota sampling, with samples of around 1,500, and crucially with questionnaires of 30 or even 40 minutes in length. The questionnaire gave comprehensive coverage to the strengths and weaknesses of the two main parties and thus provided the oppor-tunity for a very real test of whether the ITC poll was part of a consistent trend. For reasons of analysis, each interview always started off with a question to establish people's underlying feeling of attachment to one party rather than another, as this was seen as more important for long-term strategic purposes than simple voting intention, so our cold-start version had voting intention not as the very first question but as the fifth question in the interview. A random half of the sample was assigned to this condition, while for the other half the voting-intention question was moved from the fifth question in the interview to the very last question before the demographics. Other than this the two versions of the question were identical.

The first test suggested that we may indeed have been seeing the same effect again. In the version where the voting questions came at the beginning of the questionnaire, the Conservatives scored 26%. In the version where it came at the end of the questionnaire they scored 29% – a change in the same direction as that seen in the ITC poll. However, closer inspection revealed an immediate divergence from the ITC figures: whereas the ITC poll had shown Labour with a much lower vote than all the opinion polls, in the first wave of our tracking study Labour also scored 3% higher in the version where the question was asked at the end of the interview than in the version where it was asked at the beginning. The victim of this swing to both Conservative and Labour was not surprisingly the Liberal Democrats, whose vote was 7% lower in the warm-start version than in the cold-start version.

While conflicting with the ITC findings, this was still not inconsistent with the same basic thesis. The tracking questionnaire concentrates almost exclusively on the Conservative and Labour parties, and thus one might hypothesise that having suggested so strongly to respondents that the election was a two- rather than a three-horse race, that less firmly attached Liberal Democrat supporters switched to one of the two main parties after answering a whole series of questions about one or other of them.

Unfortunately this theory too fell by the wayside after the second survey. Here there was no significant difference between the cold and 'super-warm' starts for any of the three main parties. We carried out the experiment for one further wave and here the results were quite different again. The Conservatives scored 3% higher in the version where the voting-intention question was asked first, but Labour scored exactly the same in the two versions. The experiment thus gave no support to the theory that placing the voting-intention question at the end of the survey has a significant impact on the results, though this is not to say it never exists.

It still seems likely that question-order effects played a major part in the difference between the ITC poll and all the other pre-election polls in 1992. However, the subsequent analysis suggests that if this were the case it was due to factors which were either particular to an election situation as opposed to the gap between elections; or was specific to that particular election, for there is no sign of any consistent pattern of a similar trend in the years after 1992.

The interviewer's task

Once the sampling points have been drawn, the quotas set, and the questionnaire written, a poll then becomes dependent entirely on the skills of the interviewer. Who then are these people, on whom the reputation of the polling companies ultimately depends?

Fieldwork management

Interviewers are almost invariably freelances, rather than full-time employees. They work varying numbers of hours, from no more than one day a fortnight on a particular survey, to more than fifty hours a week. They are offered work on an assignment-by-assignment basis, either by an area manager or by head office. The agency does not guarantee to offer any amount of work, and the interviewer is free to accept or refuse each assignment. However, an interviewer who repeatedly turns down work will be offered less and less, while if the agency does not offer enough work, the interviewer will go to other agencies to look for work. Indeed, many interviewers do work for more than one agency, to achieve the balance of work they want.

The traditional image of the interviewer is that of a middle-aged, middle-class woman, working for pin money. This was always a caricature, and now bears virtually no relation to reality. Interviewers are increasingly likely to be male, frequently young, and many are working as the main income-earner of their household. As the requirements of their task have become more demanding, interviewers have become increasingly professional. At the same time, legislation, mainly from the European Parliament, which aims to give part-time workers the same rights as full-time staff on matters such as sick pay and holidays, is hastening a process which will probably culminate in full-time, employed field forces.

All interviewers receive comprehensive training before starting work, and interviewers moving from one company to another have to retrain. Training covers the different techniques of random and quota sampling, ways of dealing with respondents, the importance of asking the questionnaire exactly as written, plus company-specific matters such as administrative procedures. All new interviewers are also accompanied by field supervisory staff on their first day's work, and again at six-monthly intervals thereafter, to ensure that they are following the rules correctly.

Working on their own, dispersed across the whole country, there is always a temptation for interviewers to cheat, and to make up interviews altogether, or else to conduct them, but only ask a few of the questions, and then make up the other answers later. All market research companies take steps to ensure that if interviewers are cheating they are detected, and fired, as soon as possible. The big companies check up with each other when taking on interviewers who have worked for other agencies, so that those who are caught cheating can be effectively blacklisted. The main weapon against cheats is a constant process of checking back on a sample of interviews. This is done by a mixture of postal checks, telephone calls, and personal visits by field supervisory staff.

Because so much rests on it, most field managers will prefer to use their most experienced interviewers on opinion polls, and there certainly are advantages in using interviewers who are familiar with the system. Also, because opinion polls are widely viewed as providing interesting and rewarding work, they are also often used as 'reward' to interviewers who have helped out by taking on other difficult or unpopular assignments.

On a typical opinion poll each interviewer has twenty interviews to conduct, and typically a single day in which to conduct them. There have been experiments with two-day polls, or weekend polls, but they have not tended to produce significantly different results, and have meant that at least some of the results are an extra day out of date when published. Depending on the publication deadlines of the client, and in particular whether it is a newspaper or broadcast media client, it is sometimes possible to start fieldwork on one evening and finish it the next morning.

Getting the work out

Twenty years ago, the norm was for questionnaires to be posted out to interviewers, who would in return post the completed questionnaires back, thus giving a minimum turnround time of three days. Since then the reliability of the postal service seems if anything to have declined, and it would be a brave or foolish pollster who expected 100 packs posted on one day all to arrive the next. Also, demands for results to be ever more up to date mean that even a three-day turnround is not considered satisfactory.

The solution has been the use of the telephone or the fax, either as the main means of transmission, or as back-up. For despatch of work, the post is still the main means, since the great majority of interviewers will receive their work the next day, and it is not a major task to take emergency steps for the few who do not. At first this was done by telephone, with the head-office field staff, or the local area field manager, ringing the interviewer and dictating the questionnaire. This is not as terrible a task as it first sounds, since the questionnaire is fairly short, for the reasons discussed above.

Writing out the questions and answers may not be that difficult, but there remains the problem of being able to cope with twenty respondents. For the interviewer with reasonable access to a photocopier (not so common fifteen years ago as it is today) this was not a major problem, but one could hardly expect an interviewer to write out the questionnaire twenty times. The solution was to redesign the questionnaire so that the answer categories appeared on the extreme left of the page, with space for the answers from twenty respondents to be recorded each in a separate column across the rest of the page. This reduces the printing and faxing time, but also means that interviewers who work regularly on opinion polls can be sent a supply of blank forms, with the columns already marked. In the case of a requirement for a really rush job, all the interviewer then has to do is write out the questions and the answer categories once, and that is enough for the whole assignment. Figure 7 shows two pages from an example of this kind of questionnaire, used for a *Sunday Times* survey in 1997.

Using this approach, NOP conducted a poll soon after the Argentine invasion of the Falklands. An executive of the client, the *Daily Mail*, rang me at home at about 8 p.m. on the Sunday evening after the invasion, wanting a very urgent poll. I was able to phone some of the area field managers at home, and asked

Figure 7 *Sample opinion-poll questionnaire*

Q6 Who would you trust more to make you and your family better off: a Conservative government under Mr Major, or a Labour government under Mr Blair?

	1	2	3	4	5	6	7	8	9	10	11	12	13	14	15	16	17	18	19	20	21	22
Conservative government	1	1	1	1	1	1	1	1	1	1	1	1	1	1	1	1	1	1	1	1	1	1
Labour government	2	2	2	2	2	2	2	2	2	2	2	2	2	2	2	2	2	2	2	2	2	2
Neither	3	3	3	3	3	3	3	3	3	3	3	3	3	3	3	3	3	3	3	3	3	3
Don't know	4	4	4	4	4	4	4	4	4	4	4	4	4	4	4	4	4	4	4	4	4	4

Q7. The general election is on 1 May. Have you definitely made up your mind about who you will vote for?

	1	2	3	4	5	6	7	8	9	10	11	12	13	14	15	16	17	18	19	20	21	22
Yes	1	1	1	1	1	1	1	1	1	1	1	1	1	1	1	1	1	1	1	1	1	1
No	2	2	2	2	2	2	2	2	2	2	2	2	2	2	2	2	2	2	2	2	2	2
Will definitely not vote	3	3	3	3	3	3	3	3	3	3	3	3	3	3	3	3	3	3	3	3	3	3
Don't know	4	4	4	4	4	4	4	4	4	4	4	4	4	4	4	4	4	4	4	4	4	4

Q8. Regardless of who you will vote for, who do you think will win the general election?

	1	2	3	4	5	6	7	8	9	10	11	12	13	14	15	16	17	18	19	20	21	22
Labour	1	1	1	1	1	1	1	1	1	1	1	1	1	1	1	1	1	1	1	1	1	1
Conservatives	2	2	2	2	2	2	2	2	2	2	2	2	2	2	2	2	2	2	2	2	2	2
Liberal Democrats	3	3	3	3	3	3	3	3	3	3	3	3	3	3	3	3	3	3	3	3	3	3
Others	4	4	4	4	4	4	4	4	4	4	4	4	4	4	4	4	4	4	4	4	4	4
Don't know	5	5	5	5	5	5	5	5	5	5	5	5	5	5	5	5	5	5	5	5	5	5

Q9. **SHOWCARD A** Which of the parties do you think has the best policies on these issues?

a) Keeping taxes down

	1	2	3	4	5	6	7	8	9	10	11	12	13	14	15	16	17	18	19	20	21	22
Conservatives	1	1	1	1	1	1	1	1	1	1	1	1	1	1	1	1	1	1	1	1	1	1
Labour	2	2	2	2	2	2	2	2	2	2	2	2	2	2	2	2	2	2	2	2	2	2
Liberal Democrats	3	3	3	3	3	3	3	3	3	3	3	3	3	3	3	3	3	3	3	3	3	3
Other party	4	4	4	4	4	4	4	4	4	4	4	4	4	4	4	4	4	4	4	4	4	4
(Don't know)	5	5	5	5	5	5	5	5	5	5	5	5	5	5	5	5	5	5	5	5	5	5

Figure 7 (*continued*)

b) Managing the economy

	1	2	3	4	5	6	7	8	9	10	11	12	13	14	15	16	17	18	19	20	21	22
Labour	1	1	1	1	1	1	1	1	1	1	1	1	1	1	1	1	1	1	1	1	1	1
Conservatives	2	2	2	2	2	2	2	2	2	2	2	2	2	2	2	2	2	2	2	2	2	2
Liberal Democrats	3	3	3	3	3	3	3	3	3	3	3	3	3	3	3	3	3	3	3	3	3	3
Other party	4	4	4	4	4	4	4	4	4	4	4	4	4	4	4	4	4	4	4	4	4	4
(Don't know)	5	5	5	5	5	5	5	5	5	5	5	5	5	5	5	5	5	5	5	5	5	5

c) Improving the National Health Service

	1	2	3	4	5	6	7	8	9	10	11	12	13	14	15	16	17	18	19	20	21	22
Conservatives	1	1	1	1	1	1	1	1	1	1	1	1	1	1	1	1	1	1	1	1	1	1
Labour	2	2	2	2	2	2	2	2	2	2	2	2	2	2	2	2	2	2	2	2	2	2
Liberal Democrats	3	3	3	3	3	3	3	3	3	3	3	3	3	3	3	3	3	3	3	3	3	3
Other party	4	4	4	4	4	4	4	4	4	4	4	4	4	4	4	4	4	4	4	4	4	4
(Don't know)	5	5	5	5	5	5	5	5	5	5	5	5	5	5	5	5	5	5	5	5	5	5

Q10. If Europe goes ahead with the single currency, Britain could adopt it, and give up the pound, or it could remain outside the single currency. Do you, in general: **READ OUT AND CODE ONE ONLY**

	1	2	3	4	5	6	7	8	9	10	11	12	13	14	15	16	17	18	19	20	21	22
Support the idea of Britain joining the single currency	1	1	1	1	1	1	1	1	1	1	1	1	1	1	1	1	1	1	1	1	1	1
Oppose it, and believe we should retain the pound	2	2	2	2	2	2	2	2	2	2	2	2	2	2	2	2	2	2	2	2	2	2
(Don't know)	3	3	3	3	3	3	3	3	3	3	3	3	3	3	3	3	3	3	3	3	3	3

Q11. From what you have seen and heard, do you think the Conservative Party, if re-elected, would take Britain into the single currency over the next five years?

	1	2	3	4	5	6	7	8	9	10	11	12	13	14	15	16	17	18	19	20	21	22
Yes	1	1	1	1	1	1	1	1	1	1	1	1	1	1	1	1	1	1	1	1	1	1
No	2	2	2	2	2	2	2	2	2	2	2	2	2	2	2	2	2	2	2	2	2	2
(Don't know)	3	3	3	3	3	3	3	3	3	3	3	3	3	3	3	3	3	3	3	3	3	3

Q12. And do you believe that the Labour Party, if elected, would take Britain into the single currency over the next five years?

	1	2	3	4	5	6	7	8	9	10	11	12	13	14	15	16	17	18	19	20	21	22
Yes	1	1	1	1	1	1	1	1	1	1	1	1	1	1	1	1	1	1	1	1	1	1
No	2	2	2	2	2	2	2	2	2	2	2	2	2	2	2	2	2	2	2	2	2	2
(Don't know)	3	3	3	3	3	3	3	3	3	3	3	3	3	3	3	3	3	3	3	3	3	3

Q13. Many Conservative candidates, and some ministers, have said they would not support taking Britain into a single currency. John Major says that his party's policy is to 'wait and see' whether to join. Do you think this shows that (a) The Conservative Party is divided between those who are for and against Europe; (b) the Conservative Party is overwhelmingly anti-European but Mr Major will not admit it; or (c) most people in the Conservative Party are genuinely behind the party line of 'wait and see'?

	1	2	3	4	5	6	7	8	9	10	11	12	13	14	15	16	17	18	19	20	21	22
a) The Conservative Party is divided on Europe	1	1	1	1	1	1	1	1	1	1	1	1	1	1	1	1	1	1	1	1	1	1
b) The Conservative Party is anti-European but Mr Major will not admit it	2	2	2	2	2	2	2	2	2	2	2	2	2	2	2	2	2	2	2	2	2	2
c) Most follow the party line	3	3	3	3	3	3	3	3	3	3	3	3	3	3	3	3	3	3	3	3	3	3
Don't know	4	4	4	4	4	4	4	4	4	4	4	4	4	4	4	4	4	4	4	4	4	4

Q14. The Conservatives are putting forward different policies on Europe. Some people say this is good because individual Tory Party candidates are allowed to make up their own minds. Others say this just shows John Major is a weak leader, unable to control his party. Which of these come closest to your views?

	1	2	3	4	5	6	7	8	9	10	11	12	13	14	15	16	17	18	19	20	21	22
a) Major is unable to control his party	1	1	1	1	1	1	1	1	1	1	1	1	1	1	1	1	1	1	1	1	1	1
b) It is good Major is allowing debate	2	2	2	2	2	2	2	2	2	2	2	2	2	2	2	2	2	2	2	2	2	2
Neither	3	3	3	3	3	3	3	3	3	3	3	3	3	3	3	3	3	3	3	3	3	3
Don't know	4	4	4	4	4	4	4	4	4	4	4	4	4	4	4	4	4	4	4	4	4	4

Q15. Do Conservative disagreements on Europe make you: READ OUT AND CODE ONE ONLY

	1	2	3	4	5	6	7	8	9	10	11	12	13	14	15	16	17	18	19	20	21	22
More likely to vote Conservative	1	1	1	1	1	1	1	1	1	1	1	1	1	1	1	1	1	1	1	1	1	1
Less likely to vote Conservative	2	2	2	2	2	2	2	2	2	2	2	2	2	2	2	2	2	2	2	2	2	2
It makes no difference	3	3	3	3	3	3	3	3	3	3	3	3	3	3	3	3	3	3	3	3	3	3
Don't know	4	4	4	4	4	4	4	4	4	4	4	4	4	4	4	4	4	4	4	4	4	4

Q16. Who do you think is the stronger Prime Minister, John Major or Tony Blair?

	1	2	3	4	5	6	7	8	9	10	11	12	13	14	15	16	17	18	19	20	21	22
John Major	1	1	1	1	1	1	1	1	1	1	1	1	1	1	1	1	1	1	1	1	1	1
Tony Blair	2	2	2	2	2	2	2	2	2	2	2	2	2	2	2	2	2	2	2	2	2	2
Neither	3	3	3	3	3	3	3	3	3	3	3	3	3	3	3	3	3	3	3	3	3	3
Don't know	4	4	4	4	4	4	4	4	4	4	4	4	4	4	4	4	4	4	4	4	4	4

Figure 7 (*continued*)

Q17. The Conservatives say it is hypocritical of Tony Blair to send his son to a grant-maintained school, when Labour opposes them. Mr Blair says parents have always chosen, like him, to send their children to church schools. Do you (a) believe Mr Blair is being hypocritical, and should have sent his son to the nearest school to his home; (b) think Mr Blair is right, because he is only doing the best for his son; or (c) think that, whether . . . private matter which should not feature in the election?

	1	2	3	4	5	6	7	8	9	10	11	12	13	14	15	16	17	18	19	20	21	22
(a) Believe Blair is hypocritical	1	1	1	1	1	1	1	1	1	1	1	1	1	1	1	1	1	1	1	1	1	1
(b) Think Mr Blair is right	2	2	2	2	2	2	2	2	2	2	2	2	2	2	2	2	2	2	2	2	2	2
(c) It is a private matter	3	3	3	3	3	3	3	3	3	3	3	3	3	3	3	3	3	3	3	3	3	3
(d) Don't know	4	4	4	4	4	4	4	4	4	4	4	4	4	4	4	4	4	4	4	4	4	4

Q18. Do you think, in general, that politicians are telling you the truth in this election?

	1	2	3	4	5	6	7	8	9	10	11	12	13	14	15	16	17	18	19	20	21	22
Yes	1	1	1	1	1	1	1	1	1	1	1	1	1	1	1	1	1	1	1	1	1	1
No	2	2	2	2	2	2	2	2	2	2	2	2	2	2	2	2	2	2	2	2	2	2
Don't know	3	3	3	3	3	3	3	3	3	3	3	3	3	3	3	3	3	3	3	3	3	3

Q19. **SHOWCARD B**. I would like you to think ahead to the day after the election. If you wake up on 2 May and find out that the Tories are still in power, how will you feel?

	1	2	3	4	5	6	7	8	9	10	11	12	13	14	15	16	17	18	19	20	21	22
Very pleased	1	1	1	1	1	1	1	1	1	1	1	1	1	1	1	1	1	1	1	1	1	1
Fairly pleased	2	2	2	2	2	2	2	2	2	2	2	2	2	2	2	2	2	2	2	2	2	2
Not pleased but I could live with it	3	3	3	3	3	3	3	3	3	3	3	3	3	3	3	3	3	3	3	3	3	3
Fairly disappointed	4	4	4	4	4	4	4	4	4	4	4	4	4	4	4	4	4	4	4	4	4	4
Very disappointed	5	5	5	5	5	5	5	5	5	5	5	5	5	5	5	5	5	5	5	5	5	5
Don't know	6	6	6	6	6	6	6	6	6	6	6	6	6	6	6	6	6	6	6	6	6	6

each in turn to ring one or two more. Each supervisor was asked to find three or four interviewers who could work the next day. They rang round their interviewers all evening, and told the ones who could do it to stand by their phone at 10 a.m. on Monday, by which time NOP and the *Daily Mail* would have agreed the questionnaire.

At 10 a.m. prompt, a great team of NOP executives, field staff, and anyone else available began ringing the interviewers, and all had the questionnaire by 11 a.m. As the area managers already had copies of all the quota sheets, they were able to give out the quota information on the Sunday night as the interviewers were booked. The interviewers were told they must phone back to give details of their results by 5 p.m., and the full results were with the *Daily Mail* by 5.30 p.m., less than twenty-four hours after the survey was commissioned, for publication in Tuesday's paper.

As technology has continued to spread, this somewhat crude technique of transferring the information by laborious reading-out and writing-down has been increasingly replaced by the less laborious faxing of questionnaires. At first only one or two interviewers had a fax at home, usually in connection with their spouses' business, then a few more found local offices which had a fax which they could use for a small fee, and now even interviewers in rural Scotland have a fax within reach. Nowadays, if work sent out by post has not arrived the next day, any interviewer can receive an emergency copy by fax. Presumably there will come a time when every interviewer will have fax or e-mail capabilities at home, and the post will no longer be used at all.

Within the constraints of the quota system, interviewers have complete freedom to choose their respondents, although they may have to operate under various geographical constraints, as discussed above, and there may be other rules as well. Some agencies insist that all interviewing is done in the street, on the grounds that many people who are not easily available at home can be intercepted near shops or railway stations. Others insist that all interviewing is conducted in people's homes, to ensure those who rarely go out, or who only travel by car, have a chance to be interviewed. Still others insist on a mixture of the two, and in this case it is common for there to be a particular control on interviewing working men, such as that all working men in the sample must be interviewed at home and after 5 p.m. The logic behind this is a theory that samples of working men obtained in the street are likely to be biased towards shopkeepers, delivery workers, traffic wardens, and so on. However, as with the polls conducted at different times of the week, or over different numbers of days, there seems to be no consistent differences between in-home, in-street or mixed polls.

Getting the results back

Their quotas complete, the interviewers' last task is to get their results back to head office. This too was all done by post in the past, but the need for speed is even greater for the return of results than the sending-out of work, and so the post is now hardly used at all. One reason is the relative effect of delay on out-going and returning post. If an interviewer's pack does not arrive by the day fieldwork is due to start, it is not difficult to get blank questionnaires out to the interviewer by phone or fax, as described above, and the delay is only an hour or so. If a pack of completed work posted back by the interviewer does not arrive at head office the next day, there is nothing that can be done to access those results until the post eventually turns up.

If results are required the next day, then post is simply not an option, but there are a number of alternatives. One of the easiest is to get interviewers to phone back their results, so that they can be tallied up, and this used to be common practice, although it only really worked if all that was required were answers from the total sample, with possibly one crossbreak. Having completed their quotas, interviewers would add up the answers from all their twenty respondents to produce tallies. Thus at Q1 there might be ten 'yes', six 'no', and four 'don't know', at Q2 seven 'Conservative', six 'Labour', seven 'both equally', and 1 'don't know', and so on.

If the interviewers collected the answers for men and women separately, they could do separate tallies for men and women. The answers or the total sample could then be created in the office by adding the two together, and in this way the client could have answers for all adults and could analyse the differences between men and women. Alternatively, interviewers could produce a tally for all their twenty interviews, and then two additional ones, for Labour and Conservative supporters. The choice would vary from survey to survey, depending on the subject matter, and any variable could be used for the extra count if it were seen as particularly important. Thus if the survey were about education, there might be a separate count for those with school-age children. It would not matter what the variable was, so long as the interviewers never had to do more than three counts in all. At the end of a day's interviewing, patience tends to wear thin.

If there were twelve questions on the questionnaire, and interviewers did tallies for the total, plus separate tallies for Labour and Conservative support-ers, then each interviewer would have thirty-six sets of question answers to read out, with each question typically having four responses. Taking 144 sep-arate figures from each of 50 interviewers (a total of 7,200 data items) would be desperately time-consuming, so to speed the process up, interviewers phoned their tallies not to head office, but to a team leader. For a poll with fifty inter-viewers there might be eight team leaders, each taking results from around six interviewers. When they had received calls from all their team, they would create their own tallies of the sum of all their team's results. These eight inter-mediate tallies would then be phoned through to head office, where the calls could easily be handled by a team of three or four researchers in a short period of time. Finally, the intermediate tallies would themselves be summed to produce the final totals, usually within two hours of the end of interviewing.

This approach was fine so long as only simple totals, or totals plus one analysis variable, were required, but if full analysis is required – analysing by age, sex, past voting behaviour, current voting behaviour, and so on – then it is necessary to analyse each respondent's answers separately, rather than as just part of a subtotal tally, and some means of getting data from each questionnaire in turn into the computer is necessary.

In the halcyon days whilst it was still part of a state-run industry, and before hours and outlets were dramatically cut back, Red Star Parcels offered a very effective way of getting completed questionnaires to London. Provided interviewers could get to the local Red Star office before it shut (and in big cities they never shut), then the work would be in London either later that evening or, in the case of the more remote areas, by early the next morning.

In the 1983 general election NOP polled for the *Mail on Sunday*, with fieldwork taking place on a Friday, and detailed tables required by the middle of Saturday afternoon. Interviewers worked until 5 p.m., which gave most of them plenty of time to get to a Red Star office. As the executive in charge of the survey, it was my task, at about 11 p.m. to drive in a loop round all the London Red Star termini collecting packages, take them home, serial-number them and batch them up ready for punching on to cards. (These were the days when the punched card was still the main way of entering data on to the computer for analysis.) At about 8 a.m. on Saturday I did the rounds again to collect the stragglers, and the whole job would be ready for a taxi to take it to the punch company by around 10 a.m. By early afternoon the cards all came back to NOP by taxi, they were run through the card reader, and by mid-afternoon the tables were ready to go to the client.

Such simple, almost primitive, methods offered the best way to get full tables quickly, until the spread of telephone interviewing, and in particular of computer-assisted telephone interviewing (CATI). Although it took a long time for the pollsters to consider *interviewing* by telephone on opinion polls (see Chapter 9), the technology was used to get answers from field interviewers on to a head office computer system more quickly.

With CATI the telephone interviewers all have computer screens in front of them, on which the question wording and answer options appear. They simply enter the code number beside the answer each respondent chooses, and that result is immediately stored in the computer. One of the principal attractions of CATI for research in general is that all instructions for filtering and so on are handled automatically by the computer, thus removing the major source of interviewer error. The attraction of CATI for the pollsters is that it allows field interviewers to get their data entered on to a computer by using the telephone.

An equivalent version of the field questionnaire is set up on the CATI system, and a number of telephone interviewers stand by at the appointed time. As the field interviewers complete their quotas, they phone in, and read out each in turn from the first respondent, then each answer in turn from the second respondent, and so on through all twenty respondents. All the field interviewer needs to read out is the question number, and the answer code which has been ringed – there is no need to read out 'Conservative': reading out '1' is all that is needed.

In about twenty minutes all the answers from a quota of twenty can be read out and entered into the CATI system and, once all the interviewers have done this, the effect is just the same as sending the questionnaires back for normal data entry. The full data set from each respondent is available, and any question can be analysed against any other. The cost is much greater than posting work back, as the field interviewers have to be paid extra for the extra task, and there is the additional cost of telephone interviewers, but since it allows full analysis to be available on a survey within a few hours of the end of fieldwork (even less time if necessary; one just adds more telephone interviewers), the benefit to the client far outweighs the cost.

Analysis

It was stated earlier in this section that it is often difficult for a media client to find space for the answers from all the questions in a typical poll, and this is true even if the only published figures are total figures for the whole population. The amount of cross-analysed data that ever gets used is very little. Nevertheless, standard practice is to analyse each question against a standard crossbreak of variables such as age, sex, class, previous voting behaviour, certainty to vote, and so on. The research team and the client both study the tables, and if there are any major differences between subgroups this can be included in the write-up of the poll.

Analysis of opinion polls is very similar to analysis of any other kind of survey, though it is worth making one particular point about the actual calculation of the final voting-intention figure, particularly since one of the main reasons why polls from organisations not accustomed to conducting them are often very different from the main run of published polls is because the standard procedure for calculating voting intention has not been followed. It has traditionally been the case for pollsters simply to add together the figures from the two voting questions (the initial question and the leaner question), remove any residual undecideds and refusals – those who didn't name a party at the leaner question – plus those who said they would not vote, and rebase the published percentages on all those who did name a party. An example of this is shown in Table 14.

The main justification for this is that it makes the party-support figures add up to 100% (give or take 1% either way for rounding), which is what the actual election results always do. There is no category marked 'undecided' or 'refused' in the actual election results, and if calculations are required of the level of swing from the previous general election to the time of the poll, both sets of figures need to be on the same base.

One of the features of polling in the USA which can be confusing when the results are viewed from this side of the Atlantic is that there is often a switch during the campaign from presenting the figures based on all respondents to presenting the figures based just on those naming a party. Even worse, polls can be published simultaneously, one of which bases the figures on all respondents, and the other on all those naming a party. If poll A on Monday shows 40% for Clinton, 30% for Dole, 10% for Perot and 20% undecided, and then on Tuesday Poll B shows 50% for Clinton, 40% for Dole and 10% for Perot, it is hard to tell immediately if this represents any change.

Table 14 *Calculation of final voting intention*

	Initial question (no.)	Squeeze question (no.)	Initial & squeeze (no.)	Those naming a party (no.)	Final voting figure (%, based on 878)
Conservative	255	27	282	282	32
Labour	322	27	349	349	40
Liberal Democrat	190	8	198	198	23
Other	45	3	48	48	5
Would not vote	15	3	18	—	—
Undecided	108	57	57	—	—
Refused	65	48	48	—	—
Total	1,000	173	1,000	878	100

Repercentaging does not have to be done by simply cutting out the unde-cideds and refusals. As will be seen in Chapter 6, this practice, like every other, came under scrutiny after the 1992 election, and this is an area where the poll-sters have begun to refine their techniques, though as yet no consensus has emerged on exactly what is the best approach.

Weighting

Weighting of the data is a common part of most survey research. There are two main reasons for weighting survey data: to correct for any imbalances in the original sample design, and to correct for any imperfections in the achieved sample. The former, known as post-stratification weighting, is the more methodologically pure of the two. As discussed in Chapter 2, the aim of any sampling process is to ensure that, as far as possible, all people have an equal chance of selection. Thus constituencies are selected with a probability propor-tional to size to avoid any bias in favour of people living in smaller constituen-cies. However, it is not always possible to achieve this, and indeed there may be times when chances of selection are deliberately set to be different.

One example of this would be a survey about attitudes to racial discrimina-tion. A representative sample of 1,000 people would only contain around 40 people of black or Asian origin – far too few to be able to comment on separately. A common practice would be to boost the number of ethnic minority respondents to a minimum analysable level of 100 black and 100 Asian respondents. This permits comment about each of these groups, but the sample of 1,000 is now no longer nationally representative, since it contains 20% ethnic minority respondents instead of 4%. Weighting is therefore applied to the full data set to restore ethnic minority respondents to their true proportion. This done by giving each ethnic minority respondent a weight of 4/20, i.e. 0.2. In effect, each ethnic minority respondent is being counted as only 0.2 of a person.

In this example, weighting was necessary to correct for deliberate oversampling of one group, but in random sampling it is often necessary to apply weighting to correct for unavoidable but undesirable differences in the chance of selection. Almost all opinion polls are sample of individuals – people are speaking about their own opinions, not on behalf of their whole household. The electoral register provides an ideal sampling frame for this, since it is a list of individuals, and it is possible to select every nth person from the list. For many years the electoral register was the main sampling frame used for random surveys of individuals, but after the introduction of the poll tax in 1990, it became clear that many people were no longer registering to vote, in the hope that by not being on the electoral register they might also escape inclusion on the poll tax register.

The electoral register thus became a biased sampling frame, and most random surveys switched to the use of the Postcode Address File (PAF) instead. This was a much more complete list than the electoral register, since it recorded only the address and not who was living there, and was thus not subject to the same problems as the electoral register, but PAF is a sample of addresses, not of people. This means that every address has an equal chance of selection, regardless of the number of people living there. This in turn means that any PAF-based sample will be biased towards people living in small households.

Consider a hypothetical population of 1,000 households, 500 of which contain 1 person, and 500 of which contain 2. Of the 3,000 people in the population, one-third live in one-person households and two-thirds in two-person households. A PAF sample of 100 households, drawn by selecting every tenth address, will include 50 one-person households and 50 two-person ones. Since the norm is to conduct only one interview in each household, the achieved sample will have 50% living in one-person households instead of 33%.

Since people living in one-person households are likely to be very different from those in two-person ones, this is a significant bias, and one that needs to be corrected by weighting. The chance of each household being selected is equal, but the chance of any individual being selected is different. Those living in sampled one-person households are sure of selection, while those living in two-person households have only a one in two chance of selection. The means to correct for this is to give each interviewed person a weight equal to the number of people in his or her household. (This also copes with households of three, four, or even more people.)

Post-stratification weighting of this kind is carried out on all surveys where chances of selection are deliberately or accidentally different, but the less scientifically acceptable weighting is corrective weighting. This is applied when the achieved sample does not match the population as a whole on any known parameters. We know from the Census that around 47% of the adult population of Great Britain is male. If a poll is conducted and the achieved sample is only 40% male, it is clearly biased. Since we know what the 'true' figure is, it is a simple matter to apply corrective weighting to restore the male proportion to 47%. It is common practice to use corrective weighting on opinion polls, the main weighting variables being age, sex, housing tenure, car ownership and social class, but while some of these are relatively uncontroversial, there is some doubt about what the 'true' figure is for others. As Chapter Six discusses, one of the problems with the polls in 1992 was that they were weighting to targets which later proved to be inaccurate.

Weighting will always be a part of sample surveys, but it should be used with care, and anyone analysing polls should in particular be wary of major changes brought about purely by weighting.

Notes

1 S. L. Payne, *The Art of Asking Questions* (Princeton University Press, 1951).
2 The British Household Panel Study is conducted by the ESRC Research Centre on Micro-Social Change at the University of Essex.
3 A. H. Barton, 'Asking the embarrassing question', *Public Opinion Quarterly*, 22:1 (1968).
4 M. Thomas, M. Bloor and A. Crozier, *Young People and International Travel: HIV Prevention and Health Promotion* (Health Education Authority, 1997).
5 There is of course no evidence that the lower level of bias is exactly half as biased as the upper one, and it would be possible to score the options as +1 and +3, or +1.0 and +1.5, but convention generally assigns value in a simple integer procession when assigning scores to scales in questionnaires.
6 In a typical week the Omnibus has 2,000 respondents, so a random half of respondents were given one version of the wording, and the other half another version. Because the two halves are drawn randomly from the same overall sample, differences between them should not be caused by sample differences.
7 It is true that there are those who are unable to vote because of infirmity, or indeed death. Since these people are also at best unlikely to be interviewed, one would expect an interviewed population to have a higher turnout than the total population, but this is not sufficient to explain all the discrepancy.
8 Barton, 'Asking the embarrassing question'.
9 H. Schuman and S. Presser, *Questions and Answers in Attitude Surveys: Experiments on Question Form, Wording and Content* (Academic Press, 1981).
10 E. Noelle-Neumann, *The Spiral of Silence* (University of Chicago Press, 1984).

5

Recent history, 1970–1992

Yesterday's gone but the past lives on,
Tomorrow's just one step beyond

As we have seen in Chapter 1, the 1970 election proved to be a major shock for the pollsters. Inevitably when the predicted polls were almost unanimous in calling the wrong winner, after the election there was both a widespread inquiry, and also widespread speculation that this meant the end of opinion polling. If the polls could get it so spectacularly wrong, the argument went, what was the point of newspapers paying for them in the first place? There were also concerns about a knock-on effect on the wider world of market research in general. Here the argument ran that if polls were unable to get something as important and as clear-cut as voting correct, what chance did surveys have of measuring far more ephemeral things, such as the intention to purchase one brand of baked beans rather than another, or the recall of an advertising campaign?

On the latter point, NOP's Frank Teer wrote a robust defence of the principles of opinion polling in a document produced for circulation to NOP's clients.

> Finally, then, what is the relevance of these results to market research? Are the techniques used in market research in any way discredited? The answer to this second question is undoubtedly not.
>
> In the first place, the degree of accuracy expected of opinion polls is far higher than that required in most marketing research. As already discussed, the line between being right and wrong in opinion polling is finer than it is in market research.
>
> Secondly, in so far as it is the object of the market researcher to measure trends, the opinion pollster has, by all the evidence previously discussed, measured those trends.
>
> Thirdly, the subject of measurement in political opinion polling seems to be more subject to change than the subjects measured in most market research enquiries. Apart from the findings of the opinion polls, the actual evidence is that there was a substantial change in allegiance between April and early June. No

brand share gains or loses at this rate, no newspaper gains or loses circulation to that degree in that period of time. In other words, there is far greater stability in the market place than there is at the polling booth, and consequently the risks of inaccurate measurement are substantially less.

Fourthly, most market research is designed to establish behaviour and attitudes as they exist at a given point in time. Very little market research work is predictive, although many people take the view that it is not predictive enough. However, as all of us know, prediction is a most hazardous activity. Human behaviour is too complex and changeable to be comprehended by more forecasting models. This is particularly true of political behaviour where the stimulus to change within a short period of time is so much greater than in any market place situation.

There are, then, problems which the political pollster faces which are not found in market research enquiries. Opinion polling is often incorrectly regarded as simple headcounting.

In fact, it is a fairly hazardous and in many ways complex operation. Because of this, opinion polls have made incorrect forecasts before in this country and elsewhere and will probably do so again in the future. This is not, however, a reflection of the techniques used, but of the hazards of the game. When things do go wrong we are bound to be scoffed at and criticised but none of this detracts from the usefulness and general reliability of sample survey research. As one of our clients said after this election: 'This won't affect our use of research, but I hope it persuades our competitors that market research is a waste of money.'

Fortunately for the market and media research industry and indeed business in general, not many people are likely to be persuaded of that.

The subsequent history of research and polling shows that Frank Teer was, of course, correct. The market research industry continued to grow, despite the setback of the 1970 opinion polls. For the vast majority of commercial market-research surveys, to be within 7% or 8% of the true finding is a far greater level of accuracy than is normally required. In choosing, for example, between two variants of a new packaging design, a manufacturer will be looking for one to have a clear lead amongst the likely buyers. Such a manufacturer does not conduct a survey to find out if one is preferred by 51% and the others by 49%, and then to proceed accordingly, but instead to establish whether one of them is preferred by 80% and the other by only 20%, and errors of $\pm$ 10% are still not a problem with data of this kind. There was inevitably a certain amount of hand-wringing about the impact on commercial survey research in the immediate aftermath of the 1970 election, but this was soon forgotten.

Commercial polls, then, carried on just as before, and, confounding all predictions, opinion polls proved to do exactly the same. In the 1970 general election there were five polls which can be regarded as prediction polls. In the election of February 1974 there were six. Nor was it a case of the old order being thrown out and replaced by new pollsters. All five of the organisations that conducted prediction polls in 1970 did so again in 1974, and there was one new entrant to the fray: Business Decisions, who polled for the *Observer*.

When it came to polling day, the pollsters learned a lesson that the American polls had learned in 1948. This was that it is not enough simply to measure public opinion as closely as it is reasonably possible to expect a poll to do, but it is also essential the get the order of candidates correct. In research terms, the improvement in the polls from 1970 to February 1974 was dramatic. In 1970 the average error on the gap between the parties across the five prediction polls was 6.5%. In February 1974, across the six prediction polls, it was a mere 2.4%. This is well within the level of sampling error one might expect, given the sample sizes used. The problem was that all but one of the polls said that Labour was going to lose the election, when of course they actually won it, in the third of Harold Wilson's four election victories.

Table 15 *Actual and predicted results, February 1974 general election (%)*

Pollster	Bus. Dec	ORC	Harris	NOP	Gallup	Marplan	
Newspaper	*Observer*	*London E. Standard*	*Daily Express*	*Daily Mail*	*Daily Telegraph*	*Ldn Wknd Television*	**Actual result**
Fieldwork	21 Feb.	n/a	26–27 Feb.	23–27 Feb.	26–27 Feb.	n/a	28 Feb.
Sample size	1,056	2,327	3,193	4,038	1,881	1,649	–
Conservative	36.0	39.7	40.2	39.5	39.5	36.5	38.8
Labour	37.5	36.7	35.2	35.5	37.5	34.5	38.0
Liberal	23.0	21.2	22.0	22.0	20.5	25.0	19.8
Others	3.5	2.4	2.6	3.0	2.5	4.0	3.4
Labour lead	+1.5	−3.0	−5.0	−4.0	−2.0	−2.0	−0.8
Error on lead	−2.3	−2.2	−4.2	−3.2	−1.2	−1.2	(2.4)
Average error on share	1.7	1.2	1.8	1.5	0.7	2.9	(1.6)

This is why the British experience matched that in the USA in 1948. If you can predict party share very close to the actual figure in a close election you will have done all you can reasonably be expected to do, but if it turns out that the party you predicted to be narrowly behind proves to be narrowly ahead, you will be forever damned as having called the wrong winner. The polls said Labour would lose; Labour won; *ergo*, the polls were wrong. Grossly oversimplistic though this analysis is, it is probably unreasonable to expect media commentators to say anything else. However, closer examination of the results from February 1974 shows that the polls were even more correct than appeared at first sight (see Table 15). The polls said Labour would lose narrowly, and lose narrowly is exactly what Labour actually did in February 1974, despite going on to form the next government. The explanation for this paradox lies in the way the British electoral system works, and in what it is exactly that the polls are trying to measure.

The polls seek to measure public opinion. They ask each member of their samples how they intend to vote, and by assuming that the small number of people they interview are representative of the great mass of voters in total, the pollsters assume that voting behaviour amongst the entire electorate will be the same as in their samples. The important words here are 'voting behaviour amongst the entire electorate'. What the pollsters are trying to do is to measure the share that each party will have of the total popular vote. But the British electoral system does not necessarily transfer the parties' relative share of the popular vote to a similar share of seats in the House of Commons. There is an intervening mechanism of over 600 individual share-of-the-vote contests, fought out separately in each constituency. In the absence of any system of proportional representation, there is no guarantee whatsoever that a party's share of the MPs in Westminster will match its share of the popular vote. It has long been accepted that the Liberals or Liberal Democrats receive a far lower allocation of seats under the first-past-the-post system than they would under any form of proportional representation, but the same problems can afflict the two main parties as well.

In the February 1974 election Labour did indeed lose as far as the popular vote was concerned, in getting 38% of the vote compared with 38.8% for the Conservatives. Despite this, because the electoral system in 1974 worked to the advantage of Labour, they ended up with a plurality of five seats. In practice it took fewer votes to elect a Labour MP than it did to elect a Conservative MP. Given that the prediction polls on average suggested a 2% Conservative lead, it would have been galling enough for the pollsters had Labour in fact won by 1% and they had taken a lot of flak for getting the parties in the wrong order. What made it even more galling was that in fact Labour did indeed lose by 1%, and they still took a lot of flak for getting it all wrong.

The February 1974 polls told a broadly consistent story. Six of them showed a Conservative lead between 2% and 5%, with the one outlier being Business Decisions in the *Observer*, who ended up showing a Labour lead of 1.5%. Closest to the actual result were Gallup and Marplan, who each had the Conservatives winning by 2% instead of the 1% they actually did win by. Then came ORC, predicting a 3% Conservative lead, followed by NOP on 4%, and finally Harris, who predicted a 5% Conservative lead. As far as methodology is concerned two of the six – Harris and NOP – used random-sampling methods while the other four all used quota sampling. The two which used random sampling were two of the three most inaccurate in terms of overestimating the Conservative lead.

The second 1974 election saw the last published general election polls based on random sampling, although random sampling's final swansong was the European referendum of 1975. In the October 1974 general election both Harris and NOP used random sampling, but by the time of the referendum NOP had made the switch to quota sampling, leaving Harris alone on random. In fact in October 1974, it was one of the random surveys that was the least reliable (see Table 16).

The average error on party share across all the pollsters was a very respectable 1.6%. All the polls underestimated the Conservative share of the vote, but most were within 3%. The real exception was NOP's random sample, which underestimated the Conservatives by 5.7%. The other pollster using random sampling, Harris, did better but was still worse than three of the four who used quota sampling.

Table 16 *Actual and predicted results, October 1974 general election (%)*

Pollster	Bus. Dec	ORC	Harris	NOP	Gallup	Marplan	
Newspaper	Observer	London E. Standard	Daily Express	Daily Mail	Daily Telegraph	Sun	**Actual result**
Fieldwork	2 Oct.	5–9 Oct.	5–9 Oct.	5–9 Oct.	3–8 Oct.	8 Oct.	10 Oct.
Sample size	2,071	1,071	678	1,978	954	1,024	–
Conservative	35.5	34.0	35.0	31.0	36.0	33.0	36.7
Labour	40.0	42.0	43.0	45.0	41.5	44.0	40.2
Liberal	20.0	19.0	19.0	19.0	19.0	19.5	18.8
Others	4.5	4.0	3.0	4.0	3.5	3.5	4.3
Labour lead	4.5	8.0	+8.0	14.0	5.5	11.0	+3.5
Error on lead	+1.0	+11.0	+4.5	+4.5	+2.0	+7.0	–
Average error on share	0.7	3.0	1.2	1.6	0.8	2.1	–

The pollsters had another chance to restore their reputation in the European referendum of 1975 (see Table 17). The referendum has already been discussed in Chapter Four, but the important thing in 1975 was the opportunity that it gave the pollsters to compare their measurements against an actual result without any intervening factors. As was stated above, in a general election there is always the chance that the polls will correctly predict the popular share of the vote but fail accurately to predict the share of seats that will result for each party. With the referendum there was no question of first past the post, no aggregation of results from individual constituencies; instead there was just a simple total of the vote expressed as percentages of all those who voted.

Whilst this of course means that the pollsters are more masters of their own fate, and less likely to be blamed for things for which they cannot really have any responsibility, it is also the case that they have no excuses if they fail to get the answer right. In fact there were five 'prediction' polls conducted shortly before the referendum, by the now established pollsters – Gallup, ORC, Harris, Marplan and NOP.

Table 17 *Actual and predicted results, 1975 European referendum (%)*

Pollster	ORC	Harris	NOP	Gallup	Marplan	**Actual result**
Yes	74	72	68	68	68	67
No	26	28	32	32	32	33
Yes lead	48	44	36	36	36	34
Error on lead	+14	+10	+2	+2	+2	–

Of the five prediction polls, three – Gallup, Marplan, and NOP – were as close to the final result as is reasonable to expect. Each overestimated the majority of the 'yes' vote by just 2%. The two others, however, were far further away. ORC massively overestimated the 'yes' lead by 14%, while Harris were not far behind, overestimating it by 10%. It was this failure that led Harris also to abandon random sampling, and from 1979 until 1997 published opinion polling in Britain was exclusively based on quota sampling.

The 1979 general election saw NOP polling once again for the *Daily Mail*, Marplan once more for the *Sun*, and Gallup yet again for the *Daily Telegraph*. This election also saw the first published poll by MORI. Market & Opinion Research International had originally been set up in 1969 by Kansan *émigré* Robert Worcester, jointly funded by the American Opinion Research Corporation and NOP. From the 1970 election onwards it had conducted private polling on behalf of the Labour Party, but it had not had a nationally published poll until 1979. MORI celebrated their entry into public polling by working for no fewer than three newspapers; the *Sunday Times*, the *Daily Express* and the London *Evening Standard*. They also continued to carry out Labour's private polling. ORC continued to carry out the Tories' private polling but were in this election without a published client. The other new – or rather returning – entrant to the polling field was RSL, who worked for the *Observer*, as they had done in 1966.

The pattern of the polls in the 1979 election was pretty clear and broadly consistent throughout the campaign (see Table 18). The one exception was RSL, which consistently showed Tory leads far higher than the other pollsters. Without exception, the other pollsters had the Tories at 48% ± 2 and Labour at 40% ± 2 over the first three weeks of the campaign. The biggest lead shown was thus only 12% and yet in their first poll RSL showed the Conservatives 21% ahead. Subsequent urgent discussions on methodology between RSL and the other pollsters led to some revisions in their methodology. Most critically they had failed to follow up the simple voting-intention question with the subsidiary 'squeeze' question to those undecided or refused. They switched to the more standard questioning for all subsequent polls but continued to be out on a limb throughout the campaign, making difficult the task of analyst Professor Anthony King, who had to write the polls up as if he believed them to be correct.

Table 18 *Actual and predicted results, 1979 general election (%)*

Pollster	Gallup	MORI	Marplan	NOP	MORI	
Newspaper	Daily Telegraph	Daily Express	Sun	Daily Mail	London E. Standard	**Actual result**
Fieldwork	30 Apr.– 1 May	29 Apr.– 1 May	1 May	1–2 May	2 May	3 May
Sample size	2,348	947	1,973	1,069	1,089	–
Conservative	43.0	44.0	45.0	46.0	45.0	44.9
Labour	41.0	39.0	38.5	39.0	37.0	37.7
Liberal	13.5	13.5	13.5	12.5	15.0	14.1
Others	2.5	3.0	3.0	2.5	3.0	3.3
Conservative lead	2.0	5.0	6.5	7.0	8.0	7.2
Error on lead	−5.2	−1.8	−0.7	−0.2	+0.8	–
Average error on share	1.6	0.6	0.5	1.2	0.5	–

After this very flat start to the campaign (RSL apart) the final week saw some signs of movement. This was begun by a MORI poll in Saturday's *Daily Express* showing the Tory lead at only 3%, followed by an NOP poll in Tuesday's *Daily Mail* actually showing a Labour lead, though one of less than 1% and statistically inseparable from the parties running neck and neck. It is possible to interpret this movement, particularly in comparison with the final prediction polls, as a sign of an electorate first reacting against the possibility of a large Conservative majority, but then having considered the dangers of flirting with another Labour government, bouncing back to support the Tories again. It is more likely, however, that polls early in the week, especially the NOP one, simply underestimated the strength of the Conservative position.

Of the five polls that were conducted in the last two or three days before the election, four predicted a Tory lead within 2% of the actual figure, and three were indeed within 1%. The outlier was Gallup, which, having been the most accurate in both the 1974 elections, was the least accurate in 1979, underestimating the Conservative lead by a little over 5%. It is noticeable that the two polls which continued fieldwork until 2 May – the day before election day – were the two which finished up closest to the actual result. NOP predicted a Conservative lead of 7% compared with an actual figure of 7.2% while MORI, who conducted all their fieldwork on the day before the election, predicted a Tory lead of 8%.

If the talk among poll-watchers during the election campaign was all of RSL, perhaps the most interesting story was one which was not even told at the time. MORI had been commissioned by the *Sunday Times* to conduct a panel survey for them throughout the campaign, selecting a sample in the normal way at the start of the campaign, and then returning to those same respondents on a weekly basis during the campaign, to see how opinions changed. However, a strike throughout the whole election period meant that the poll results never appeared. Because it was unclear whether the *Sunday Times* would resume publication before the election, the poll went ahead as originally planned, although the results were only written up after the election.

The 1979 election was the first general election I worked on, and my main responsibility was to manage the fieldwork for the MORI panel. (Since MORI did not have its own field force at that time it subcontracted interviewing to NOP.) It was a surreal experience going through the full process of conducting a poll each week without any certainty whether it would ever be published. Right up to the last moment we were making plans to supply camp beds to the office so that we could carry out and report on a post-election wave in time for the following Sunday's paper. Although the paper never appeared, the poll was written up during the campaign by Kellner,[1] and subsequently by Worcester.[2]

The principal aim of the panel study was not so much to try to predict who was going to win the election, as the other polls were broadly doing, but to try to explain why any movements detected during the campaign should have happened. After a recent run of general elections up to 1997 when relatively little has changed in the poll figures during the campaign, it is easy for us to forget that in the elections immediately preceding 1979, it appeared that the election had been decided in the last week or so of the campaign. The purpose of the *Sunday Times* panel was to try and explain why such a change should take place, and in particular, in the final wave, to ask those who had voted why they had chosen to support the party that they eventually did.

As stated above, the published polls suggested that Labour 'won' the campaign itself, finishing far closer to the Tories than the polls at the outset of the campaign had suggested. This was borne out by the MORI panel. Over the four weeks of the survey, 8.5% of the sample switched away from the Conservatives to some other party. Over the same time the Conservatives gained 4.5% of the electorate, meaning that overall they lost 4% over the campaign. Over that same period Labour both gained and lost 6.5%, leaving no net change. Labour thus gained 4% on the Tories during the course of the election campaign.

One of the most interesting things about any panel study is the way it shows how gross change is so much larger than net change. The figures quoted above represent a net gain to Labour of 4%, but this conceals a gross change involving 13% of the electorate, most of it obviously self-cancelling. Another of the interesting findings often derived from political panel studies is the extent to which indecision sets in during the campaign, with people who are supporters of a party in one week then becoming undecided in the next week. In many cases they return to the party they originally started out with, and one has to be wary of attributing too great an import to this change, but the 1979 MORI panel also shed interesting light in this respect. During the course of the campaign three-quarters of those who started off as 'don't knows' decided to support one party or another. Of these, 33% decided to vote Labour, while only 26% went to the Tories.

The most interesting feature in polling terms about the first Thatcher government was the fact that, during the course of it, all three parties were at one time shown in the polls to be supported by half the electorate. Once the usual new government honeymoon had worn off, Labour as the mainstream opposition moved into the lead in the polls, a pattern seen during the life of almost every parliament. Labour peaked at 52% in an NOP poll in February 1980, but then came the internecine rivalries which were to lead to a split and the defection of the 'Gang of Four' to form the Social Democratic Party. The subsequent accord between the Liberals and the Social Democrats to form the Alliance tapped into a major swing in the public mood. By the end of 1981 it was the Alliance's turn to win the support of half of the electorate, reaching 50% in a Gallup poll in December 1981.

This huge swing in the national polls was matched by a spectacular series of by-election victories in seats previously felt unwinnable, such as Shirley Williams's win in Crosby. However, some of the initial support wore off as the Alliance was forced to face up to the realities of being a new party, with arguments over party leadership, policy and candidate selection. By the spring of 1982 the Alliance had fallen back from its peak.

At this stage all three main parties were fairly equal at around 30%. By June of the same year the Tories were once more riding high in the polls, with MORI showing them on 48%. The obvious explanation for this dramatic return to the Tories is the Falklands War which began in April 1982, though detailed analysis by political scientists such as David Sanders of Essex University of the polling trends compared with economic indicators suggests that a rise in economic fortunes played as important a role in the rise in Conservative support.[3] (Sanders in fact subsequently took the model developed for the Falklands further, and was able to use it to predict the 1992 general election very closely, although the same model did not work in 1997.[4])

Whatever the reason for this change in party fortunes, the important point as far as the 1983 election is concerned is that the Conservatives, having initially trailed massively behind Labour, and then trailed massively behind the Social Democrats, found themselves with a commanding lead over Labour (see Table 19). Throughout 1983 the Conservatives consistently polled in the low to mid-forties while Labour found themselves in the low to mid-thirties. The Conservatives ended the election campaign roughly where they had started it, finally polling 44%, but there was a dramatic change in the fortunes of Labour and the Liberal/SDP Alliance. Having begun the campaign with little more than half Labour's vote share, by election day the Alliance had virtually caught them up, making the most interesting aspect of the election the question of who would come second to the Tories. In the end Labour's support held firm and they ended up with just 2% more of the vote than the Alliance, thus quite possibly staving off an irreversible decline. Although to all intents and purposes the parties came second equal, the psychological impact of being the one in second place rather than the one in third place was critical, and meant that it was possible for Labour after the election still to describe the Liberal Democrat/SDP Alliance as 'the Third Party'.

Table 19 *Actual and predicted results, 1983 general election (%)*

Pollster	ASL (telephone)	Harris	Gallup	Marplan	NOP	MORI	
Newspaper	Sun	Observer	Daily Telegraph	Guardian	Daily Mail	London E. Standard	**Actual result**
Fieldwork	7 June	7–8 June	7–8 June	8 June	6–7 June	8 June	9 June
Sample size	1,100	567	2,003	1,335	1,040	1,101	–
Conservative	46.0	47.0	45.5	46.0	46.0	44.0	44.0
Labour	23.0	25.0	26.5	26.0	28.0	28.0	28.0
All	29.0	26.0	26.0	26.0	24.0	26.0	26.0
Others	2.0	2.0	2.0	2.0	2.0	2.0	2.0
Conservative lead	23.0	22.0	19.0	20.0	18.0	16.0	16.0
Error on lead	+7.0	+6.0	+3.0	+4.0	+2.0	0.0	–
Average error on share	2.2	1.5	0.8	1.0	1.0	0.0	–

The final prediction polls all overestimated the scale of the Conservative victory, though for the most part not by very much. MORI succeeded in getting all three parties exactly right. Close behind, NOP had the Labour figure spot on but overestimated the Tories by 2% and underestimated the Alliance by 2%. Similarly, Gallup overestimated the Tories by 1.5% and underestimated Labour by 1.5%, getting the Alliance vote exactly right in this case. Marplan also had the Alliance exactly right, but overestimated the Tories and underestimated Labour, each by 2%. Least accurate of the mainstream pollsters was Harris, whose much smaller sample overestimated the Conservative lead by 6%.

The other notable polling feature of the 1983 election was the appearance for the first time of national published opinion polls conducted by telephone.

These were carried out throughout the campaign on behalf of the *Sun* by Audience Selection Ltd (ASL). Throughout the election the ASL telephone polls consistently showed the Alliance with a higher figure than in any of the other polls, predominantly at the expense of Labour. In their final prediction ASL overestimated the Conservative share by 2%, and underestimated Labour by 5%, with the Alliance also overestimated, by 3%. That this was the result of institutional bias rather than random error is seen from the fact that a similar overstating of the Alliance existed in each of the polls conducted by ASL.

Table 20 *Actual and predicted results, 1987 general election (%)*

Pollster	ASL (telephone)	Harris	Gallup	Marplan	NOP	MORI	
Newspaper	Sun	TV AM	Daily Telegraph	Guardian	Independent	Times	**Actual Result**
Fieldwork	9 June	10 June	8–9 June	10 June	10 June	9–10 June	11 June
Sample size	1,702	2,122	2,005	1,633	1,668	1,688	–
Conservative	43.0	42.0	41.0	42.0	42.0	44.0	43.0
Labour	34.0	35.0	34.0	35.0	35.0	32.0	32.0
All	21.0	21.0	23.5	21.0	21.0	22.0	23.0
Others	2.0	2.0	1.5	2.0	2.0	2.0	2.0
Conservative lead	9.0	7.0	7.0	7.0	7.0	12.0	11.0
Error on lead	−2.0	−4.0	−4.0	−4.0	−4.0	+1.0	–
Average error on share	1.0	1.5	1.25	1.5	1.5	0.5	–

ASL apart, 1983 was undoubtedly a good election for the polls, with four of the five being no more than 2% out on any party, and all five within the 3% level of error on parties that one might expect from sampling error. The pollsters repeated this success in 1987, when final predictions from all six pollsters, this time including ASL's telephone polls, were within 3% of the actual figure for each party (see Table 20). All the errors were once again broadly in the same direction. Five of the six pollsters underestimated the ultimate size of the winning majority, and four of the six underestimated the Conservative share of the vote. Harris, Marplan and NOP all had the Tories 1% lower than they actually were, while Gallup showed them 2% lower. ASL in fact had the Conservatives absolutely correct, but by overscoring Labour still underestimated the Tory lead. The exception was MORI, which overestimated the Conservative share of the vote, and the Conservative lead, by 1%. The significance of this consistency, with the polls being almost all in error in the same direction, is discussed in Chapter 6, but most important for the purposes of this chapter is the fact that all six polls predicted the Conservative share of the vote to within 2%, and all six polls predicted the Labour share to within 3%. Once again this is as good a result as one can reasonably expect, even from random samples of this size.

But it is perhaps significant that the pollsters who did so well in 1987 were exactly the same as the pollsters who did so well in 1983, and four of those six had also performed well in 1979. If the early days of polling in Britain were marked by a considerable degree of chopping and changing of different organisations entering and leaving the polling world, there has been some consistency since 1979. Polling since then has been dominated by Gallup, Harris, Marplan/ICM, MORI and NOP, who have joined together to form the Association of Professional Opinion Polling Organisations (APOPO), with a common set of minimum standards for the conduct of published opinion polls.

Whilst the pollsters themselves have remained constant, their relationships with their clients have not been for the most part so consistent. Gallup is the exception, having polled for the *Daily Telegraph* since 1964, but the other four have all switched between newspapers or television clients over the years. In 1987 Audience Selection polled for the *Sun*, as they had done in 1983. Harris's prediction poll was for TVAM, Marplan's for the *Guardian*, MORI's for *The Times* and NOP's for the *Independent*.

NOP's polling in 1987 was unusual in being concentrated in marginal seats. This was at the suggestion of the *Independent*, which felt that since the election would ultimately be decided in the marginal seats the most interesting story was to poll only in these seats. This undoubtedly made some interesting reporting, but there is an element of Catch-22 in this approach. The only justification for polling solely in the marginals is the belief that the marginals are going to behave differently from the rest of the country. If the marginals behave the same as everywhere else one could predict what will happen in them merely by extrapolating from the national figures. However, if the marginals do behave differently from the rest of the country then polling in the marginals cannot say anything about the position in the country as a whole.

This meant that in order to reach their final prediction of the overall share of the vote for the election, something which the *Independent* felt its readers would want, the paper had to assume that the marginals did behave in the same way as the rest of the country, rather undermining the point of studying them separately. In fact the marginals in 1987 did indeed behave the same way as the rest of the country, though this was something that could only be established after the election. One consequence of the concentration on the marginals during the campaign, and the failure therefore to produce a national share of the vote, was that the *Independent*'s polls could not easily be compared during the campaign with those from other pollsters. This in turn meant that the *Independent* received virtually no secondary reporting of its polls.

Normally secondary reporting is widespread, and is often regarded as a form of 'below-the-line' marketing. Because polls are news, polls will be reported on by news organisations other than those which commission them in the first place. If *The Times* publishes a poll on Wednesday, it is almost inevitable that the BBC and ITN news programmes the evening before will give details of that poll, attributing it of course to *The Times*. In this way the paper receives valuable and completely free air time in front of large audiences. Then the next morning the other papers will also report on the poll, again crediting *The Times* as the sponsor. It is impossible to quantify the value of this, or even to be sure that it actually has value, but even if no effect can be proved, most editors will prefer to have their paper mentioned on the *Nine o'Clock News* or *News at Ten* rather than not mentioned. It is also noticeable that no media client in the 1992 election repeated the concentration on marginals chosen by the *Independent* for 1987.

Table 21 *Actual and predicted results, 1992 general election (%)*

Pollster	Harris	MORI	Gallup	MORI	NOP	ICM	
Newspaper	ITN	Yorkshire TV	Daily Telegraph	Times	Independent/ BBC	Guardian	**Actual result**
Fieldwork	4–7 Apr.	6–7 Apr.	7–8 Apr.	7–8 Apr.	7–8 Apr.	8 Apr.	3 May
Sample size	2,210	1,065	2,478	1,731	1,746	2,186	–
Conservative	38.0	37.0	38.5	38.0	39.0	38.0	42.8
Labour	40.0	40.0	38.0	39.0	42.0	38.0	35.2
Liberal Democrat	18.0	20.0	20.0	20.0	17.0	20.0	18.3
Others	4.0	3.0	3.5	3.0	2.0	4.0	3.1
Conservative lead	−2.0	−3.0	0.5	−1.0	−3.0	0.0	7.6
Error on lead	−9.6	−10.6	−7.1	−8.6	−10.6	−7.6	–
Average error on share (±)	2.7	3.1	2.3	2.6	3.2	2.6	–

Going into the general election of 1992 the pollsters could be forgiven a certain amount of complacency. In all five elections since the 1970 debacle, the average error on each party share across all the final polls was well below 2%. Indeed over the last three elections, the average error on the party share of the two main parties has been 1.1%, 1.5% and 1.7%. It is difficult to see how the pollsters could reasonably be expected to do better than this, and yet this run of success was followed by a disaster for the polls even greater than in 1970.

As Table 21 shows, all of the polls significantly understimated the size of the Conservative vote, and overestimated the Labour vote.

Notes

1 P. Kellner, 'The voters who switch sides', *The Economist*, 27 April 1979.
2 R. Worcester, *British Public Opinion: A Guide to the History and Methodology of Political Opinion Polling* (Blackwell, 1991).
3 D. Sanders, H. Ward and D. Marsh, 'Government popularity and the Falklands War: a reassessment', *British Journal of Political Science*, 17 (1987).
4 D. Sanders, 'Government popularity and the next general election', *Political Quarterly*, 62 (1991).

6

What went wrong in 1992?

There's no success like failure, and failure's no success at all

As the previous chapter has shown, the polls were more wrong in the 1992 general election than at any other British election. Even more than in 1970, this led to widespread debate about how the polls could possibly have been so wrong, how likely it was that they would do better next time, and what the implications were for survey research in general. The opinion pollsters came in for criticism, especially from those who commissioned commercial market research, who wanted reassurance that they weren't wasting their money; and from agencies conducting commercial market-research surveys, who objected to having their own competence questioned as a result of the pollsters' error. The gist of their complaint was that the pollsters had risked damaging the whole research industry by causing this crisis of confidence among both clients and the public.

Now that a few years have passed it is clear that, as happened after 1970, the market research industry has not been damaged as a result: it has continued to grow. The pollsters have to be prepared for this criticism at any time, because it is they who so publicly put their work to the acid-test of comparison between survey results and the real thing. The vast bulk of survey research – social and commercial, random and quota, telephone and face to face – can never be tested against reality. The government spends huge sums on surveys to measure income, or hours worked, or reasons for not taking up a benefit, but can never prove whether the results are accurate or not. The big multinationals spend even huger sums finding out who remembers seeing their advertisements, or why they choose one brand over another, or what they read, again without ever being able to test the accuracy of those results. There are surveys about something which is ostensibly measurable, such as the intention to purchase a new product, but there are so many factors which may intervene between the survey and the introduction of the product – marketing effort and activity by the competition, for example – that it does not prove a survey is right if the predicted level of sales is achieved, or that the survey was wrong if it is not.

Despite the problems of 1992, the pollsters have a very good track record, and have done far more to justify the existence of survey research than to threaten it. However, because they are the ones who put their heads above the parapet, they will always be at risk of being found wrong, and of being attacked from within the industry as a result. Indeed, at the 1993 Market Research Society annual conference there was a debate on a motion suggesting that the bad publicity garnered by the polls was threatening the rest of research. The main thrust of the proposers' argument was that they would be much happier selling research to clients without any independent assessment of whether the data they were selling their clients was worth anything or not.

Whatever the rights and wrongs of the various criticisms, the industry as a whole could not just wash its hands of the whole problem by claiming that opinion polling is quite different from the rest of market research, or that it should just be written off as an aberration after a whole series of accurate general-election polls. As in 1970 the Market Research Society set up a committee of enquiry, though unlike in 1970 the committee included not just survey experts outside the opinion-polling world, but two pollsters as well. Whether because of this, or entirely coincidentally, most would agree that the committee produced a far more accomplished and useful report than that of 1970. This chapter covers much of the same ground as the committee's report, although the arguments made in it are mine rather than theirs.

Before looking in detail at any of the possible explanations for the problem, it is important to clear up any possible confusion between error in the polls and bias. When results of polls are published they are normally accompanied by an estimate of the sampling error to be expected with a poll of that size, and Chapter 2 discussed the calculation and meaning of sampling error. Looking at the results of the 1992 polls it is clear that not only were they outside sampling error for the two main parties, but they were all erring in the same direction. In any series of surveys, sampling error is as likely to lead to underestimates as overestimates. What we saw in 1992 is clearly the presence of bias at work in the polls.

Before going on to look in detail at the prediction polls and the problems within them, it is worth looking also at the exit polls conducted by NOP on behalf of the BBC, as these proved to shed some light on the pre-election polls as well. NOP conducted two separate exit polls for the BBC, which are discussed in more detail in Chapter 7. Similarly, Harris conducted two separate exit polls for ITN.

In each case the error was in the same direction as the error in the prediction polls, though to a far lesser extent. There are complicating factors in the translation from an exit-poll *vote share* into a projection of *seat numbers*,[1] but the overall pattern is clear.[2] All four polls underestimated the Conservative share by around 2% and all four overestimated the Labour vote by a similar extent. Despite the huge differences in methodology between exit polls and pre-election polls, the fact that the errors were in the same direction is significant, and will be returned to in this chapter.

One other aspect of election polling which it is worth examining as background to the 1992 final polls is the performance of the single-constituency polls. NOP conducted eight constituency polls during the election campaign. The first comment to make on constituency polls in general is that they are rarely if ever conducted so close to the election day as to be proper predictors. For example, NOP's four polls for the *Mail on Sunday* were conducted in the first week of the campaign. There is clearly plenty of scope for opinion to change in those constituencies before the election, and so one should always be wary of treating constituency polls in the same way as the final national polls, but the results are still informative.

Given that they were conducted at the beginning of the campaign, the record of NOP's *Mail on Sunday* polls is very good. Even if they had been conducted on the day before the election, only one of the twelve figures for the major parties is outside the sampling error of 4% that one would expect for polls of this size and type. It should, however, be noted that three of the four polls underestimated the Tory share of the vote, and three overestimated the Labour share. It is not strictly a scientific approach, but if the *Mail on Sunday* polls are adjusted for the factors identified by the MRS committee, such as late swing and differential turnout, then they would all have been virtually spot on.

NOP's other constituency polls were for Harlech Televsion (HTV). These were conducted over a longer period of time, which makes analysis slightly more difficult. The errors are all within sampling error apart from in one constituency, and the direction of the errors is again consistent with late swing. Thus with only one significant exception, the record of the NOP constituency polls was a very good one.

This, then, is the background to the detailed investigation of what went wrong. The investigation itself can be broadly broken down into two areas – things that the pollsters couldn't have done anything about; and things that were wrong within the polling methodology. Under each of these headings theories were put forward in the immediate aftermath of the election, some of which were subsequently proved correct, and some of which were subsequently shown to be wildly inaccurate.

In every election pollsters are vulnerable to the effects of factors outside their control, with late swing and differential turnout being the most significant.

Late swing

In trying to assess the accuracy or otherwise of any prediction poll, the first thing that one must bear in mind is that any poll can only set out to measure opinion held at the time that the poll was conducted. This was the lesson that was learnt very painfully by all the polls in 1970 when, as seen in Chapter One, polling effectively stopped the weekend before the election and pollsters missed out on a substantial swing to the Tories during the last few days of the campaign. Since then the pollsters have carried out interviewing up until the Tuesday or even the Wednesday before election day, in order to minimise the risk of failing to detect late swing. However, even with polling carrying on until the Tuesday or Wednesday, there is still some time remaining after being interviewed in which people may change their mind before casting their real ballot. This is particularly likely to be the case in a close election or, as was the case in this election, where very extensive campaigning on key themes takes place in the last few days.

As far as 1992 is concerned, views differ on the impact of late swing. Most people actively involved in campaigning during the election, especially those on the Labour side, say they detected an ebbing-away of Labour support during the last week of the campaign, but simple statistical analysis of the polls throughout the campaign offers little support to this view. There are a number of different ways of measuring the presence or otherwise of late swing, and different approaches produce slightly different results. Clifford and Heath, on the basis of detailed statistical analysis, concluded that there was little or no evidence of movement during the campaign.[3] Anyone studying the election-day newspapers would have had a different impression, for as is shown in Figure 8, almost all referred to a narrowing gap or a Conservative surge. The MRS enquiry used a different approach from Clifford and Heath.[4] It broke all the national polls down into five clusters, based on the first day of fieldwork, as shown in Table 22.

Table 22 *National published polls, 1992, grouped by first day of fieldwork*

	No. of polls		Con.	Lab.	Lib. Dem.	Other	Labour lead
11–13 Mar.	8	%	39.3	40.6	15.3	4.9	1.3
15–21 Mar.	11	%	39.1	40.5	16.5	3.8	1.4
22–30 Mar.	14	%	38.0	40.3	17.5	4.2	2.3
1–6 Apr.	13	%	37.1	39.4	19.3	4.2	2.3
7 Apr.	4	%	38.4	39.2	19.2	3.1	0.8

Although the differences are not statistically significant, the table does suggest a swing to the Conservatives in the very last days of the campaign, and the MRS enquiry concluded that 'there were signs of a swing in the week preceding the election' and 'despite some appearances to the contrary, the British electorate *was* more than usually volatile in 1992'.[5]

Analyses of the kind shown in Table 22 and the kind undertaken by Clifford and Heath can only investigate changes that might have been going on between one poll and the next. What they cannot do is measure any change which occurred *after* the final polls. Having learned from 1970, the pollsters carried

Figure 8 *Election-day newspaper headlines, 1992*

The Daily Telegraph

Polls put parties neck and neck

Polls put parties neck and neck

Role of power-broker beckons for Ashdown

Late surge by Tories closes gap on Labour in final hours of campaign

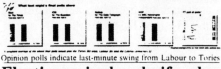

Opinion polls indicate last-minute swing from Labour to Tories

Election poised on knife-edge

Final polls put parties neck and neck   Labour strategists look to tactical voting in marginals   Lib Dems fear 'drift' in South

Tory hopes rise after late surge

out their interviews as late as possible, but they had to have results ready in time for the first editions of Thursday morning's papers, which means by quite early on Wednesday evening. In NOP's case the final poll was conducted for the *Independent* and BBC *Newsnight*, with interviewing being conducted on the Tuesday afternoon and evening and the Wednesday morning. It is estimated that at least 75% of the interviewing was completed by the Tuesday evening. This still leaves over twenty-four hours for people to have a final change of heart – as much as forty-eight hours if they didn't vote until the Thursday evening.

Normally one can only speculate as to the presence or otherwise of swing after the final polls, but in 1992 there were two separate panel studies running which conducted a final wave of interviewing immediately after the election, and because of the error in the final polls, ICM, MORI and NOP all conducted recall interviews by telephone with respondents from the final prediction poll. On the Friday, Saturday and Sunday after the election NOP re-interviewed by telephone 705 of the 1,746 respondents on the final *Independent* survey. For various reasons it is somewhat difficult to interpret these recall polls in detail, but a broad conclusion can be reached.

The NOP recall survey suggested that there had been a swing of 2% from Labour to the Conservatives among our sample between the data of interview and the election itself. NOP also re-interviewed 800 of the panel of voters who had been interviewed on a weekly basis throughout the election on behalf of the *Independent on Sunday*. One has to be even more careful in interpreting the evidence from re-interviews of a panel survey because by the time of the election the panel members will inevitably have been to some extent conditioned by having been part of the panel, and may not behave in exactly the same way as the rest of the electorate. The recall on the panel did, however, also reveal a swing to the Conservatives.

NOP were not alone in going back to their respondents after the election, and by drawing on results of recall surveys by other pollsters as well as NOP, the MRS enquiry was able to reach slightly more definitive conclusions. ICM and MORI both showed net movement to the Conservatives between the final pre-election poll and the recall, and the enquiry concluded that the swing to the Tories after the final polls 'was the cause of a significant part of the final error'.[6]

This suggests that a substantial part of the discrepancy between the polls and the actual result can be explained not by any errors as such in the polls but by an inevitable consequence of the gap between the end of polling and election day itself. There is nothing the pollsters can do about this – given the publication deadlines of our clients, we already continue interviewing as late as we possibly can – so it cannot be said to be the result of error on the part of the pollsters, but it does mean that the predictive powers of the polls are not necessarily as great as has recently been assumed. In future both pollsters and their clients must be more sensitive to the possibility of last-minute swing.

With the benefit of hindsight, we can look back to the 1970 election, where the only poll correctly to predict a Conservative lead did so not by having a Conservative lead in the poll itself, but by extrapolating a trend from its previous poll to its final poll and then concluding that, if that trend continued until polling day, the Conservatives would just edge into the lead. Had a similar technique been used in 1992 the final polls would have been more accurate, but it would be dangerous to assume that such trend-following would work at every election, and there have been elections between 1970 and 1992 when it would have made matters worse. Nevertheless, in the future we can perhaps be more sensitive to the possibilities of further post-survey swing. Again, with the benefit of hindsight, one might argue that the very powerful campaign waged by the main Conservative-supporting tabloid newspapers over the last couple of days of the campaign succeeded in cajoling waverers back into the Conservative fold, and such last-minute changes could happen in any future election.

Differential turnout

Late swing, then, is a shortcoming rather than a fault of the polls and the next area to be addressed is of a similar nature. The polls can set out only to measure people's claimed intentions, and will inevitably interview many people who say they will definitely vote but do not actually do so on the day. Failure by one party to get its vote out to the full extent has often been the cause of lost elections, and it is very difficult for the polls to predict whether the supporters of one party will prove more apathetic than those of another. The MRS enquiry included differential turnout as part of the overall 'late-swing' hypothesis, but it is really a different category of explanation. Late swing is about people changing their minds between being interviewed and voting. Differential turnout encompasses both those who fully intended to vote but in the end didn't, and those who had no intention of voting but did not want to admit as much to an interviewer, for the reasons discussed in Chapter 4.

The pollsters do ask people how likely they are to vote, and the final predictions are often based only on those who said they were certain to vote, but more people say they are certain to vote than actually vote, so even this measure is far from foolproof. To the extent, then, that the difference between the poll findings and the actual result can also be explained by the differential propensity for Conservatives to get out and vote compared with Labour supporters, this too can be described in the category of shortcoming rather than failure. If people tell the pollsters that they will vote but then in fact don't this can hardly be construed as a failure in the *methodology* of the polls, though, as with the problem of late swing, it can be seen as a problem of interpretation. If there is likely to be a considerable difference in turnout between Conservative and Labour supporters, even among those who told pollsters they would definitely vote, then this is another area where one may need in future to exercise some caution in looking at the poll results.

It is possible to look at the impact of differential turnout in two ways: from the evidence of the recall surveys, and from the more objective evidence of actual turnout constituency by constituency. The recall surveys suggest that those who in the prediction poll were Conservative supporters were slightly more likely than Labour supporters to say they had indeed gone and voted on election day, but it must be remembered that claimed voting is a far from reliable measure. For example, of the NOP recall on the *Independent*/*Newsnight* survey, some 92% of those we spoke to claimed to have voted on election day.

As we know, the actual turnout was in fact under 80%, and even allowing for a higher 'effective' turnout once the dead and incapable have been removed from the calculation, there is a considerable degree of overclaiming among our respondents (although we must allow for the fact that people who take part in opinion polls must be more likely to vote than the population at large). If, for example, all the Labour voters were honest about whether they had voted or not, but Conservative supporters who had not in fact voted were more likely to claim that they had, then this would be merely a measure of people giving what is seen to be a socially acceptable answer to the interviewer rather than a true measure of differential turnout. For this reason the recall surveys should not be seen as the main source of evidence of any differential turnout, and the actual turnout figures should also be considered.

Turnout in the 1992 general election at 77.9% was 2.4% higher than in 1987. There were considerable differences in the way in which turnout changed from the last general election over the different regions of the country. Broadly speaking, the increases in turnout were much higher in the Conservative heartlands of the South of England than they were in the Labour strongholds of the North, Scotland and Wales. Turnout in those seats held by the Conservatives in 1987 increased by 3.5% in average from 1987 to 1992. In those seats that were held by Labour in 1987 the increase in turnout in 1992 was an insignificant 0.1%. These figures refer to changes in turnout from 1987 to 1992, and a similar pattern emerges if one looks at absolute levels of turnout.

To take a very simple measure, if all the constituencies in the country are ranked in order of turnout from the highest to the lowest, then a mere glance at the list shows the enormous concentration of Conservative seats at the high-turnout end of the list, and Labour seats at the low-turnout end of the list. The same pattern is seen in the marginals. In the forty most marginal Tory seats – the ones they just succeeded in holding on to – turnout was 1% higher than in the forty most marginal Labour gains – the ones they just managed to win. One should be wary of assuming too much about individual behaviour from these constituency aggregate figures, but it does seem that higher turnouts benefited the Conservatives.

The evidence from the recall surveys and from the actual turnout levels suggests some differential turnout effect, and overall there seems no doubt that had all of those who told the pollsters that they were going to vote actually gone and done so then the election result would have been closer, and the error on the polls lower.

Expatriate voters

One of the more fanciful explanations for the error of the polls was that the government's well-publicised drive to enlist expatriate voters after the change in registration rules for those living abroad. This was said to have had an effect by bringing in considerable numbers of votes for the Conservatives (usually said to be targeted in marginal seats) from people who could not possibly be interviewed by opinion polls. This is an attractive argument from the pollsters' point of view, since no one could reasonably expect the pollsters to measure the expatriate vote, but there is no evidence for it whatsoever. There were only 32,000 overseas voters on the 1992 electoral register, and in only two constituencies were the numbers of expatriate votes cast greater than the size of the winning party's majority. These are thus the only two out of 651 seats which could have been won by the expatriate vote, and one of these was won by the Liberal Democrats.

The poll tax and deregistration

One aspect of the election which received much comment throughout, and which has also been put forward as a possible explanation of the problems of the prediction polls, is the extent of non-registration by people trying to avoid the community charge. There is no doubt that many people did indeed fail to put their names on the electoral register in the hopes of thus becoming hidden from the poll-tax collectors. The 1992 electoral register contained only 20,000 more names than the 1987 register, whereas the population estimates from the Registrar General suggest that the number of those over eighteen in fact grew substantially during the same period.[7] Whereas in 1987 the total number of electors was 97.4% of the estimated adult population, in 1992 this proportion had fallen to 95.7%.[8] The case has been put forward by some people that it is the 'missing voters' who explained the pollsters' error. Their theory runs that the pollsters interviewed people who said they intended to vote Labour but who either knew already, or subsequently discovered, that they were unable to vote because their names were not on the electoral register.

This is not the same category of error as the theory about expatriate voters, since one can argue that before asking anyone how they will vote the pollsters should check that respondents are eligible to vote. Were this theory true it would represent an avoidable failure by the polls, but again, there is no evidence to support it. First, there was an increase in the efficiency of the electoral register in 1992 compared with 1987. Electoral registration officers had been bringing registers more up to date by ending the previous practice of leaving on the register people who did not return a registration form. To the extent that returning officers were thus clearing out 'dead wood' the register would be expected to shrink as a result, and much of the decline between 1987 and 1992 could be explained in these terms. This argument is supported by the MRS committee, and by Jowell *et al.*,[9] although Smith and McLean[10] disagree and argue that poll-tax deregistration could have had a marginal but significant effect on the size of the Conservative victory. Apart from the ques-

116

tion of the absolute numbers, one can also make a plausible case that many of those who did indeed deregister themselves were people who were far less likely to turn out and vote than the average elector. Overall the evidence seems to suggest that, as an explanation of the error of the polls, poll-tax deregistration is insignificant.

Because of the attention which had been paid to this whole issue of deregistration, NOP made some attempt in its early polls to take account of it. At the end of the interview respondents were asked if, as far as they knew, they were on the electoral register and eligible to vote. We found on average that around 95% of our respondents claimed that as far as they knew they were, but the more important finding was that there was virtually no difference between Labour voters and Conservative voters on this question. Because we could see no evidence that it could have an impact on the result, we stopped asking this question in our last polls in the campaign. ICM and MORI continued to use this extra filter throughout the campaign, but there was no consistent difference between their figures and those of the other pollsters who did not use the filter, suggesting that it made no difference.

The main reason why it made no difference is that the numbers involved are simply not enough for non-registration to have had any impact on the election result. One figure seized on by several commentators after the election was the gap of 1.9 million between the size of the electorate and the size of the adult population as estimated by the Registrar General. Had all these been Labour supporters they could have changed the election completely. However, what this theory ignores is the fact that in the previous election in 1987 there was a gap of 1.1 million between the register and the population. The maximum level of deregistration is thus 800,000 rather than 1.9 million, and it is almost certainly less than this because of the process of modernisation of the register discussed above.

When allowance is made for the fact that many of those who dropped off the register were those who were least likely to vote, then the possible impact of deregistration on the overall election result is minimal. The MRS committee concluded that even if as many as 75% of the deregistered were Labour voters, they would only have raised the Labour share by 0.5% had they actually voted.[11]

Residual error

The points discussed above all concern factors outside the pollsters' control, and which suggest that the polls were correct in what they were measuring at the time they measured it, but that this was not necessarily the best way of predicting the result of the general election. Thus if people genuinely do intend to vote Labour at the time they are interviewed by the pollster, but subsequently change their mind the following day, then the poll is perfectly valid as it stands, though not as much use a predictive tool. The same is largely true of differential turnout. If people genuinely believe when they speak to a pollster that they will go out and vote, but then for various reasons on the day do not in fact do so then the poll is again correct at the time it was conducted, but of limited predictive value. In both these cases the polls are as correct as they possibly could be, and the problem lies in the interpretation placed upon them.

When we come to the issue of the anti-poll tax, Labour-supporting, deregistered voters, we start to move on to a different category of issue. If the polls correctly reflect the views of the population, but the views of that sub-sample of the population which is the valid electorate are subtly different, then the poll is again correct as far as it goes, but it is in fact the wrong kind of poll. If the registered electorate is significantly different in behaviour from the total population over eighteen then the polls should be interviewing only the electorate and not those over eighteen. We can then go a step further than this and look at areas which suggest the polls may actually have been inaccurate even in what they set out to do: that is to say, they were not in fact accurate pictures even of the population they were surveying.

Taking late swing and differential turnout together, the MRS report, while shying away from actual figures, estimated that they may have accounted for between a fifth and a third of the discrepancy between the polls and the actual result. Splitting the difference and calling it a quarter means that around 6% out of the average error of 8.4% on the Conservative lead must be down to other factors. Since the other factors outside the pollsters' control – expatriate voters and deregistration – have been shown to be insignificant, this still leaves a discrepancy of the order of 3% on each party share still to be explained. Again it must be remembered that, whilst we have now reduced this level of error to something within the levels of sampling error expected, because all the polls showed an error in the same direction it cannot be explained away in terms of sampling error. It is also worth noting at this point that the level of this residual error is not much higher than that found in all the exit polls, suggesting there may be some common causes.

Broadly speaking, there are two main ways in which the polls could have been at fault. The first is that there may have been deficiencies in the sampling approach, that is to say that the people interviewed in the polls were not in fact a representative cross-section either of the population or more specifically of the voting population. The second possibility is that even if the polls were a perfect sample of the electorate they failed accurately to record what people intended to do.

These possibilities are by no means mutually exclusive, and within these two broad headings are a large number of possible causes of bias. Whilst each individually may have been relatively minor, what seems to have been important in 1992 is that all of these possible sources of bias seem to have been operating in the same direction, that is, against the Conservatives.

Sampling

The first area that must inevitably be looked at is the quality of the samples used in the opinion polls. If the polls are not interviewing a representative sample of the population then the possibility for bias will inevitably be considerably increased. At the extreme, Jowell *et al.* have argued that there is something inherently wrong with the whole method of quota sampling which means that it is less reliable than random sampling, and that therefore quota sampling should never be taken seriously as a means of measuring public opinion.[12] However, it must be remembered that the record of the polls from 1974 to 1987 was extremely good, and the polls managed to predict all of those elections with an acceptable level of accuracy by using quota samples. Given that the methodology used in 1992 had changed little since 1974, and that in the previous five elections before 1992 the polls managed to predict the Conservative share of the vote on average to within 0.0% and the Labour share to within 0.3%, it cannot possibly be argued that there is anything fundamental within the *methodology as a whole* which could explain the errors in 1992. Explanations based on quota sampling *per se* are insufficient. What is needed is an explanation why quota sampling should suddenly have failed in 1992, having succeeded before. In his analysis of why the polls got it wrong, Ivor Crewe made this very point.[13]

> Firstly, the fairly impressive record of the polls until 1992 sets limits to possible explanations. To be convincing an explanation must specify what was *different* about either the polls or the electorate in 1992 compared with earlier elections. Any account in terms of the general principles or normal practices of opinion polling (e.g., quota sampling, in-street interviews, etc.) immediately bumps up against the objection that the same procedures operated at previous elections without leading to inaccuracies.[13]

By this criterion, Jowell *et al.* fail to come up with a suitable explanation, and their analysis is longer on theory than on fact. Key to their argument is an analysis of the random-sample British Election Study, where they look at those people interviewed on the interviewer's first visit to the address. They argue that these people are the same people who are found on quota surveys, since there is no need to make a recall visit on a quota survey. Having found that these people, even when weighted to the demographic norm, are more Labour than the rest of their sample, they pronounce this as evidence of the fundamental flaw in quota sampling. However, not only does this fail to explain the success of quota sampling in the elections up to 1992, but the 'first-call' random respondents are not a true surrogate for quota respondents because no account is taken of some of the other controls on quota sampling.

It does seem likely that availability bias, which always affects quota sample more than random ones, played some part in the polls' failure in 1992, but not to the extent claimed by Jowell *et al.* An alternative view of a weakness of quota sampling argument was put forward by the political journalist Peter Kellner.[14]

119

Arguing from the geography of his home town, he suggested that random sampling may be more likely to find hardened Tory loyalists, while although quota sampling will find people who voted Tory in 1992, it is relatively more likely to find those who have now switched to another party. In the area where he lives there are many ABs, living in large houses fronting the street, and occupied largely by those in the liberal professions who are not likely to be strong Tories. Round the corner is a road with very large houses, all with long drives, and often entryphones on the gates, and likely to be occupied by staunch, lifelong Tories. Faced with an AB quota to fill, an interviewer is far more likely to interview in Peter Kellner's own area than round the corner, and thus quota sampling will tend to get ABs who are less Tory. At the moment this is no more than speculation, and would be very difficult to test, but it does suggest that weighting by past voting (as discussed in Chapter 9) is not a panacea for the problems of sampling bias.

As discussed in Chapter 2, the first stage of the sampling process is the selection of primary sampling units: constituencies, in the case of the 1992 opinion polls. All the pollsters except Gallup, who drew a new sample for the 1992 election, used samples they had been polling in since 1987. They were representative of the 1987 election result at the time they were drawn, but had become less so by 1992. It would appear at first sight to be easy to judge the representativeness of the sample – one would just compare the overall share of the vote in the sample with the result in the country as a whole. This would mean that larger constituencies in the sample would contribute more to the overall figure than smaller ones, but the pollsters conduct equal numbers of interviews in each seat, as explained in Chapter 2. This means that to give each constituency equal weight, one should average not the raw votes from each constituency, but the percentages from each one.

Also, a comparison of this figure with the actual election result in terms of party share would be influenced by differences in turnout. Since the pollsters already attempt to deal with this by the question on how likely people are to vote, differential turnout should be eliminated from the comparison by recalculating the election result as if turnout were the same in every seat.

The MRS committee made all the necessary calculations, and concluded that there was a small discrepancy between the pollsters' samples and the electorate as a whole. One reason for the discrepancy is that between 1987 and 1992 Conservative-held seats grew larger, in terms of numbers of electors, while Labour seats shrank. Given that the initial selection of seats was with a probability proportional to size, by not resampling the pollsters were oversampling Labour seats and undersampling Conservative ones. Like so many of the other possible causes of the pollsters' errors, the impact of this would have been minor, but yet again any resultant bias was in the same direction – against the Conservatives.

Another possible cause of the difference between all seats and the sampled ones was that the swing to the Conservatives was lower in the sampled seats than in the country as a whole. The MRS committee again made the necessary calculations and concluded that there was no significant difference in the levels of swing. As far as sampling points are concerned, there was thus a small amount of bias against the Conservatives, which had probably been present since the seats were first selected.

Moving from primary sampling units to sampling individuals, the choice of the correct quota variables to use for setting the sample is generally believed to be crucial in the success of any quota survey. It is because there is this element of choice of which variables to use that the hardline proponents of random sampling see quota sampling as inevitably flawed. In view of this it is informative to note that there were small but significant differences between the types of quota controls set by the different pollsters during the election. Some of the agencies did not interlock their quotas at all, whilst the others interlocked them in different ways. Some agencies allowed all interviewing to be conducted in the street, and some had no controls on interviewing by time of day. Perhaps most significant in theoretical terms is that some agencies had no quotas on working status.

Despite these differences, which one would have expected to lead to significant differences in the data collected, the similarity of the polls throughout the entire campaign is very striking. It has been noted above that the NOP final prediction poll differed slightly from the other main prediction polls, but apart from NOP the other final prediction polls were very close together. It does seem difficult therefore to argue that the bias could lie in the choice of quota controls set. There is, however, another area of quota sampling where the error could lie. Having decided what variables should be used for the quota controls, the next stage is to put numerical values on each of them: to decide exactly how many of the sample should be males working full time, exactly how many should be 18–34-year-old C2s, and so on. If there is any error in this, that is to say the quotas set do not reflect the actual balance of the total population in these various sub-cells, then again there will be considerable possibility for bias.

Because the 1981 Census figures were too out of date, and the 1991 Census had not been published by the time of the 1992 election, the pollsters used other surveys as the basis for their quotas. NOP, for example, derived its figures for the age and sex make-up of the population, plus the regional breakdown, from the Registrar General's mid-year population estimates. These were then used as weighting controls on the regular weekly random omnibus survey, and having been weighted in this way the omnibus data were then used to provide information on social class and other variables. The other pollsters also used the mid-year estimates, but for the other data they tend to use demographic information from the NRS.

The NRS (National Readership Survey) is a very large-scale random-sample survey, and is generally held to be one of the most reliable sources of commercial market-research data, but its response rate is still lower than that achieved on the big government surveys such as the General Household Survey (GHS) or the Labour Force Survey (LFS), and is likely to be less reliable as a result. Because the government surveys use a different social class schema from the AB, C1, etc., system used in commercial market research, the pollsters did not look to the GHS or LFS for demographic information, but these surveys do include other demographic information which could be used.

Comparison of the GHS figures with the profiles of the election-poll samples reveals at least one significant difference. Although none of the pollsters used housing tenure as a quota control, most used it as a weighting variable, and whether weighted or not, all the poll samples contained more council-house tenants than the GHS, and therefore probably more than the population as a whole. Since council-house tenants are more likely to be Labour voters, this was another cause of pro-Labour bias in the polls.

Comparison with the NRS after the election also suggested that the pollsters had set quotas which contained too few ABC1s, and too many C2DEs. Since council-house tenants are mainly C2DE the error in the class quota was probably interlinked with the inaccuracy of tenure figures. The pollsters were at fault for not making use of surveys such as the GHS, and as a result ended up with a skewed sample. The effect on the overall results was small, but as argued above, the pollsters' error was more the result of a number of small biases rather than a single large one.

The impact of non-response

Whilst there may be some impact caused by the quota and weighting controls, it is likely to have had less effect than differences between those people who chose to take part in the polls and those who did not, and between those who answered the voting questions and those who did not. Response rate is not normally seen as relevant for a quota sample since the whole basis of quota sampling is that one person in a particular age and sex category is pretty much the same as another, and so it is not measured in the same way as in random samples. On some quota surveys records have been kept of the number of people who were approached by the interviewer, but declined to take part in the interview. Typically the refusal rate found has been of the order of 50%, compared with 20% or less on a typical random sample. At first sight this difference looks as if it could be significant, but the level of refusals where measured in 1992 was no higher than it had been in the 1987 election, when the polls succeeded in measuring the actual Conservative vote very accurately.

This is a problem we keep coming back to with so many of the possible explanations of the bias in 1992. It is entirely plausible that people who choose not to take part in a political opinion poll may be more likely to be Conservative than Labour. It is quite possible, for example, that people with more old-fashioned views believe more in the secrecy of the voting process and are therefore much more reluctant to discuss politics with a stranger, and we would of course expect the more old-fashioned people to be more likely to be Conservative. However if this is the case, one would have expected this to show up as a *consistent* anti-Conservative bias, and to reiterate this point yet again: there is no evidence of consistent anti-Conservative bias in the elections covered by quota sampling.

It is difficult to estimate the impact of differences between those who refuse to take part in polls and those who agree, because almost no information exists about those who do refuse, for fairly obvious reasons. A slightly different aspect of the same issue which does lend itself to further investigation more easily, is the impact of those people who agreed to take part in the survey, but refused to answer the voting-intention question. A small proportion on any voting-intention survey refuse to answer that particular question, and although they *are* only a small proportion, if they were all actual Conservative supporters this would have an effect on the reliability of the poll. On NOP's final poll for the *Independent* and *Newsnight* 2% of respondents refused to say how they would vote, even after the 'squeeze' question, which asks those who are undecided or who refused to answer the first voting question which party they are most likely to support.

As was shown in Chapter 4, British polling practice has been to ignore those who do not answer the voting question – they are removed from the figures, and voting intention calculated on a base of those do vote. In effect, this assumes that the non-answerers have exactly the same political distribution as those who do answer. In the past this has tended to make the result more reliable.

In other countries this repercentaging approach is known to be unreliable, because for cultural reasons supporters of one party may be much less likely to disclose their intention to an outsider, and a paper at the 1992 World Association for Public Opinion Research conference by Dimitras and Basanez covered this very issue.[15] That concerned surveys where over a third of survey respondents did not answer the voting question. Any impact of differential item non-response is bound to be far higher in that situation than it is in the UK, where fewer than 10% of respondents do not give a voting intention, but having previously felt that this was a problem which did not affect the UK, it appeared after 1992 that this would be a valuable area of investigation.

NOP conducted some research on aggregate data from all its 1992 pre-election polls, looking both at those who were undecided and those who refused.[16] The investigation looked separately at those who were undecided or refused to answer the voting question, and those after the squeeze question, and created a category called 'final not say' – a composite of all those who were ultimately excluded from the voting figures because they were undecided or refused after the squeeze question.

It should be noted that there are far more undecideds than refusals. The aggregate sample from the eight polls was 9,978, of whom 2,072 were initial undecideds (21%) and 612 final undecideds (6%), compared with only 260 initial refusals (3%) and 173 final refusals (2%). This means that in the combined cells, such as 'final not say', the undecideds account for the great majority, and so the average will tend to be close to that for the undecideds.

There were few consistent differences by sex or age, and little by class. Those who refused or were undecided at the first question, but who then answered the squeeze question, give the first clue that there was a political component to non-response. This group was noticeably more likely to say that they would vote Conservative, and the effect of asking the squeeze question was to reduce the Labour lead in NOP's last poll from 5% to 3%. Had the 'final not say' category split in the same way, the parties would have been virtually neck and neck.

This highlights something the pollsters had technically been doing wrong for years, but which had always worked before. The squeeze question was introduced because those who did not answer initially were not the same as those who did, but the pollsters then assumed that those who did not answer the squeeze question either were the same as everyone else. Even assuming this latter group was the same as those who *did* answer the squeeze question would have helped in 1992, and one could argue that they ought to be the same, only more so. That is to say, if those who answered the squeeze question were more Conservative than those who answered the original question, then those who answered neither were likely to be even more Conservative still.

Analysis of refusals and undecideds against claimed voting behaviour at the previous general election is complicated by the fact that while we are predominantly interested in differences in non-response categories between previous Labour and Conservative voters, a high proportion of our target group did not give an answer.

Thus of the initial refusals, 46% refused to answer about 1987 as well, and among final refusals this figure was as high as 62%. The undecideds were quite different, with only 6% of initial undecideds, and 11% of final undecideds, not saying how they voted in 1987.

If we look just at the final undecided or refused group, and within them look only at those who named a party they voted for in 1987, then the claimed past vote among this group was much the same as that of the sample as a whole. However, these figures were heavily influenced by the undecideds, as there were so many more of them, and because so many of the refusals in 1992 refused the 1987 question as well. There are so few refusals in 1992 who did say how they voted in 1987 that data from them can at best be considered as illustrative, but the figures are striking. Of the 110 people who refused the initial voting question, but said how they voted in 1987, 52% said they voted Conservative in 1987, compared with 46% of the total sample. Among the even smaller group of just 45 who refused the second voting question, fully 64% said they voted for the Conservatives in 1987.

Another way in which we can assess the likely voting behaviour of those who did not express a party preference is to look at their answers to other questions within the interview. It is only feasible to look at questions which appeared on several surveys, in order to ensure a reasonable sample size of the unde-cideds and refusals. The most suitable questions are those on satisfaction with the party leaders, which appeared in some form or other on seven of the eight surveys.

The question wording differed between the surveys, but the principle was the same, and the two versions were both scored with mean scores from +2, meaning a very good rating, to −2, meaning a very poor one. On the total sample, John Major was rated at 0.20. Conservative supporters rated him at 1.14, Labour ones at −0.56, and Liberal Democrats at 0.06. Apart from those who said they would not vote, all the different undecided and refusal groups rated him higher than the average, but the differences were slight, and the scores never even approached those given by Conservatives. Perhaps more important is the fact that there was a gap between the final refusals and the final undecideds, with the former rating John Major higher than the latter.

A similar pattern was seen in the question on Neil Kinnock, where the refusal and undecided groups all rated him lower than the sample as a whole. The combined refusal and undecided group scored Neil Kinnock 0.16 worse than the average, and John Major 0.13 better than average. The similarity of the two figures implies there is some consistent effect.

Further support for this comes from questions asked on all four of the polls for the *Independent* about how much people trusted the two main parties to run the economy. For the Conservatives, the sample as a whole rated them at −0.05, very close to the neutral point, with their own party supporters rating them at 1.16, and Labour supporters at −0.96. Final undecideds were the same as the average at 0.01, but final refusals were more supportive of the Conservatives, rating them at 0.37. The mirror image was again seen in the rating of Labour for economic confidence.

Perhaps the most powerful evidence that refusals are more likely to be Conservative supporters comes from the exit polls. The great advantage the exit polls have over the prediction polls is that the problems of late swing, differential turnout, nonregistration and accuracy of quota profiles do not affect the exit polls at all. They are simple random samples of all those who vote at the selected polling stations. Assuming we can rule out lying, which seems particularly plausible in the case of the secret-ballot approach used by the exit polls, then there are two ways in which we could explain the error on the exit polls (which, as shown above, is a consistent underscoring of around 2% of the Conservative vote in both the Harris and NOP polls). The first possibility is that the sample of polling stations used is not representative of the whole country, and the second is that the sample of those who actually fill in the exit-poll ballot form is not rep-resentative of all voters at that polling station.

In the absence of localised records of voting behaviour of the form available in the USA and other countries, it is impossible to measure the reliability or otherwise of the sampling of locations. However, the fact that a similar bias was seen in both the marginal polls and the national polls, and in polls carried out by another organisation using a different sampling method, it seems to us that the error is more likely to lie in the sample of individuals rather than the sample of locations. Given that the sample of individuals is carried out according to a pure probability model, the only source of error (assuming the interviewers correctly apply the sampling rules) lies in the people who refuse to take part in the exit poll.

Both NOP and Harris found that around 16% of those approached refused to take part in the main-projection exit poll. As the poll involved only answering two questions, lack of time is unlikely to be a factor in refusal, and we can safely conclude that those who refused were the ones who feel it is not right to tell others, however anonymously, how they actually voted. In our early experience of conducting exit polls at by-elections for the BBC we produced results which were definitely within sampling error, but which tended to show the Conservatives being underestimated by around 1% and Labour being overestimated by around 1%.[17]

Although this level was small, it was clear again that it was consistent and therefore that there was some form of bias. In those early elections we were conducting exit polls by means of interviewers actually asking respondents as in a normal survey, and as a result we had refusal rates in the mid- to upper twenties. Convinced that if we could reduce the refusal rate we could reduce this anti-Conservative bias, we changed our methods and switched from interviewing to the use of self-completion forms, on which the respondents could mark anonymously how they voted and then put the form in a box with all the others. The three by-elections where NOP carried out exit polls using this approach showed lower refusal rates, and also the removal of the anti-Conservative bias, though it should be noted that even after this we did not on any occasion overestimate the Conservatives. Despite our success in these by-elections the bias seems to have returned in the general election exit polls, and this reinforces the view that those who refused to disclose how they voted are more likely to be Conservative supporters.[18]

As well as those who refuse to say how they will vote, there is always a proportion in every survey who, even after the second 'squeeze' question, say that they are undecided how they will vote, and these people are a further source of possible bias. In NOP's final poll they accounted for 6% of the sample. It is often argued, particularly in the USA, that the 'don't knows' are actually 'won't says' who are too polite to refuse outright. As far as this is the case, one would expect them to exhibit the same behavioural patterns as the outright refusals.

Some preliminary evidence from polls conducted during 1991 shows that those who were initially undecided at the voting question did indeed have more negative views on the Labour party than the samples as a whole. In particular they gave a lower rating to Neil Kinnock, and had a less favourable view of Labour's economic competence, and if the undecideds in the election polls had been allocated more to the Conservatives than to Labour, the final polls would have been slightly closer to the actual result.

There is, however, always a danger in such interpretative use of data, and Gallup in the USA made their final prediction for the 1992 presidential election much worse by disproportionately allocating 'don't knows' to Bill Clinton, although they were using a different approach from the one discussed above.

Telling the truth?

All the points that have been discussed so far in this chapter have assumed that the people whom we have interviewed were telling us the truth in terms of how they intended to vote, and that the errors arose either because the people we interviewed were an inaccurate sub-sample of the total population, or because they changed their minds about how or whether to vote after being interviewed. There is, however, another area of investigation and this is into the whole question of whether people are actually telling us the truth at all. It is no good having the most perfectly designed sample if respondents give untruthful answers to the questions. At its most straightforward this simply consists of respondents who deliberately lie to the pollsters, either just for the hell of it or to cause confusion in which they may see some political advantage for their own party. This was another theory put forward by several people after the election, mainly, it must be said, on letters pages and by people with very little knowledge of the polls. It was encapsulated by Robert Harris in the *Sunday Times*: 'I have reached the reluctant conclusion that ours is a nation of liars. People lied about their intentions up to the moment of voting, and went on lying even as they left the polling stations.'[19] Such was the pervasiveness of this argument that Crewe uses it in the title of his own analysis of the election, but he concludes that deliberate lying is not a plausible explanation for the error.[20]

In my own view it is extremely unlikely that deliberate lying was a factor of any significance. Firstly, if it existed to any extent I would expect it to be self-cancelling: there would be as many Labour supporters who lied and said they were Conservatives as there were Conservatives who said they were Labour. Also we again come back to the point about recent history. There is little reason to suppose that people should be deliberately trying to mislead the pollsters in 1992 when they had not done so in 1974, 1979, 1983 or 1987.

A much more profitable line of enquiry is to ask why, if people *were* lying, they were all lying in the same direction. This then leads to a more plausible hypothesis – rather than deliberately lying, people were giving an untruthful answer to the interviewer because they were seeking to conceal to what they believed to be an unpopular attitude. This is the so-called 'spiral of silence' – a hypothesis

put forward by a researcher named Elizabeth Noelle-Neuman, who first suggested it was operating in Germany.[21] The basis of the theory is that people who
hold views they perceive to be unpopular are often reluctant to express them to
friends or colleagues (or indeed to survey interviewers). Since they do not
express the views the impression is created that even fewer people hold these
views than actually do, and thus that view is seen to be even more unpopular,
and so even more people are reluctant to mention it (hence the spiral).

Whilst supporting the Conservatives could hardly said to be an extreme position, there are reasons why some people may have been reluctant to admit so to
a pollster. To take a rather simplistic view of the election, it is possible to see that
the Tories' continual concentration on Labour tax plans and the financial
impact a Labour victory would have on individuals, mean that one very important reason presented to voters for voting Conservative was that they individually would be better off. On the other hand Labour, in trying to draw attention
away from the argument over tax, concentrated on its own strong points on
health and education, and thus tried to give the impression that the Labour
campaign was about making a better society for everybody. The media coverage
of the election certainly reinforced this split. Any voters who saw the election
in these uncompromising terms, but who still intended to vote Conservative,
may well have felt guilty about putting their own personal wellbeing above that
of society, achieved through a better health service and education system. Then
if they do feel guilty about their voting intentions they will be less likely to admit
them to an interviewer. The Conservatives themselves certainly were aware
that this might have been happening, for in one of his key speeches in the final
days of the election Mr Major actually told people that there was no reason for
them to feel guilty about voting Conservative. Robert Harris, in the *Sunday
Times* piece quoted above, certainly agreed with this view. 'The cynics were
right after all. People may say they would prefer better public services, but in the
end they will vote for tax cuts. At least some of them had the decency to be too
ashamed to admit it.'[22]

In the chapter on the polls in the Butler and Kavanagh on the election, Denis
Kavanagh quotes a 'central figure in Labour's campaign' on this subject:

> Labour's campaign, the pollsters, the broadcast media and the press all sub-
> merged the Tory vote. Submerged it because people were guilty and because a
> kind of social dynamism had been established that made Labour more acceptable
> than the Conservatives. This led people to be publicly embarrassed and uncertain
> about expressing support for the Conservatives. But it was also submerged and in
> the sense that many people hid from themselves their real intentions, feelings and
> view of where their self-interest lay.[23]

If people had lied to the pollsters in this way out of any feelings of guilt the
problem is that it would be virtually impossible to measure this through polls,
since they are almost certain to lie at any recall interview.

There is a similar problem in trying to locate through recall interviews another category of voters similar to the 'spiral of silence' voters. Festinger first expounded the theory of cognitive dissonance in 1957.[24] The theory has it that there is a tendency for individuals to seek consistency among their cognitions (i.e. beliefs or opinions). If there is any inconsistency between attitudes or behaviours, people will attempt to eliminate the dissonance. The application of this theory to the 1992 election is that some people felt a dissonance between wanting the kind of society Labour was offering, and being concerned about the personal financial implications of a Labour government. These voters are people who told the pollsters they would vote Labour and probably genuinely felt that they would, and if they were lying they were lying to themselves as much as to the pollsters. These would be people who felt that a vote for Labour was the correct thing to do because of the important issues like the National Health Service, but who found it impossible to go through with this once it actually came to the moment of putting a cross on the ballot paper.

One can then argue that they resolved the dissonance in an interview by saying they would vote Labour, but resolved it in the voting booth by actually voting Conservative. If this behaviour pattern was occurring at all, the polls themselves do share some blame for it, in that by suggesting that a Labour government was a very likely possibility they made people confront the reality of that rather than just protesting against the government. Provided one could argue that voting Conservative was more 'shameful' in 1992 than in earlier elections both the spiral of silence and cognitive dissonance theories meet Crewe's criterion of explaining why there was an error in 1992 but not in the 1980s.

Another theory which seeks to explain people not actually lying to the pollsters, but still voting differently from how they said they would vote, is based on a comparison of opinion polls to by-elections. It has long been argued that a by-election provides people with the opportunity for a cost-free protest vote. By voting against the government they can register their disapproval of its policies or performance, in the hope of causing it to change either or both of these, but without having to risk the upheaval of an actual change of government. It is difficult to view some of the huge swings against the Conservatives in the 1992–97 Parliament, such as Newbury or Christchurch, in any other light, and it could be said that the electorate was becoming more sophisticated in this way. In a similar vein, it can be said that a reply to an opinion pollster is similar to a vote in a by-election. By helping produce a massive government deficit in the opinion polls, respondents were able to express their dissatisfaction to the government, without necessarily meaning they would actually vote against it when it came to the crunch. If true, and it is very difficult to test it, this theory would have significant implications for the interpretation of opinion polls, if not their conduct.

With the benefit of that wonderful science known as hindsight, we can see some signs in the election polls that something of this sort of dissonance between expressed voting intention and probable likely voting behaviour was present. It has generally been held that whatever people may say about the key issues in an election their views on the different parties' competence to handle the economy are absolutely crucial in determining their final voting behaviour. Except in extreme circumstances most people would not vote for a party they think will make them worse off. Because Labour was doing relatively well in the voting-intention question this tended to draw attention away from the fact that on these key economic issues they were doing very badly throughout the campaign. Labour scored well on voting, and they also scored well on the 'soft' issues of NHS and education, but throughout the election they were outscored by the Conservatives on quality of leader, taxation policy, competence to run the economy in general, and ability to deal with economic specifics such as inflation. Here the pollsters can definitely be accused of having been oversimplistic in interpreting their data. Having argued for some time that economic competence was a key determinant of voting behaviour, the pollsters did not hear the alarm bells which should have rung when two key indicators pointed in an opposite direction from the voting question.

More than just voting intention

This leads on to an issue which has been raised frequently by my colleagues in commercial market research, and which other media commentators raised after the election. If, they argue, one is about to launch a new chocolate biscuit on to the market, and conducts research in advance of this, one would not assume just because 60% of the survey sample say they would buy this chocolate biscuit then in fact 60% of the population would go ahead and do so. In purchasing research one would look at intention to buy merely as one factor alongside a whole variety of others, such as general attitudes to biscuits, type of chocolate preferred, previous purchasing behaviour, frequency of eating biscuits generally, and so on. With the vast amount of data that are available on purchasing behaviour it is possible to generate some form of model, but this is not the case for voting behaviour. Even if one were to look at all the various attitudes on economic issues, compare them with the voting-intention figures, and produce a model which then predicted the actual election result, it is extremely unlikely that the same model would work in the next general election. The overall experience of modelling general elections is that, as with generals always fighting the last battle, it is a lot easier to 'predict' the result of the last election than it is to predict the result of the next one.

There is also a flaw in the basic analogy that researching future purchasing behaviour is the same as researching future voting behaviour. One of the reasons why complex models exist to predict consumer behaviour is that often quite a long time elapses between someone being interviewed and them making the purchase, and during this interval there are plenty of stimuli such as competitive advertising, price changes, and so on, which might lead to a change of mind. If one could guarantee a sample of people who could be interviewed the day before they made their purchase, one would be much more likely to take stated intention at face value.

Also, much consumer purchasing is of relatively low-priced items, where product differentiation may not be very great, and relatively superficial factors may have a major impact on the decision. A shopper may visit the supermarket intending to buy chocolate biscuits, and expecting to buy digestives, but if there is a new brand of chocolate creams on offer, or if a previous favourite is on display next to the digestives, then the alternative may be bought instead. Any model which helped relate claimed intention to purchase in a survey to actual behaviour for a market such as that, would not work for a market where there is likely to be far more prior consideration of the product alternatives, leading to a careful choice along the lines of a *Which?* report. Buying a car, for example, comes into the latter category, and if it were possible to interview a sample of people the day before they were going to sign the purchase agreement for a new car, then it is very likely that the model they told an interviewer they intended to buy would be the one they actually bought the next day.

My contention is that voting for a government is much more like buying a car than buying chocolate biscuits, and that given the advantage of being able to interview so close to the decision time a simple 'how will you vote?' question is likely to be satisfactory, as it had been in all the elections from 1974 to 1987. It is also worth noting that the prediction polls in the 1992 American presidential election came very close to the actual result, using exactly such a simple voting question.

All this is not to say that the voting question must remain the be-all and end-all of political polling, and one benefit to have come out of 1992 is that pollsters realised that in future they would need to look closely for any clear disparities between voting intention and views on key issues. Whilst it may not be possible to produce a modified voting intention figure based on a formal model, it can at least be made clear that there are other factors suggesting that the voting intention may not be the only story. It would in any case be no bad thing if media coverage of the polls concentrated less on the simple horse-race element of who was ahead and more on people's opinions on the issues of the day.

Conclusion

To conclude, then, the pollsters have to accept a considerable part of the blame for what happened in 1992. Late swing may have accounted for a significant part of the error, but even though this is outside the pollsters' control, it is not something we can simply shrug off. Polls may be perfect representations of the state of opinion at the time they were conducted, but if last-minute shifts mean they are consistently out of date by the day they are published then one would have to question their value, and newspapers would soon cease paying for them.

The pollsters can be blamed for not using better data on which to set their quotas, and slightly less so for relying too much on the voting-intention question, but in my own view the biggest problem lay with the refusals, especially those who refused to take part altogether. Since refusal rates are unlikely to go down, the challenge is to find ways of compensating for the problem, and the various attempts made by the pollsters to do this are examined in Chapter 9.

It also seems to me likely that the problems lie not in any difficulty in research in general, but in the difficulties in researching such a personal and crucial issue as party choice. A failure of the polls does not necessarily mean that other research surveys will be wrong in the same ways.

Notes

1 J. Curtice and C. Payne, 'Forecasting the 1992 election: the BBC experience', in I. Crewe and B. Gosschalk (eds), *Political Communications: The British General Election of 1992* (Cambridge University Press, 1994).

2 G. Mathias and D. Cowling, 'The ITN exit poll', paper presented at EPOP conference, Essex, 1992.

3 P. Clifford and A. Heath, 'The election campaign', in A. Heath, R. Jowell and J. Curtice with B. Taylor, *Labour's Last Chance?* (Dartmouth, 1994).

4 Market Research Society, *The Opinion Polls and the 1992 General Election* (Market Research Society, 1994).

5 *Ibid.*

6 *Ibid.*

7 Population Monitor, Office of Population Censuses and Surveys, published annually.

8 Boundary Commission for England, Newsletter No. 5, July 1993.

9 R. Jowell, B. Hedges, P. Lynn, G. Farrant and A. Heath, 'The 1992 British general election: the failure of the polls', *Public Opinion Quarterly*, 57:2 (1993).

10 J. Smith and I. McLean, 'The poll tax and the electoral register', in Heath *et al.*, *Labour's Last Chance?*

11 Market Research Society, *The Opinion Polls and the 1992 General Election*.

12 Jowell *et al.* , 'The 1992 British general election.

13 I. Crewe, 'A nation of liars? Opinion polls and the 1992 election', *Parliamentary Affairs*, 45:4 (1992).

14 P. Kellner, 'The spiral of truth?', *British Journalism Review*, 7:1 (1996).

15 P. Dimitras and M. Basanez, 'The art of "second-guessing" undecided voters', paper presented at 1992 conference of World Association for Public Opinion Research, St Petersburg, FL.

16 N. Moon, 'If I did know why the polls got it wrong I wouldn't tell you: a case study in item and unit non-response', paper presented at Market Research Society Conference, 1994.

17 N. Moon and R. McGregor, 'Exit polling: developing a technique', *Journal of the Market Research Society*, 34:3 (1992).

18 *Ibid.*
19 R. Harris, 'We are a nation of liars', *Sunday Times*, 12 April 1992.
20 Crewe, 'A nation of liars?'
21 E. Noelle-Neumann, *The Spiral of Silence* (University of Chicago Press, 1984).
22 Harris, 'We are a nation of liars'.
23 D. Butler and D. Kavanagh, *The British General Election of 1992* (Macmillan, 1992).
24 L. Festinger, *A Theory of Cognitive Dissonance* (Stanford University Press, 1957).

7

Exit polling:
a special case

Now, the man on the stand he wants my vote,
He's a-runnin' for office on the ballot note.

One of the most specialised forms of opinion polling is the exit poll, conducted on the day of the election itself, among actual voters, in order to enable a media client to predict the result of the election a bare few hours before the official result is known. Both in its purpose and in its methodology the exit poll is completely different from a predictive opinion poll, and is worth discussion in its own right. Although both an exit poll and a prediction poll seek to measure voting behaviour and public opinion on the parties, the fact that the former can only take place on one day and at a very limited number of locations imposes restrictions that require significant differences of approach.

With access to no more advanced technology than the simple telephone system it is possible for results from an exit poll to be available within half an hour of the end of interviewing. Given that, in the UK at least, relatively few people vote in the last hour of polling, it is possible to produce an estimate based on all polling conducted up until an hour before the close of the poll. This estimate is likely to be very close to the final estimate produced after the very last interviews have been conducted, but it can be made available to the media client during the last hour of polling. This gives the client time to assess the results of the opinion poll, translate this into the final prediction, and broadcast that prediction the moment the polls close.

The broadcasters are not permitted to publish any opinion-poll information on election day whilst the polls are actually open. Thus it has become traditional for both BBC and ITN to broadcast their prediction of the election result on the stroke of ten o'clock. Given that in Britain the first constituency results start coming in soon after eleven, and a good estimate of the overall result is usually available by soon after midnight, this means that the lifespan of a predictive exit poll is no more than an hour or so. This makes it seem like somewhat expensive television, but as we will see, the broadcasters clearly feel it is worth it, and indeed an exit poll typically has more than just a predictive purpose. It may well also set out to try to explain the result rather than just predict it, and this extra analysis can be used throughout an election-night programme, and indeed into the coverage which continues the following day. Since the last results are not usually available until Friday afternoon, there is an awful lot of airtime to be filled, and the more detailed exit-poll analysis helps to serve this purpose.

Development of exit polling

As with pre-election opinion polls, the history of exit polling begins in the USA. It is not as difficult to date the first appearance of an exit poll as it is to be sure about the first appearance of an opinion poll, but it is harder than one might first imagine, given that exit polls are a product of the television age. Part of the problem is in deciding exactly what constitutes an exit poll. This confusion stems largely from the difference between the USA and Britain in the way elections are conducted.

In Britain the electorate in each constituency is subdivided into a number of wards, as discussed in Chapter 3 above, and then within each ward further broken down into polling districts. The electorate from each polling district votes at a particular location, the polling station. At the close of polling the presiding officer seals the ballot boxes from the polling station, and they are then transported to a central location for the count. In local elections, where councillors are elected to serve particular wards, counting must of necessity be on a ward-by-ward basis. However, for general elections counting is not carried out separately by ward, but only at the level of the whole constituency. This means that there is a major counting process to be undergone before the constituency result can be declared.

By contrast, in the USA and in some European countries, counting is carried out at the polling places themselves, and results produced separately for each precinct – the precinct being a rough US equivalent of the polling district. The much smaller numbers involved in the precinct mean that it is much easier and therefore quicker to count the results from a precinct. The use of voting machines in some precincts makes the process even quicker. Producing the final official results obviously takes a lot longer, as the individual results from each precinct need to be verified and then added together to produce city-, county- or state-wide figures. While the official result has to wait until every single vote has been counted, one possibility for the television networks is to produce a projection of results based on only some of the precincts. Thus in 1962 Louis Harris, working for CBS News, used a quota sample (or as he called it a 'recipe') of precincts within states to project the winning candidates in thirteen contests for Senator and Governor.

This is a very efficient means of calling the result of an election in advance of an official announcement, and the fact that it is based upon actual results rather than opinion polling gives it an advantage over polling-based methods. Of course there is no guarantee that such a method will get the result right, for there is still potential sampling error. Although the results from each precinct are based on the official returns for all people who voted, rather than from interviews with a mere sample of them, and are thus more of a census than a sample, the results are only derived from a small number of precincts. The sampling of these precincts from all those across the country therefore introduces an element of sampling error. Effectively the sample size is the total number of the precincts covered, and the universe is the total number of precincts in the country. With this method of exit polling, therefore, the skill lies entirely in the selection of precincts themselves.

If the main aim of an exit poll is simply to call the result of an election before the official results come in, then this precinct-based approach is fine. However, there are two things it does not do. It does not give any indication of differential voting patterns among different parts of the population, and it does not give any indication as to why voters made the decisions that they did. In the 1960s attempts were made to resolve this problem in the USA by producing demographic portraits of the precincts themselves. Based on census information, precincts would be classified as black precincts or white precincts, rich precincts or poor precincts, and many other similar types. An attempt was thus made to analyse the voting behaviour of black voters, blue-collar voters, or whatever, by looking at the pattern of votes in black precincts as opposed to white precincts, and in blue-collar precincts as opposed to white-collar ones.

Unfortunately this approach is far too simplistic. Examination of the data in detail shows that most blacks do not live in black precincts, nor do most rich people live only in high-income precincts. This form of classification based on geography is fine for categorising areas into urban or rural but it is not a good method of analysing individual demographics. Arguments such as this are what is known as the ecological fallacy – the assumption that correlations that exist at the aggregate level exist also at the individual level as well.

Warren Mitofsky, the doyen of US exit polling, describes one example of how broadcasters can reach the wrong conclusion from precinct data.[1] In 1972 CBS News conducted an exit poll collecting information from a sample of voters as they left the polling stations, and also used vote returns from a sample of predominantly black precincts. However, according to the US Bureau of the Census, only about a third of all black voters actually lived in predominantly black, inner-city areas, and the exit poll showed that blacks living in predominantly black precincts do not necessarily vote the same way as other blacks. The sample of precincts recorded a 13% vote for Nixon in the black precincts, and yet the exit poll showed that 17% of all black voters actually voted for Nixon. The weakness of the precinct-based approach is shown from the exit poll data, which revealed that the level of blacks voting for Nixon varied from 6% in the inner cities to 34% in the more affluent suburbs.

After these early experiments it quickly became clear that classifying precincts was not a satisfactory way of classifying voters. This, plus the desire to have some form of explanation as to why voters behaved the way they did, led to the development of an alternative form of election-day information-gathering.

Mitofsky again quotes an anecdote illustrating how the modern exit poll was developed almost by accident. During the 1964 Maryland presidential primary a Louis Harris interviewer in Baltimore, told to talk to voters in their homes to find how they had or would vote, said she got tired of climbing up and down stairs in tall apartment buildings to find her voters, and instead went along to the local school where the voting was taking place. After asking permission from the polling officials, she interviewed voters as they came out of the polling station. When Louis Harris heard what she had done he liked the idea and put it into wide-scale use for the 1964 California Republican primary.

At a similar time Mitofsky himself was directing a new research team at CBS News, charged with resolving the two problems of providing an explanation as to why voters had behaved the way they did, and of providing an analysis of voting behaviour by demographic type. This unit experimented with a number of different approaches of which the exit poll was but one. It was used in conjunction with precinct returns, the larger county returns which were available a little later, and pre-election polling. Experiments were also tried with using election-day telephone calls to voters at home, but it proved impossible to interview a reasonable-quality sample in a single day.

The various experiments showed that the exit-poll approach was sufficiently reliable to be pursued. After initial experiments at the 1967 Kentucky gubernatorial election proved accurate, exit polls were used throughout the 1968 primaries and in the 1968 presidential election itself. The exit polls produced early estimates for presidential, senatorial and gubernatorial elections which were then amended by combining them with the actual returns from sample precincts. Information on the sex and race of each voter was also collected during these exit polls, but there was at this time no means of getting results from precincts scattered all over the country back to a central computer for analysis. Therefore the only way in which cross-analysis by sex or race could be carried out was if it was done manually by the interviewer at each precinct, and the results of this cross-tabulation aggregated back in head office.

The next major step was the development of the exit poll as an analytical tool, using much longer questionnaires aimed at establishing the key issues in the voters' minds and their perceptions of the different candidates. In the 1969 New York City mayoral race the local CBS affiliate developed a lengthy questionnaire about issues to go along with the simple voting question. The information from this poll allowed CBS to give a detailed analysis of the election issues throughout its election night programme. Indeed, between 1970 and 1980 CBS used exit polls only for such analysis purposes, relying on early precinct returns for the actual projection. From 1982 onwards CBS used a mixture of exit-poll figures plus early precinct returns for their predictions.

The other networks in the USA were proceeding in much the same way. NBC conducted its first real exit poll in 1973 though NBC, like CBS, at first used exit polls solely for analysis rather than for projections. ABC came later on to the scene, not conducting exit polls at all until 1980, though by 1982 it was using its exit-poll results for projection purposes. Thus throughout the 1980s the three main American networks were all conducting exit polls, using broadly similar methodology.

The way the networks' exit polls for presidential elections accumulate and use the results is quite different from the method used in Britain, as will be discussed below. This is because the American presidential election is based on the concept of electoral votes. Each state has a fixed number of electoral votes equal to the number of people it sends to Congress (its representatives in the House, which are proportional to its electorate, plus its two Senators). There is thus a vast imbalance in the electoral votes between the huge states such as California, which has fifty-four votes, and sparsely populated states such as Wyoming or South Dakota, which have only three each. Within each state all the electoral votes are awarded to the candidate who wins the popular votes in that state. Thus whether candidates beat their opponents by a mere 1% or by a landslide makes no difference: they still receive all the electoral votes for that state.

This means that the US presidential election is effectively a composite of fifty-one separate statewide elections (the fifty states plus the District of Columbia). Predicting the result of a US election is therefore a matter of predicting the result of these fifty-one separate statewide races. For each state either the exit poll, or the early precinct returns, or a mixture of the two, allow predictions to be made of who will win that state. If a candidate appears to have a clear majority, above any allowance of sampling error, that state will be 'called' for that candidate. At the same time the relevant number of electoral college votes will be added to that candidate's pile. Once any candidate has a clear majority of the electoral votes, the result of the entire election can be called.

Of course there are elections in individual states where the two candidates seem to be running very close together. Again, whether this is based on exit polls or early precinct returns, or a combination of the two, if the projections are that the two parties are closer together than the gap necessary for sampling error, the state will be declared as 'too close to call'. In this case the electoral votes for that state will not be allocated to either candidate until enough actual returns are in for it to be clear that one candidate can be reasonably safely assumed to be the winner.

Because there are so many different races and it is not necessary to 'call' each one in order to come up with a final prediction, there is an inevitable tendency towards conservatism in deciding whether a race is 'too close to call' or not. This extends even into the later stages of an election broadcast, when most of the results are in. In 1992, for example, some races were not being called by the networks even with well over 90% of the vote in, because it was just theoretically possible that if the candidate in second place gained all of the votes outstanding, then he or she could still emerge as the winner. This may serve to delay slightly the declaration of one candidate as the ultimate winner, but it does minimise the risk of false predictions being made.

Although the British parliamentary general election also consists of a series of separate first-past-the-post races, the difference between 51 separate races in the US and 659 separate races in Britain means that in Britain it is essential to treat the process much more in overall terms, rather than try to predict each seat separately. This is why the British methodology, as described in detail below, differs in a number of respects from that used in the USA.

Because the US networks were all carrying out exit polls in much the same way, and using much the same rules to decide whether it was safe to call an individual state or not, there was a lot of pressure on them to save money by pooling their resources rather than each conducting their own separate exit poll. On the one hand one can argue that, since the methodology is so similar and since so much is also reliant on early precinct returns rather than exit polling, the networks are likely to have similar results and are thus duplicating each other's effort. On the other hand, having its own poll allows the network a chance to put new methodology to the test, and possibly come up with a different approach which will lead to a more accurate result. It also allows them to choose their own questions to use for analysis purposes. Sheer commercial pressure of competition between the networks also encourages the use of separate polls by each one. However, by 1992 the networks decided that it would be more sensible for them to work together and commission a single organisation to conduct an exit poll which would be used by all of them. Thus it was that the three networks plus Cable News Network (CNN) effectively created a new polling organisation called Voter News Service, under the direction of Warren Mitofsky, to conduct exit polling for the 1992 presidential election, and the same organisation worked in the same way for the 1996 election, now under the direction of Murray Edelman.

While the development of the exit poll in the USA was closely linked to the use of other methodology such as samples of actual precinct returns, in Britain there is no such choice available. In the absence of any early declaration of results at a polling-station level, the only way in which a British election can be predicted on election night in advance of the actual result is by some form of polling. This is why, in contrast to the pre-election opinion poll, the exit poll as we know it today was used in Britain before it was used in the USA on anything like a comparable scale.

Pioneers of exit polling in Britain were ITN and their pollsters Harris. The first election in which ITN carried out and announced the result of an exit poll was that of October 1974.

ITN's basic approach has been to concentrate polling in the marginal constituencies, and, in particular, marginal constituencies held by the party currently behind in the polls. There are, of course, exceptions to this, and in fact in
the first ITN exit poll in October 1974 there was no clear indication which party
was going to win, so both Conservative and Labour marginals were polled.
ITN's first foray into exit polling was successful. They predicted a Labour majority of fifteen seats, compared with an actual majority of just three seats, which
is within the level of sampling error one would expect. The BBC used pre-election predictive polling rather than exit polling for its own projection and was
wildly wrong with a projection of a Labour lead of 137 seats.

In 1979 ITN and the BBC continued with their respective exit-poll and predictive-poll techniques. ITN were again reasonably close to the actual election
result, having predicted a 63-seat Conservative win as opposed to the 43-seat
majority actually obtained. The BBC this time were far more accurate than in
1974, with a prediction of a 14-seat Conservative majority. In 1983 the BBC's
improvement, still based on predictive polling, continued, as they were within
2 seats of the actual Conservative majority of 144 seats. ITN, keeping faith in
their exit-poll technique, underestimated the Conservative majority by 28
seats. In 1987 both broadcasters did much worse than in 1983. Set against an
actual Conservative majority of 102 seats, ITN's exit poll prediction of 68 seats
was much worse than one might expect, though still far more reliable than the
BBC's projection of a mere 26-seat majority.

It was after this further failure of the predictive-poll technique to produce a
reliable projection that the BBC changed their approach. In 1987 they had
commissioned Gallup to conduct a large-scale on-the-day exercise, interviewing people in the street and at home. People who had already voted were asked
how they had voted, while those who had not yet voted were asked if they
intended to vote and, if so, for which party. In addition there were a large
number of questions about the issues of the election. In retrospect it appears
that mixing results from those who actually had voted with those who had not
yet done so was an unsatisfactory technique, and it also appears that the length
of the questionnaire – far higher than a typical predictive poll, and certainly
longer than an exit poll – led to a high refusal rate and response bias. Thus in
1992 both the BBC and ITN made use of exit polls for their projections.

ITN continued to use Harris, as they had done for every one of their exit
polls, while the BBC for the first time commissioned NOP. Sadly, the switch from
predictive polling to exit polling did not benefit the BBC greatly, for its predictions were once again considerably adrift from the actual result. However, this
cannot be blamed on the switch to exit polling alone, for ITN's exit poll was
almost as far adrift. Both predicted clear Labour majorities compared with a
final actual Conservative majority of twenty-one seats. *Post hoc* analysis made
it clear that the exit polls in 1992 suffered from some of the same problems as
the predictive polls, as already discussed in Chapter 6 above. That the errors in

the exit polls, whilst large, were still considerably lower than the errors in the predictive polls, is itself a partial explanation of the problems of the polls in 1992. In order to appreciate these differences we now need to look in more detail at the ways in which exit polls are actually carried out.

Exit-poll methodology

After its inaccurate seat-forecast in the 1987 general election, the BBC decided to investigate alternative approaches. It commissioned NOP to write a paper discussing the various options open for election-night forecasting, and making a justified recommendation for one method. The paper concluded fairly firmly that exit polls were the right approach, although there was scope for discussion as to the exact means of conducting them. Following this, the BBC commissioned NOP to undertake a development programme of an exit-polling strategy, with the aim of having a settled, agreed method in place in time for the next general election.[2]

It was a slightly strange situation, in that while NOP and the BBC could spend as much time as we liked discussing various approaches, they would only ever get the chance to put them to the test at an actual election. Other than the European elections (which were over two years away) and local council elections (which were less than ideal because their low turnout raises severe doubts about their representativeness), we were reduced to waiting somewhat ghoulishly for by-elections to occur.

The discussion of the theory of exit-poll sampling which follows is intermingled with some of the practical experiments used by NOP and the BBC during the development programme. It must be remembered that all the early testing was in single constituency by-elections, and although the principles are exactly the same, some of the maths in the examples would be very different in a national election exit poll.

Exit polls enjoy two crucial advantages over prediction polls, and as a result have tended to be more accurate. The first is that they involve interviewing only people who have actually voted. Chapter 4 discussed the problems in pre-election polls of distinguishing those who are likely to vote from those who are not, and the bias that can result if they do not. With an exit poll this problem simply does not arise. If Labour supporters are more likely to tell an opinion pollster that they will definitely vote, while knowing that it is in fact unlikely, or if Liberal Democrat supporters tell interviewers that they will vote, and genuinely mean it, but in fact are more likely then to fail to do so, then this would cause bias in an opinion poll, but not in an exit poll. If they do not actually vote, people will not be interviewed on the exit poll: it is as simple as that.

This same principle also takes care of the problem of non-registered voters. Chapter 6 discussed the extent to which the opinion polls' problems in 1992 were caused by their interviewing people who were not on the electoral register, and thus not eligible to vote. Although this was dismissed by the MRS enquiry as a very minor problem, it still accounted for some part of the polls' errors, and yet cannot have accounted for any of the error in an exit poll.

The other great advantage that exit polls have over pre-election polls is simply one of timing. Throughout this book examples have been given of the importance of polling as close as possible to election day itself, in order to avoid missing out on any last-minute swing. There is less agreement about the impact of last-minute swing in the 1992 election than there is over the impact of non-registration, but there is no doubt that it accounted for some of the error, and more than non-registration. Since the polls all interviewed on the day before the election, they could not have done much more to catch any late movement, and yet they still suffered to some extent from late swing.

With an exit poll it does not matter how late people make their final decision about which party to vote for. Since voters cannot ask for a replacement ballot paper to have another go if they change their minds after voting, the exit-poll interviewer approaches voters only after they have made that irrevocable decision. Voters may still choose to dissemble, or just to refuse differentially, which is partly why exit polls are not guaranteed to get it right, but at least an exit poll has these two great advantages over pre-election polls.

One other key difference between exit polls and the prediction polls in 1992, which on that occasion contributed to the better result achieved by the exit polls, is that they were conducted using random rather than quota sampling. As Chapter 6 has probably made clear, I am not at all convinced by the argument that quota samples *must necessarily* be worse than random samples – the evidence from earlier elections is too strong to be ignored – but in 1992 a major part of the error in the polls arose from the fact that they were quota samples. This is not to say that they were inevitably wrong as a result, merely that they happened to be wrong as a result. Because of the lack of accurate information on which to set quotas, the pollsters all set quotas in 1992 that were biased towards the demographic groups most likely to favour Labour.

With exit polls the question of random versus quota sampling does not even arise – there is no point in using anything other than random sampling of voters. Even if one wanted to use quota sampling it would be impossible, because no one knows what the demographic profile of voters is. We know from the Census, and from large-scale surveys, what the *population* as a whole looks like. With a bit of extrapolation we can use the OPCS survey of the Census against the electoral register to produce a reasonable estimate of what the *electorate* looks like. The one thing we do not know is what, for want of a proper word, I will call the *voterate* looks like. Not only is there no source of information available (apart from other exit polls, which makes the whole thing a bit circular), but even if there were, there would be no guarantee that those who vote in one election are the same people as those who vote in the next election.

Fortunately, given the above, we do not actually want to use quota sampling for exit polls because there is no point. Even a hardened user of quota samples such as I is happy to accept that, all other things being equal, random samples are preferable to quota samples if the means exist to conduct each properly. The problem with pre-election polls is that it is not possible to conduct them properly using random samples, mainly because of the problems of timing. The main difficulty with random sampling is the need to return several times to many of the selected respondents in order to catch them at home. In an exit poll this is not a problem, since all potential respondents are by definition present when the interviewer wants to interview them.

There is no possibility of availability bias with an exit poll, and the only serious possibility of response bias arises from possible differential refusal rates. From the interviewer's point of view it is thus no harder to apply random sampling to select voters for interview than it is to select people to fit quotas. Indeed it is easier, because with random sampling the interviewer knows that everyone approached is eligible for interview. With quota sampling there is always the risk of approaching someone who appears to fit the quota but in fact proves not to. It is also easier from the research executive's point of view to give an instruction to interview every nth person leaving the polling station rather than to draw up quota sheets.

This is not to say, however, that sampling for exit polls is a simple matter. Whereas the selection of respondents at the end of the sampling process may be a simple task, the process by which some polling stations are covered in the exit polls and some are not is an immensely complex one. In devising a strategy for selecting primary sampling units there are a number of both theoretical and practical issues to be resolved. Since the selection of respondents is fairly straightforward, an exit poll stands or falls on the quality of the first-stage sampling.

The sampling variables

In either pre-election or exit polling one is measuring at the individual level: either claimed future intention or claimed actual behaviour. In either case the individual is the source of the survey data and the selection of individuals is, therefore, key to its success. However, economics rules out a simple random sample of individuals across the whole population being surveyed, and some form of clustering is inevitable. Clustering is normally considered as a geographical variable: one interviews a number of individuals in each of a number of selected locations, be they constituencies, wards, postcode sectors, or whatever. The starting point for almost all survey sampling is the selection of these geographical clusters; in a national survey this would be the selection of constituencies, followed by the selection perhaps of wards within constituencies, and possibly even the selection of polling districts within wards. The use of sensible stratification in the selection of these clusters can help to offset the increase in survey error caused by the clustering effect, and this is why selection of clusters is such a key element in the success of any opinion poll.

It can also be argued that a survey sample is clustered by time as well as by place. An opinion poll taken during an election campaign will probably be undertaken on only one or possibly two days and so can only set out to demonstrate how people were feeling on those days. As well as sampling people in particular places it has sampled them at a particular moment in time.

In the case of predictive polling, time is not a significant element in the reliability of the survey, provided one realises what is going on. As long as commentators do not assume that a poll conducted on one day will inevitably predict the result of an election carried out ten days hence, there is no critical role for time to play in the sampling process of an ordinary opinion poll. It is setting out to measure people's opinions rather than their behaviour, and although opinions do change over time they are longer-lasting than a single act which takes place at one moment only.

So long as the poll is not spread out over such a large number of days that the people interviewed at the beginning could well have given different answers had they been interviewed at the end of the fieldwork period, and so long as the fieldwork period is not so short that people who are only available at certain times of the day have no chance of being interviewed (the most obvious example of this latter being the stipulation in many opinion polls that working men have to be interviewed after 5 p.m. to ensure that those who are confined in office or factory during the day can still have a chance of being interviewed), then all that reasonably needs to be done on the time front has been done.

The situation is very different, however, when it comes to an exit poll. Exit polls measure a single act which electors carry out once only at a specific moment during the voting day. Although some of the received wisdom on the way supporters of different parties are more likely to vote at certain times of the day than others is inaccurate (not all early-morning or late-evening voters are Labour supporters, nor are Tory voters always most likely to turn out in the middle of the day), it is undoubtedly the case that there are differences in voting behaviour at different times of the day. This makes it imperative that as well as representing the whole of the geographical area correctly, an exit poll must also represent the whole of the polling day.

One way to resolve this is simply to say that those polling stations selected for coverage in the exit poll will be covered continuously from the moment the polls open to the moment the polls close. This was in fact the approach adopted by the BBC for its by-election exit polls conducted prior to NOP's involvement, and by Harris for ITN. Taking a fairly arbitrary figure of 150 interviewer-hours (which was the amount expended on the BBC's previous by-election exit polls), one could cover 10 polling stations for 15 hours each, or 25 for 6 hours, or 50 for 3 hours each. (In theory a national poll could cover 150 for 1 hour each, but since almost no constituencies have 150 polling stations, this extreme end of the scale was not considered.) The choice between approaches depends on the different levels of variability. There are three types of variability to consider:

A variability between polling districts
B variability between hours of the day
C variability by time of day between polling districts.

The aim of any sampling system is to ensure the maximum coverage of the maximum variability. Type B is clearly covered by interviewing all day at ten polling districts, and provided the three-hour slots are allocated properly it is also covered by interviewing at fifty polling stations for three hours each. The difference between an approach which sets out to cover a small number of places each for the whole day, and one which interviews at more places for less time each, comes down to a question of whether variability of Type A is greater than variability of Type C.

The key assumption behind the 'more places for less time each' approach is that provided the time slots are allocated carefully, then it doesn't matter which places are covered at which time. Variability by time of day is assumed to be constant across the different polling places. If in some polling stations Conservatives are most likely to vote between 9 a.m. and 11 a.m., while in others these are times of peak Labour voting, this strategy will miss out on the resulting variation. On the other hand, by going to more places, this approach covers more of the variability between one place and another.

All the evidence available from polling and other sources is that variability between polling districts can be enormous, as party allegiance is such a geographically clustered variable. Though there is little or no evidence, we believe that variation by time of day is likely to be fairly consistent across all polling districts. We are therefore convinced that variability of Type A is likely to be far greater than variability of Type C, and this is why our approach was to cover more places, but only for part of the day each.

If this alternative approach is adopted, maximising the number of polling districts included by covering each one for only part of the day, then time has to be built into the initial sampling system in just the same way that any form of geographical stratification is carried out, and will be just as important to the success or failure of the exit poll. If some times of day are used more than others, or if all the places covered during the 'dead' early-afternoon time periods are strong Tory seats, then bias will almost inevitably result.

Primary sampling units

The first stage of any clustered sampling process is to identify what are to form the primary sampling units (psus). Normally this simply is a matter of deciding how small the geographical area to be considered at the primary sampling stage should be. In the case of a constituency poll the psus would be wards, polling districts, enumeration districts or postcode sectors. Whilst there may be some discussion as to which of these four is the most appropriate, there would be no doubt as to what options were available. In the case of an exit poll, however, even the identification of the psu is a complex issue. On the geographical front, first of all, wards are too crude a geographical level for political work and one is therefore moved towards polling districts, but immediately there is a problem – because voting takes place at polling stations the final sampling unit needs to be a polling station, and in many areas a polling station can serve more than one polling district.

It is therefore necessary to treat polling districts which share the same polling station as effectively the same unit, though this can then cause problems if they come from different wards, and should therefore be in different parts of the stratification list (or, as happened in a double by-election in Paisley North and Paisley South in 1990, come from a different constituency altogether). The situation is further complicated by the need, as discussed above, to include time as part of the sampling frame. The position is analogous to that of interviewing visitors to an exhibition, or any other moving population. The basic sampling unit has to be one of both time and place. This may seem on the surface a relatively simple task, and several academic statisticians of my acquaintance insist that it should be, but once the practicalities are examined it becomes clear that this is not the case.

Before looking at the link between time and place it is necessary to consider one further element of the process of selecting psus, and this is the role of population size. In any form of clustered sampling one has to choose between giving each psu an equal chance of selection regardless of population size, and then holding the sampling interval constant so that larger psus generate more final interviews; or alternatively selecting psus proportional so size, and then varying the sampling interval so that each psu produces the same number of interviews. The choice between these two options will vary from survey to survey and will depend on the variables being examined. Sheer practicality will also play a part and this is of crucial importance in exit polling.

Variations of size between different polling districts, even in the same constituency, can be enormous. If a constant sampling interval were to be used it would have to be set large enough to enable interviewers in the biggest polling districts to be able to keep up with the flow of required interviews. An interval set this large would mean that in the smallest polling districts interviewers may be conducting only one or two interviews in an hour, and in extreme cases could end up not doing any interviews at all. To have only a small number of interviewers working at a sensible capacity, and some of the rest producing only one or two interviews from an entire day's work, cannot be a sensible use of interviewer resources. The choice is thus easily made that for exit polls one has to select psus with a probability proportional to size and then vary the sampling interval.

146

In a pre-election poll one can achieve selection with a probability proportional to size by the simple means of listing population size against each unit in the stratified list, accumulating population down the list, and then applying a constant sampling interval (as explained in Chapter 3). In the case of exit polls, however, we have seen that time as well as place should play a part in the stratification system. This means that in an ideal world the selection of psus would be a function of voters within time and within place. Selection by place would be by polling station, and as for selection by time, it seems at first sight logical to split the fifteen-hour polling day into fifteen separate hours. What we should then do is ensure that the chance of any of these resulting polling-station hours being selected for inclusion in the sample is in proportion to its population, that is to say the number of people who would actually vote at that polling station during that hour. This would then give us a sampling frame of the kind shown in Table 23.

Table 23 *Example polling station by time by voters matrix*

Ward	Polling station	Hour	Voters	Cumulative
Speedie	AA	7–8 a.m.	75	75
		8–9 a.m.	180	255
		↓	↓	↓
		9–10 p.m.	90	1,575
	AB	7–8 a.m.	60	1,635
		↓	↓	↓
		↓	↓	↓
Dixon	ZZ	9–10 p.m.	100	65,500

The problem with this approach is that we are not in a position to estimate what proportion of the voters in a particular polling district will vote during a particular hour of the day. There is a body of evidence from previous exit polls which suggests that there is a general pattern of distribution of votes during the day. Broadly speaking it is a two-peak distribution, with a small peak in the early morning and a much larger peak in mid-evening. However, individual by-elections have failed by a considerable extent to conform to this pattern, and also we have no information as to whether the pattern of voting by time of day is likely to be different from one part of a constituency to another. Any errors in estimating the number of voters who actually go through a polling station in a particular hour will have to be corrected by weighting at the analysis stage, and this could easily involve the use of some very large weights indeed.

In developing an exit-polling strategy the BBC and NOP agreed that they simply did not have accurate information on which to make reasonable estimates of the number of voters who would have voted at a particular polling station during a particular hour, and indeed that by trying to do so they were more likely to make the situation far worse rather than better. This then led to the conclusion that one has to drop the link between voters and time of day from our sampling matrix. Instead, one should assume for the purposes of sampling that one-fifteenth of the voters would vote during each hour of the day. By assuming that each hour is equal, any actual variation from one hour to another will be taken care of by holding the sampling interval constant throughout the day so that busier periods will simply generate more interviews.

This system produces a similar matrix to that of Table 23, but instead of having separate voter estimates for each hour the estimated number of voters is simply divided by fifteen and that number filled in each of the cells. This then gives a frame similar to that shown in Table 24.

Table 24 *Example polling station by time matrix*

Ward	Polling station	Hour	Voters	Cumulative
Speedie	AA	7–8 a.m.	105	105
		8–9 a.m.	105	210
		↓	↓	↓
		9–10 p.m.	105	1,575
	AB	7–8 a.m.	220	1,795
		↓	↓	↓
		↓	↓	↓
Dixon	ZZ	9–10 p.m.	113	65,500

This still does not solve all the sampling problems, however, for there is another area in which the demands of theoretical statistics clash with those of the real world. If we assume a target of 150 polling station-hours, then the total electorate of the constituency will be divided by 150 and from a random start point that sum applied all the way down the list. This means that each polling station may be selected for one hour, two hours or more, depending on the size of the polling station, but except in the case of enormous polling stations it would not be selected for two consecutive hours. This, in turn, means that either interviewers would have to be employed on the basis of only one hour's work at a time or interviewers would have to move from one polling station to another at the end of each hour.

Even if it were possible to find 150 separate interviewers prepared to accept a one-hour shift, the cost of travelling time relative to interviewing time would make the whole exercise uneconomic. In practice interviewers wish to work for several hours during the day, and if they have to be allowed a break in order to move from one polling station to another at the end of every hour, then the amount of time they spend interviewing compared to the amount of time they spend travelling will again be highly cost-ineffective. It is simply not possible to

treat each hour within a polling station as a separate unit for sampling purposes, and so time has to be clustered somewhat further.

Given that a typical interviewer-day involves six hours' interviewing and
one hour travelling, the most practically sensible approach is to allocate interviewing into three-hour shifts. This means that an interviewer can take on just
one three-hour shift, or two three-hour shifts with a break in between for a full
day's work, and if any interviewers wish to put in a longer day to earn some
extra money then at an extreme they can do four shifts. It would seem at first
sight that this involves only a slight amendment to the frame as laid out in Table
24. If three-hour shifts are to be required, then instead of listing each hour from
7 a.m. to 8 a.m., 8 a.m. to 9 a.m., and so on down the sampling frame, one
simply breaks the day up into three-hour shifts from 7 a.m. till 10 a.m., 10 a.m.
till 1 p.m. and so on, and then samples from this list using a constant interval
as before. The problem with this approach is that it fits in only with the idea of
interviewers doing single shifts, or doing a three-hour shift followed by a three-
hour break. These problems are discussed in more detail below, but for the
moment we can simply rule out the idea of breaking the sample into five constant three-hour sections.

The only solution to this problem is to divorce time from place as far as the
sampling process is concerned, and to treat them as two entirely separate tasks.
What happens as far as sampling of polling stations is concerned is that we
revert to the idea of sampling as used in predictive polling. Each polling station
is simply sampled in proportion to its own population. This then produces a
sampling frame as shown in Table 25, and applying a constant interval down a
cumulative list will simply specify that each polling station is to have none or
one or more shifts conducted at it.

Table 25 *Example polling station by size matrix*

Ward	Polling station	Electorate	Cumulative
Speedie	AA	1,575	1,575
	AB	3,300	4,875
	↓	↓	↓
Dixon	ZZ	1,695	65,500

Once 50 polling-station shifts have been allocated, there needs to be a secondary sampling of time. With our by-election design assuming that 150 interviewer-hours were to be used on the day, and given that the polls are open for
15 hours, then the aim of the time sampling was to ensure that each hour was
covered by ten interviewers. This seems on the surface a simple process: you
simply start with ten interviewers working from 7 a.m. until 10 a.m. and when
they come to the end of their three-hour shift another ten interviewers start
work to cover the period from 10 a.m. to 1 p.m. At 1 p.m. there will be need of

a further ten interviewers, and at this stage, of course, one can bring back the interviewers who started the day.

Unfortunately, because they have had to wait three hours whilst the second team of interviewers did their shift, their break is two hours longer than they need and is almost certainly two hours longer than the client is willing to pay for. Since the most efficient way to use interviewers is to give them a three-hour shift followed by a one-hour break, or at worst a two-hour break, a different approach is needed to time allocation. We have ten interviewers starting work from 7 a.m. till 10 a.m. and they will then have a one-hour break before resuming at 11 a.m. Because every hour of the day needs to be covered we must then start another team of ten interviewers at 10 a.m. to fill in that 10 to 11 gap.

This then generates a different problem. Because they too have to work a three-hour shift if they are to used efficiently, then after they have worked for one hour the first team will come back, and the two teams will both be working at the same time. If the number of interviewer-hours is to be kept at 150 we will run out of interviewer-hours long before the end of the day.

In fact, once we began putting the theory of sample design into practice, it soon became apparent that any straightforward, systematic application of sampling points by time would not be possible and some form of compromise would be necessary. Unfortunately it took a lot longer to find a solution than it did to identify the problem, and despite many iterations I am still far from convinced that I have *the* answer. I have certainly found *an* answer, but there may be better ones.

The compromise is based on an acceptance that it is impossible to achieve even close to an average of ten interviewers for every hour of the day, but that it is possible to achieve this for *almost* every hour. Provided those time slots which are most different from the target are the ones during which least voting takes place, then at least the effect on the quality of the survey will be minimised. It is clear from the evidence of previous by-elections, and from the ITN/Harris exit polls, that the slackest times of the day are the first hour, the last hour and the hour from 2 p.m. to 3 p.m. By introducing considerable variation in the number of interviewers who start work each hour it is possible to achieve a time-sampling frame which closely matches the target for twelve of the fifteen polling hours.

Because each hour of the day has a number of shifts which are different from the target of ten hours, weights need to be applied to interviews conducted during each hour of the day to bring them back into line. The weight is calculated simply by dividing the target number of interviewers in each hour – ten – by the actual number. The by-election sample design we ended up with kept the range of weights down from 1.67 in the three quietest hours, to 0.82 in the most oversampled hour. Given that the three hours with the 1.67 weights account for probably no more than 6% of all voting, then we can fairly safely ignore them, and treat the range of weights as being from 0.82 to 1.06. This range is so narrow as to mean that, to all intents and purposes, the survey is as reliable as it would be had each hour indeed had the ten interviewers theoretical statistics says it should.

We now have two entirely separate samples: a sample of fifty polling-station slots, and a sample of fifty three-hour time slots, and the final stage of the sampling task is to marry these two together. This is simply done by allocating time slots systematically down the stratified list of polling stations. By linking the two separate samples in such a systematic way it would seem that the resulting sample of polling station by time must be free from any biases. However, in just the same way that even the most meticulously designed stratified sample of constituencies can produce a sample in which only safe Conservative seats and only marginal Labour seats are selected, so this method can produce a sample which is seriously skewed by time of day.

As stated above, it is assumed for the purposes of sampling that the flow of voters is equal throughout the day, and the actual very considerable discrepancy between different times of day is taken care of by holding the sample interval constant throughout the day. Our sampling method ensures that the busiest hours are selected no more or less often than the quietest hours, but what the matching of time to polling station can unwittingly achieve is a situation in which, for example, polling stations in strongly Conservative areas are selected only at the quietest times of the day, while interviewing at the busiest times of the day is concentrated in Labour strongholds. Given that something like one-third of all voting tends to take place between the hours of 6 p.m. and 9 p.m., concentrating on Labour areas during these hours will introduce a very strong element of bias into the final sample. We discovered this fact the hard way in our first by-election exit poll, in Kensington, which is of course perfectly designed to produce such an effect, being a constituency with a solidly Labour northern part and a solidly Conservative southern part. Fortunately we realised in time on the day of the Kensington by-election and were able to correct the polling stations' varying chances of selection at different times by use of last-minute weighting, but the lesson had been learnt and in all subsequent by-elections we took care to validate the sample before the survey began.

The exact way in which the validation was carried out depended on the ways in which the constituency subdivides; in some there were obvious geographical subdivisions, while in others there were obvious subdivisions by party strength, or both. The number of interviewing slots is not large enough for this geographical or political breakdown to be mapped on the basis of individual hours, but what we can do is to break the day down into four separate segments: early morning, middle of the day, afternoon and early evening, and late evening. Then we can check that if a particular geographical or political subdivision of the constituency contains 40% of the total electorate, it also makes up 40% of all early-morning slots, 40% of all middle-of-the-day slots, and so on. Again, because of the relatively small number of sampling units, a perfect match is rarely achieved by the first sampling allocation and some reallocation is necessary. If, for example, the area of the constituency identified as the most Conservative has too many sampling points late in the day and too few in the middle of the day, while the reverse is true of the Conservative/Labour marginal wards, then time slots have to be switched between wards until the required balance is achieved.

All the development work on sample design was for by-elections, but the requirements are different for a general election because there is less flexibility about how the interviewers work. For a general election, each interviewer has to work two shifts – it is inefficient for them to work only one, and the physical distance between constituencies makes it impossible for them to do three or four shifts. Imposing this extra degree of rigidity makes the organisation of time samples far more complex.

There was a further pressure on the design in that while it is easy to move from one ward to another in, say, Camden during a one-hour break, it is far from easy to do so in Penrith and the Borders, where the distance between sampled polling stations can involve twenty miles of driving over hill roads. Since the interviewer also has to sort out all the completed questionnaires from the first shift and report the results during this period, we decided that for the general election design we would have to have a one and a half-hour gap between shifts for a national election. This, in turn, led to the use of shifts starting on the half-hour as well as on the hour, which gave some much-needed flexibility.

Selection of individuals

The final stage of any exit-poll sampling process is the calculation of the sampling interval which determines the selection of the individuals as they leave the polling station. As explained above, we chose to disregard differential flow of voting by time of day; and also, having selected polling stations with a probability proportional to size, it is necessary to aim for the same number of interviews in each shift. The first stage in achieving this is to estimate the likely turnout on the day which, in our case, was done by conducting an informal survey of the pundits at the BBC and at various newspapers.

Once a turnout estimate was settled on, the interval for each polling station was calculated by multiplying the electorate for the relevant polling district(s) by the turnout, dividing the result by five (since three hours of interviewing represents one-fifth of the total day) and then finally dividing that result by forty (the target number of interviews). At each polling station we have a team of two working throughout the three-hour shift, one interviewing and one simply keeping a tally of voters by means of a mechanical hand counter. The counter's job is to let interviewers know who is the next person targeted for selection, and also to keep track of the total number of voters. If for any reason the number interviewed is not what it should have been (most probably because at the busiest times it is impossible for interviewers to keep up with the flow), then simple weights can be applied to bring the number of interviews achieved back to what it should have been. There seems inherently no reason to suppose that those people missed by the interviewer simply because she was already interviewing someone else when they left are anything other than a subset of all people who left the polling station at that time. Because changes in voting behaviour by time of day can be significant, the process of counting total voters and subsequent weighting are conducted on the basis of every individual hour rather than across the whole three-hour shift.

Because the variation in voting by time of day can be so extreme, experience has shown that it is better to modify this pure sampling method in two ways to take account of the practicalities. First, rather than interviewers being told to interview every *n*th person (which sometimes meant them interviewing no one at all if only a few people passed during that hour), they are instructed to interview the first person who leaves the polling station during each hour and then every *n*th person thereafter. This may seem to have only a trivial effect on the total number of interviews achieved, but its effect on interviewer morale should not be underestimated: interviewers are generally not happy about spending time nominally interviewing when there are people available to be interviewed whom they cannot interview because of the rules.

To improve the situation still further we commonly reduce the sampling interval at the very quietest times and then restore it to its correct level at the stage of weighting. If only twelve people leave a polling station where the interview is one in ten, it is better to interview six of them and weight those down to only two respondents than to stick rigidly to the rules and only interview two in the first place.

The final consideration in the whole sampling process is how refusals are dealt with. There are two basic ways of doing this, and we started off using one before deciding that the other was preferable. The initial approach was to deal with refusals by means of replacement. For every selected individual, whether actually interviewed or not, the interviewer made a note of her estimate of their age and sex. In this way a demographic record of refusals (albeit crude) was kept. Under the replacement method, if a woman aged eighteen to twenty-nine refuses, a record is made of this and the next women aged eighteen to twenty-nine who is not already targeted for interview will be approached as a replacement. The theory behind this is thus just the same as that behind weighting, that is to say that eighteen- to twenty-nine-year-old women who are interviewed are the same as eighteen- to twenty-nine-year-old women who are not interviewed.

We have found two difficulties with this approach. The first is that it is not the easiest method to explain to interviewers or indeed to ensure that they are correctly following. If the next sampled person is also an eighteen- to twenty-nine-year-old woman there is a tendency for interviewers to interview her and also to treat her as a replacement for the refusal. More worrying, we felt, was the impact on the interviewers' overall approach of the whole idea of replacing refusals. Once interviewers know that a refusal can easily be replaced by another person they lose the incentive to exert their normal persuasive skills on the refusal in the hopes of converting it into an interview. We therefore switched from a replacement approach to a weighting approach and were thus able to stress to interviewers the importance of getting as many interviews as possible, which can only be achieved by persuading the initially reluctant to take part in the survey.

The mechanics of the weighting itself are very simple. Analysis of the actual questionnaires completed gives us a demographic breakdown of the inter-viewed sample, while analysis of the separate records kept of refusals gives us a breakdown of the refused sample. Adding these two together gives us a demo-graphic breakdown of the population *target*. It is then simply a case of weight-ing the achieved sample so that each of the eight age-by-sex groups is set at its correct proportion of the total sample.

Data collection

In our first experiments in exit polling, data were collected by means of personal interview. Each selected respondent was asked how he or she had just voted, and also how they had voted, if at all, in the 1987 general election. A subset of respondents (around one in four) was then asked four further questions on issues of the election, the results of which were used in the panel discussions on the election-night programme. One attraction of this approach was that it allowed the BBC to target respondents for the follow-up attitudinal questions. Thus in one by-election all those who said they voted Liberal Democrat were asked the extra questions, while in another it was all those who had voted Conservative in 1987 but not in the by-election.

However, as discussed in more detail in the section below, there were con-cerns about the impact of the questionnaire method on response rates, and thus on the reliability of the results. There was concern that people were reluc-tant to say openly for whom they had just voted, with the possibility of being overheard by other voters (especially their partners). We therefore experi-mented with a numbered showcard listing the parties, so that the respondent did not have to name the party they voted for aloud, but could instead just read the number from the showcard. This seemed to be an unhelpful compromise, and it appeared that the problem may have been that respondents did not even want the interviewer to know how they had voted, let alone passers-by.

The solution to this was to adopt a self-completion methodology, as was already used by Harris/ITN, and in the USA. With this method the respondent is just handed a sheet with the two questions – current vote and past vote – on it, plus a clipboard and a pen. Just as in the polling station itself, respondents can fill in the form in privacy, then fold it up and put it in the special NOP ballot box without anyone knowing how they have answered. Interviewers continued recording their estimates of respondents' age and sex, but as they were written on the questionnaires as unidentified codes by the interviewer before the questionnaire was handed to the respondent, the respondents were unaware of it.

With a self-completion questionnaire it is also possible to replicate the actual ballot paper as closely as possible. Thus the full name and party attribution of each candidate is shown on the questionnaire, in the same order as they appear on the actual ballot. This requires separate versions of the questionnaire for each constituency in a national poll, but we consider the effort well worth while.

Although the evidence about the impact of refusal rates discussed below is inconclusive, we decided fairly early in the development process that rather than give everyone a long questionnaire including the analysis questions used during the programme, there would be two separate samples – one which was given the two-question questionnaire, and which was used for prediction purposes, and one which was given a much longer questionnaire, and which was used only for analysis.

There is evidence that the length of the analysis questionnaire has some effect on response rate, but not on the reliability of the results. It is thus possible to use either a one- or two-side questionnaire, but psychologically it is important that the questionnaire consists of no more than one sheet of paper, or it risks appearing too off-putting to respondents. It is, however, possible to use a two-column layout on the questionnaire, and this means a large number of questions can be included. An example of an analysis questionnaire is shown in Figure 9.

As stated above, counting and weighting is done separately for each hour, rather than for the whole shift. To facilitate this the questionnaires are printed on three colours. By using one colour for each hour the interviewer can assign each questionnaire to the correct hour without needing to keep emptying the box.

Analysis

It is obviously essential for the exit-poll results to be processed instantly. With such a short gap between the end of voting and the actual result becoming known, the media client needs to be able to broadcast its prediction almost immediately after the polls close. This means that the results must be processed throughout the day.

Originally, in the series of NOP/BBC by-election exit polls, this was done by a series of tallies. As each shift was finished the interviewer brought the questionnaires back to the hotel serving as a local base, where a summary was made of the results from that shift – twenty Conservative, eleven Labour, seven Liberal Democrat, for example. This tally was entered into a computer program (on a

Figure 9 *Sample exit-poll analysis questionnaire*

BBC Television
National Opinion Polls

The results of this survey will be broadcast on the Election Night Special on BBC1 tonight. Your answers are completely confidential. We do not want to know your name. Please answer all questions with a tick (✔) and put this paper in the box.

---

1) **Which party have you just voted for in today's general election?**
1 ☐ Conservative
2 ☐ Labour
3 ☐ Liberal Democrat
6 ☐ Referendum Party
7 ☐ Other

2) **When did you make up your mind how you would vote today?**
1 ☐ Today
2 ☐ During the last week
3 ☐ Since the election was called six weeks ago
4 ☐ Some time before the election was called
5 ☐ Not sure

3) **Which of the following comes closest to your view:**
1 ☐ It's time for a change: the Conservatives have done a bad job
2 ☐ This is no time to change: Labour wouldn't do any better
3 ☐ No matter how well or badly the Conservatives have done, after 18 years it's simply time for a change

4) **Which party do you trust most to take the right decisions about . . . :**

MARK THE PARTY YOU TRUST MOST ON EACH ISSUE

	TRUST MOST		
	Con	Lab	Lib Dem
	1	2	3
a) The economy	☐	☐	☐
b) Schools/education	☐	☐	☐
c) Income tax	☐	☐	☐
d) Dealing with "sleaze"	☐	☐	☐

5) **Compared with five years ago, at the time of the last election, have the living standards of you and your family got worse, got better, or stayed the same?**
1 ☐ Got worse
2 ☐ Got better
3 ☐ Stayed the same

6) **And compared with five years ago, at the time of the last election, is Britain's economy weaker now, stronger now, or about the same?**
1 ☐ Weaker now
2 ☐ Stronger now
3 ☐ About the same

7) **If the Conservatives win the election, do you think taxes overall will go up, go down, or stay about the same?**
1 ☐ Taxes go up
2 ☐ Taxes go down
3 ☐ Stay about the same

8) **And if Labour win the election, do you think taxes overall will go up, go down, or stay about the same?**
1 ☐ Taxes go up
2 ☐ Taxes go down
3 ☐ Stay about the same

9) **Regardless of how you voted, do you think that the Labour Party is**
1 ☐ united   *or*   divided ☐ 3
2 ☐ good for one class *or* good for all classes ☐ 4

10) **Regardless of how you voted, do you think that the Conservative Party is**
1 ☐ united   *or*   divided ☐ 3
2 ☐ good for one class *or* good for all classes ☐ 4

11) **There are proposals for the pound to be replaced by a new single European Currency throughout Europe - the Euro. What do you think the government's policy on this should be?**
1 ☐ To say now that Britain will never join the Single Currency
2 ☐ To say now that Britain will join the Single Currency
3 ☐ To wait and see what happens

12) **Regardless of how you voted today, who do you think would make the best Prime Minister?**
1 ☐ John Major
2 ☐ Tony Blair
3 ☐ Paddy Ashdown

13) **How much do you agree or disagree with the following statements**

a) The government should redistribute income from the better-off to those who are less well-off

Agree strongly	Agree	Neither agree nor disagree	Disagree	Disagree strongly
1	2	3	4	5
☐	☐	☐	☐	☐

b) Private enterprise is the best way to solve Britain's economic problems

Agree strongly	Agree	Neither agree nor disagree	Disagree	Disagree strongly
1	2	3	4	5
☐	☐	☐	☐	☐

14) **Whoever wins today's election do you think the new government should or should not increase income tax by 1p in the pound and spend it on Britain's schools?**
1 ☐ Should
2 ☐ Should not

15) **How did you vote, if at all, in the last general election in 1992?**
1 ☐ Too young to vote
2 ☐ Did not vote
3 ☐ Voted Conservative
4 ☐ Voted Labour
5 ☐ Voted Liberal Democrat
6 ☐ Voted SNP/PC
7 ☐ Voted for some other party
8 ☐ Can't remember

16) **Are you:**
1 ☐ Male
2 ☐ Female

17) **To which age group do you belong?**
1 ☐ 18–29
2 ☐ 30–44
3 ☐ 45–64
4 ☐ 65+

18) **Do you own or rent the accommodation you live in?**
1 ☐ Home-owner with a mortgage or loan
2 ☐ Home-owner (no mortgage)
3 ☐ Rented - from council
4 ☐ Rented - from housing association or trust
5 ☐ Rented - from private landlord
6 ☐ Other

19) **Please indicate the type of work which *best describes* the job of the person who is head of your household. If that person is unemployed or retired, please indicate the type of work which best describes his/her work before unemployment/ retirement.**
1 ☐ Skilled manual worker *(e.g. plumber, electrician, cook, hair dresser, foreman, welder)*
2 ☐ Semi-skilled or unskilled manual worker *(e.g. assembler, postman, waitress, cleaner, labourer)*
3 ☐ Office worker, junior professional worker *(e.g. clerk, secretary, salesperson, social worker, nurse)*
4 ☐ Manager/administrator/senior professional *(e.g. company director, manager, headteacher, doctor, lawyer)*

20) **Do any of the following apply to you?**
PLEASE TICK AS MANY AS APPLY
1 ☐ In a paid job for more than 30 hrs/week
2 ☐ Retired on a State Pension
3 ☐ Unemployed or seeking work
4 ☐ Member of a trade union
5 ☐ A share owner
6 ☐ Have children at school
7 ☐ Self-employed
8 ☐ Been made redundant in the past five years
9 ☐ Have a university/polytechnic degree
0 ☐ Become home owner in past five years

BBC micro!) which applied the weights and added the results to the sum of all the previous tallies. In this way a running total was always available to the client. However, the drawback of this approach is that, because it relies on tallies, it does not permit any analysis at the individual level.

Once we had decided to switch from replacing refusals to weighting to compensate for them, it became important to know the results from each individual respondent. Also, there was pressure for analysis of current vote by 1987 vote, in order to set up change matrices which would help interpret the results.

The mechanisms used by the BBC and ITN to get from the exit-poll figures to their predictions are many and complex, and are outside the scope of this book, particularly as the models are designed to work with both exit-poll data and the early declared results. Curtice and Payne[3] and Mathias and Cowling[4] have described the 1992 election, though in the BBC's case at least the method used is broadly unchanged since its inception in 1974.[5]

One would not necessarily expect past voting from the sample to match the actual 1987 vote in that constituency. It is quite common for government supporters to stay at home at a by-election they are likely to lose because of normal 'mid-term blues', and this means that the past voting figures will be much lower for the government than was actually the case. However, while the absolute figures are unreliable, one can learn a great deal from looking at the extent to which supporters from one party have now switched to another. It is common for the government to attribute by-election defeats simply to their supporters staying at home, and they can usually use a much lower turnout to back them up. If an exit poll can use the change matrix it can show that $x\%$ of all government supporters who voted had switched to one of the opposition parties.

To be able to provide this change matrix, individual results have to be recorded just as on other surveys, and the technique we use for doing this is exactly the same as that now used for almost all face-to-face pre-election polls. At the end of each shift the interviewer empties the ballot box, sorts the questionnaires out into the three hours, and then phones back to NOP in London. Here a telephone interviewer takes details of the time of day (for the hour weighting); the location and the count for each hour (for flow weighting); the details of refusals (for demographic weighting); and finally the answers from each individual questionnaire, including the two codes indicating age and sex. For the prediction poll this is very quick, with only four data items per respondent, but for the analysis poll the much longer questionnaire makes it a far longer (and more boring) task.

This is a labour-intensive process, but even with advances in technology no alternative has yet been found. There is no shortage of companies in the cellular data-transfer or computing business who continually try to sell us new ways of getting data back to the central computer, but none are suitable for exit polls. With a small hand-held computer equipped with a cellular modem it would be possible to give the computer to the respondent so they could mark their vote (using a pen on a touch-based screen) in privacy. The result could then be fed instantly via the mobile phone network back to head office.

The drawback to this method is that each interviewer is currently given four or five clipboards and a dozen pens, so that at busy times more than one person can be filling in the questionnaire at once. The interviewer can just give a brief explanation, hand over the questionnaire clipboard and pen, and leave the respondent to it, allowing the next respondent to be approached very quickly. If interviewers had to wait before one respondent had finished before approaching the next one – not to mention the extra time for explaining how the computer works – the number of interviews achieved would drop markedly. The cost of equipping each interviewer with several computers, however small, would quite simply be prohibitive.

Interviewing

One of the most nerve-racking elements of conducting an exit poll – apart from the obvious one of having one's prediction put to the test so publicly and so immediately – is the lack of scope for troubleshooting if something goes wrong. On a pre-election poll, if an interviewer falls sick at the last moment it is usually possible to find a replacement who could work in an alternative constituency. If someone fails to complete their assignment through illness or other reason but fails to notify their supervisor, the problem is not too great because most agencies oversample slightly to allow for a proportion of drop-out.

The mechanics of exit-poll sampling make it much harder to oversample on an exit poll. Apart from the problems of the sample being so homogenous by sampling point, there are very limited alternatives available. On a by-election any replacement interviewer must live close to the constituency, and even on a national poll it may be hard to find someone in the right area.

It is therefore vital that interviewers fulfil their commitments, or at the very least let us know as soon as possible if they cannot. The first stage in realising this aim is to emphasise the importance of their role, and their irreplaceability, to the interviewers. In NOP's case this is done through the written interviewer instructions, and is reinforced by the area manager when the interviewers are first booked, and again when a check is made on the day before the election. NOP are proud that in the 1992 general election there were 550 interviewing shifts, and the interviewers turned up at every one when and where they were supposed to. The same was true, though for a smaller number of shifts, in 1997.

For the later by-elections NOP experimented with personal briefing of the interviewers. Since they all lived fairly near the constituency it was not a major expense to get them to come along to the hotel for an hour or so the evening before the election so the executives could run through the procedures with them. Where we ran experiments briefing only half the interviewers we could not detect any subsequent difference in performance between briefed and non-briefed interviewers, but briefing nevertheless provided important reassurance for both the executive team and the client.

For a national exit poll there is no question of personal briefing of interviewers. The briefings would need to be held in regional centres, which would still require each interviewer to travel some distance. This would have resulted in incurring effectively an entire day's cost for each interviewer, and since they were only doing one day's actual interviewing this would have doubled the field costs. As a compromise we decided for the 1992 general election to make an instructional video, showing how each aspect of the exit poll worked. We spent an interesting day at a school in west London, mocked up with 'Polling Station' signs, with interviewers performing their allotted tasks and a team of BBC staff, plus passers-by recruited to act as respondents. The video was produced by a BBC team, and so looked very professional, and the air of authority was enhanced by topping and tailing the exposition with an appearance by David Dimbleby, stressing the importance of the whole exercise to the BBC. Subsequent feedback from interviewers showed that the video was felt to be very useful, and that the Dimbleby exhortation made them feel part of an important process. Such was its success that another video was made for the 1997 election.

Whilst we were well aware before the 1992 election of the opportunity for disaster if interviewers failed to turn up, we had not fully appreciated the opportunity for disaster caused by mechanical failure at NOP – of the phone system, for example, or the computer system. There would quite simply be no time to effect repairs if anything did go wrong. Fortunately nothing did, but in a new spirit of awareness, we drew up a comprehensive disaster recovery plan for the 1997 exit poll.

There was an entire second telephone interviewing centre on standby in case the first one suffered a power failure or a bomb scare. All telephone switches were backed up with duplicates, and the field interviewers were given emergency numbers to call if the main ones failed to work. All data were backed up on to a second computer system at fifteen-minute intervals, with the second computer able to be patched in almost immediately if the first failed. About the only back-up we decided against was a standby generator, because the cost far outweighed the risk. (Though we did have all the electrics checked the week before.)

We spent a large amount of money on these back-ups. In the end none were needed, but they gave us valuable peace of mind on what is inevitably a very tense day.

Exit-poll performance

The first four by-elections covered in the development programme for the BBC were Kensington (July 1988), Glasgow Govan (November 1988), the Vale of Glamorgan (May 1989) and Mid-Staffordshire (May 1990). The mix of urban and rural seats provided a good test of the sampling methodology, and as Table 26 shows, the results were within the expected sampling error, although some judicious weighting to counter perceived refusal bias was necessary in Mid-Staffordshire to produce the final result.

Table 26 *Errors in first four by-elections for BBC/NOP exit-polling strategy, 1988–1990 (%)*

	Kensington	Govan	Glamorgan	Mid-Staffordshire
Conservative	−2	−2	0	−1
Labour	+2	+1	+2	+2
Liberal Democrat	0	−2	−1	−1

Although the results were within sampling error there was a consistent over-estimation of Labour support. Even though this was only 1% or 2% percent, its consistency suggested bias rather than simple error. With a small number of observations we could not, however, be sure this was simply a pro-Labour bias. In all cases except Kensington the poll showed a bias in favour of the winning party. In all cases the poll showed a bias towards the party which had 'surged' during the campaign.

What made investigation of the problem more urgent was the exit poll for the 1990 European Parliament elections, where an error of 4% in favour of Labour (outside sampling error) confirmed our earlier suspicions, and understandably made us determined to find out why it had happened so that we could stop it happening again at the next exit poll.

Every possible aspect of the European exit poll was examined in great detail. We proved that the sample of wards was not socially or politically biased. We investigated the size of polling districts selected and made the interesting discovery that there were was no consistent relationship between voting behaviour and polling-district size. We considered the possibility of interviewer effect: whether, for example, the interviewers did not correctly apply the sampling rules, and instead operated some form of conscious or unconscious selection of respondents. While initially attractive, this theory relied on there being something about Labour voters which made interviewers more likely to select them, and we fairly quickly came up with convincing reasons as to why the opposite was just as likely to be the case.

This left us with the whole question of refusals as a possible source of bias. Examination of refusal rates showed some clear patterns, with older people, and especially older men, much more likely to refuse. However, it appeared that the replacement had compensated for this, and demographic differences among refusals seemed not to be the cause of the bias, although one consequence of this stage of the investigation was the decision to switch from replacement to weighting in future exit polls.

While the demographic mix of refusals was not the answer, we were still convinced, mainly in the absence of any evidence of bias elsewhere, that refusals were the source of the problem. What we concluded was that there must be some direct link between voting behaviour and refusals – Conservative voters are simply more likely to refuse to take part in exit polls. (This was exactly the same problem which affected pre-election polls in the 1992 general election, as discussed in Chapter 6.) If this politically correlated refusal is happening, then neither replacement nor weighting to correct demographic imbalance will solve the problem, and can easily make it worse. Unfortunately this is a largely untestable hypothesis as we could hardly do a follow-up interview with refusers to ask how they had voted! We did, however, use a somewhat tangential method to address the problem, and while far from reliable, our tests suggested we were on the right track.

On three consecutive weeks we asked respondents to NOP's Random Omnibus Survey whether they would take part or refuse if approached by an exit pollster, and all respondents had earlier in the questionnaire been asked for their voting intention. Overall, 57% said they would refuse. This is far higher than the 29% we had actually found in our exit polls, which is why the results cannot be fully relied on, but there was a consistent pattern on all three surveys, with Conservative supporters being much more likely to say they would refuse to answer an exit poll.

Table 27 *Errors in second four by-elections for BBC/NOP exit-polling strategy, 1990–1991 (%)*

	Eastbourne (Oct. 1990)	Bradford (Nov. 1990)	Paisley North (Nov. 1990)	Ribble Valley (Mar. 1991)
Conservative	−1	0	−2	0
Labour	0	−1	+1	0
Liberal Democrat	+1	+1	0	0

This is why we agreed with the BBC that we should switch to weighting rather than replacement, and at the same time made other attempts to reduce refusals, including the change to self-completion questionnaires. A series of tests was undertaken with different lengths of questionnaire, different interviewer workloads, and so on, though what emerged as the main approach was to use a very short self-completion instrument for predictive purposes, and a longer one for analysis. Refusal rates to the short self-completion questionnaire were much lower than had been found for personal interviewing, and as Table 27 shows, the results were much more accurate when this approach was applied to four more by-elections. Most noticeably, the consistent pro-Labour bias had disappeared.

Refusal rates were higher for the longer analysis questionnaires, though the results were not significantly less accurate. We therefore concluded that there is a politically-related element of refusal based on secrecy, which can be reduced by use of self-completion, and an entirely separate 'too busy' element of refusal which has no political component.

A national exit poll methodology

The success of the last four by-elections understandably gave us confidence going into the general election. The sampling issues for a national election are quite different, but we had settled on a methodology for polling in practice which we were happy with. As ITN had done before, and were to do again, the BBC concentrated its predictive poll in 1992 in the marginal seats, while the separate analysis poll was in a nationally representative sample of seats.

The first stage of the sampling was the selection of marginals to cover. A team of psephologists agreed on a list of all seats which might possibly change hands at the 1992 election, and from these, 100 were selected with probability proportional to size, after the list had been stratified by region and type of seat. Our strategy of using more places for less time each meant that we then needed to select four wards in each constituency. Some experts argue that the best way to sample wards is to choose those which, in demographic or political terms, most 'look like' the constituency as a whole. However, we rejected this 'typical ward' approach as unsuitable, especially for marginal seats. Many marginals do not have any 'typical' wards – they have equal numbers of strong Tory and strong Labour wards, which together almost cancel each other out.

We therefore decided to select wards via probability sampling, with one key variation. The wards in each constituency were listed in order from most to least Conservative, using ward-level local election results as the best available indicator. Electorate sizes were listed against each, the total cumulated down the list, the overall total divided by four to give a sampling interval, and a random number chosen between 1 and the sampling interval, all exactly as normal in probability sampling. Under normal procedure we would then have just applied the sampling interval three times to select the four wards required.

However, we were concerned that if the random number was very low, then all four wards chosen would be relatively high up the list, and therefore relatively more Conservative. Of course there would also be constituencies where the random number was at the upper end of the range, in which case all the wards would be relatively more Labour, but given the differences between seats we could not be sure that these errors would be self-cancelling. To solve this problem we used a 'mirror-image' approach to sampling. The random number identified the first ward as usual, by counting down the cumulative list, but we then applied the same random number counting back up from the bottom of the list to select the fourth ward. Adding the sampling interval to the random number produced the second ward, and again counting the sampling interval back up from the fourth ward gave us the third.

This meant that if the first ward chosen was right at the top of the list, and therefore the most Conservative, it would be matched by the one at the very bottom of the list, and thus the most Labour. The second would be more Conservative than average, and the third more Labour. If, on the other hand, the random start point was a high number, then all the wards selected would cluster more towards the middle of the range.

Having selected four wards per constituency we finally selected one polling station in each one, using simple probability sampling from a randomly sorted list. Again, there are those who argue for a purposive approach to polling district selection, choosing the median one from a list sorted by size. The theory behind this is that polling districts with smaller electorates, being more rural, are more Conservative, while larger urban ones are more Labour. There is an element of logic behind this, since the electorate size of a polling district is mainly determined by how far people can reasonably be expected to travel in order to vote. In country areas this distance may encompass only one or two small villages, whereas huge inner-city council estates can be within reach of a single polling place. Since rural areas are more Conservative than the inner city this approach sounds sensible, but our analysis of the European elections suggests that there is no consistent relationship between polling-district size and political complexion.

In the event all this effort came, if not to naught, to less than we expected on election day. The first BBC election-night forecast, broadcast at 10 p.m., was for a hung parliament, with the Conservatives only three seats ahead of Labour. The final forecast, once all the exit-poll data were in, was for an eleven-seat gap between the parties, while the final result saw the Conservatives with an absolute majority, and with sixty-five more seats than Labour. The BBC's seat projection was based not just on the exit-poll figures, but on other factors as well. Some seats were considered to be special cases that need to be measured by other expert opinion rather than by means of an exit poll. These included all those seats which had changed hands at a by-election during the course of the Parliament, and one-off seats of a special type which cannot be used to generalise into other seats, such as seats where rebel major party candidates were standing, or seats where the SNP were in contention.[6]

Because of this multifaceted approach to the actual projection it is difficult to assess the reliability of the exit poll itself from the final projection. It is, however, possible to measure how accurately or otherwise the prediction poll represented the overall voting behaviour of those constituencies polled. Table 28 shows the share of the vote measured by the exit poll in those constituencies, and the actual results across those 100 constituencies. The error level of around 2% on each of the two main parties is outside the range of sampling error that one would expect from a sample of this size and design, but it was considerably closer than any of the prediction polls.

Table 28 *Exit poll results, 1992 general election prediction poll (%)*

	Exit-poll figures in 100 Conservative marginals	Actual result in 100 Conservative marginals	Error
Conservative	42.7	44.8	−2.1
Labour	38.9	37.2	+1.7
Liberal Democrat	16.2	16.1	+0.1
Others	2.1	1.9	+0.2

The national analysis poll suffered the same problem, with the Conservatives clearly underestimated. The poll is compared in Table 29 both with the total election result – which is what it was trying to measure – but also with the actual result just in the seventy-five seats covered. This gives a test of the polling method apart from the selection of seats, and reveals a slightly better performance. The errors are, however, again outside sampling error, as Table 29 shows.

Table 29 *Exit-poll results, 1992 general election analysis poll (%)*

	Exit poll results, 75 constituencies	Actual result, Great Britain (overall)	Actual result in 75 constituencies
Conservative	40.0	42.8	42.5
Labour	36.3	35.2	35.5
Liberal Democrat	18.3	18.3	18.4
Other	5.4	3.7	3.6

The aberrant figure for 'other' is probably a function of the small number of sampling points, with the distribution of 'other' votes being very uneven between constituencies.

The 1992 exit poll was thus much less wrong than the pre-election polls, but it was more inaccurate than either we or the BBC would have liked, and the fact that all four exit polls underestimated the Conservative vote made the BBC wary of commissioning an exit poll for the next election without reasonable indication that the problems had been both identified and solved. In the years between 1992 and 1997 the BBC and NOP undertook another programme of research to find an improved method. Following the European Parliament exit poll discussed above, NOP and the BBC had agreed that refusals were the main cause of bias, and the examination of the 1992 pre-election polls had made it clear that this was still likely to be the case.

Although the level of refusal on exit polls is fairly low at around 16%, it is high enough to cause significant errors if supporters of one party are more likely to refuse than those of another. It is unlikely one could reduce the already low level of refusal, so if there will always be a small but significant minority who will not say how they voted, the alternative approach is to try to estimate how the refusals did in fact vote.

The work done on the pre-election polls on ways of estimating the vote of don't knows and refusals had the advantage that people who refused the voting question may well have answered a whole series of other questions. Because an exit poll is virtually a one-question questionnaire, those who refuse the voting question refuse the whole survey, and there is no information about them other than the interviewers' estimates of their sex and age. If it were possible to get some other information about refusals, it might be possible to reallocate the refusals in a sensible way between the parties. Given the circumstances of an exit poll, an interview of any length is out of the question, and so the focus of the experimentation was to try to discover a single question which those who refused the voting question would answer in reasonable numbers, and which would give a reasonable indication of how they had voted.

Such experimentation can only be carried out at an election, and thus the opportunities are limited. An initial, exploratory exercise was carried out in the parliamentary by-election in Newbury, though the experimental programme proper did not begin until the by-election in Dudley West. This first stage was followed by separate experiments at the Scottish and English local government elections in 1995 (fortunately there was a gap between the two in which the results of the first could be assimilated before finalising the design for the second), and a final round of experiments at the English local election results of 1996.[7] The experiments can be split into two types – those which involve asking respondents an extra question, and those which involve interviewers estimating something about voter characteristics. The first method tested, in two polls, was an additional question on newspaper readership.

In each case the experiment did little more than broadly confirm our earlier suspicions about refusals. Because many people who refused the voting question also refused the question on readership, and because many of those who did answer did not read a national daily newspaper regularly, the base sizes were very small. All that we could conclude was that readers of Conservative-supporting newspapers were more likely to refuse than readers of other papers, suggesting again that Conservative voters were more likely to refuse. This was useful, but we needed something we could use actually to weight the raw data so we could come with a new, estimated result.

One variable which we knew from our experiments on opinion polls to be strongly correlated with vote was the question on who would make the best Prime Minister. If the refusals were a random subset of the electorate, their rating of John Major would match that of all respondents, while if they were much more likely to be Conservatives the pattern of their answers should be close to that of Conservative voters. In fact, refusals were indeed slightly more

Conservative than the whole sample, but their answers were much closer to the figures from the total sample than to the Conservatives. Any weighting of the results based on this data would have had only a marginal effect.

Another question which we knew correlated well with voting was that of which party would be best at running the economy. As a discriminator this question proved much better than the rating of John Major, since in Dudley 95% of Conservative voters thought the Conservatives were better at running the economy, and 98% of Labour voters thought Labour were better, with similar figures obtained in the other tests. In each experiment where this question was used, the weighted results were better than the unweighted, but the differences were small and the unweighted ones had been acceptably close to the actual result anyway.

In the 1992 general election interviewers had estimated the age, sex and class of all voters, so that demographic weighting could be applied to compensate for refusals. Age and sex had had no effect, and class a minimal one, so class was included in the experiments, but not age or sex.

Interviewer estimates of social class were used in the weighting by applying the voting pattern of those in each class group who did complete the ballot to those in the same class group who *did* not. Thus of those C1s who did complete the ballot in Dudley, 65% said they voted Labour, and 23% Conservative. We then assume that of the twenty-six in class group C1 who refused the ballot, 65% – seventeen people – were Labour voters, and 14% – three people – were Conservative voters. Following the same calculations for the other parties, and for the other class groups, produces an estimate of how the refusals might have voted, based on their social class. In three of the four cases, weighting in this way made the result worse, while in the final test it made no difference.

The other estimate made by interviewers was of the actual voting behaviour of all selected respondents. They were asked to classify all people approached as either Conservative, Labour, Liberal Democrat or other. It must be stressed that this was done *before* the interviewer gave respondents the ballot form. For this measure, as well as being able to look at how refusals differed from respondents, it is also possible to measure the ability of the interviewers to 'read' respondents in this way. The vast majority of people approached do fill in the ballot form, so for all of these we can compare the interviewer estimate with actual behaviour. If interviewers do not do better than pure chance, we would not use the estimate for weighting, while if they do significantly better we would use it. In fact interviewers generally did do better than pure chance, and on the three occasions this test was used it either made the poll results better or at least made them no worse.

After the 1996 English local elections it was possible that there might be another parliamentary by-election in which to carry out one further test, but as this could not be guaranteed, it was decided that no further experimentation would take place. In any case, by this time it had become fairly clear what the workable alternatives were. Of the extra questions it was clear that the only one which had any merit was the one on the economy, which had generally had a small but beneficial effect. However, there were two significant concerns about using any extra question. The first was that having interviewers ask any kind of question would put off some people who would otherwise have completed a self-completion form.

The argument that the extra question may increase the refusal rate was a powerful one, but it was reinforced by another. The whole principle behind all this experimentation was that refusals are different from respondents, and that some means must be found reliably to estimate their behaviour. All the experiments involving an extra question showed that most of those who refused the voting question also refused the extra question. In weighting the refusals using the answers to the extra question we had to weight all the refusals using the answers just from those who did answer the extra question, thus assuming that those who refused the extra question were the same as those who answered it: when the whole approach was based on a belief that this was not so for the voting question.

Either of these arguments alone would have been powerful, but together they convinced us we should not use an extra question in the general election. This left the issue of whether to use interviewer estimation, and if so, what. It was clear that estimating age and sex was of little value, and since it only added to the volume of data to be phoned back, they were not used. The experiments showed that weighting by estimated class was more likely to make matters worse than better, so the only remaining option was estimated vote.

The experimental results had been very encouraging, but there were potentially severe presentational difficulties. The whole team had visions of one of the tabloid papers running a story on how the BBC did its exit poll just by getting interviewers to guess, but it was eventually decided that because we had the ability to verify the method throughout the day, by comparing estimated vote with actual vote, estimated vote would be used to correct for refusals.

As a further check on the method a second, parallel method known as ecological inference was used by the forecasting team at the BBC.[8] This involved examining the level of refusals against the political complexion of each location. We already knew that if the level of refusals were much higher in Conservative wards than Labour ones, one could reasonably assume that refusals were more likely to be Conservative. The process of ecological inference takes this process a stage further, and aims by statistical analysis to make an actual estimate of the effect of refusals. It was agreed that weighting for refusals would only be used if both the weighting and the ecological inference produced similar figures.

As in 1992, there were two separate BBC/NOP exit polls in 1997 – a national analysis poll with a two-page questionnaire, and a two-question prediction poll. The difference from 1992 was that the prediction poll was also national, though with a marginal booster.[9] Still bearing the scar of 1992 election night, the BBC decided not to make an exact-seats projection from the exit poll, but instead to aim for a national share of the vote, from which a broad-band estimate of seats would be broadcast. ITN carried out a single prediction poll, solely in the marginals, with MORI as their contractor rather than Harris. Their poll was designed, as the BBC's had been in 1992, to produce an estimate of seats and not of votes.

As in the experiments, the NOP interviewers proved significantly better at identifying voters than pure chance, showing that the estimation method was reliable enough to be used. Table 30 shows the actual figures. Given that the election was marked by much switching by traditional Conservative voters to Labour it is not surprising that many whom the interviewers thought were Conservative in fact voted Labour. For Conservatives, the correlation between interviewer estimate and the question on voting in the previous election was much higher. Although estimation of Liberal Democrat voters was much worse than for the two main parties, this was not felt to be a major problem, because the real issue over the refusals was how many of them were Conservative.

Table 30 *Interviewer estimates of respondent voting behaviour (%)*

	Interviewer estimate		
Actual vote	*Conservative*	*Labour*	*Liberal Democrat*
Vote 1997			
Conservative	46	19	27
Labour	34	64	38
Liberal Democrat	16	12	30
Vote 1992			
Conservative	58	29	38
Labour	28	59	32
Liberal Democrat	12	10	28

The unweighted data from the NOP poll were again some way off the actual election results, which, given the effort that had been put in, was a major disappointment, and still a cause for concern. Some of this was due to the sampling of constituencies, but it is clear that differential response was again at work. In the end the broadcast figure was manipulated by the interviewer estimates, by the ecological inference, and by an estimate based on claimed vote at the 1992 election. The net effect was to move the exit poll 2% closer to the true answer for each of the two main parties (see Table 31).

The BBC 10 p.m. forecast was for a Labour majority of 'about 200', while ITN, with a poll designed for a more precise estimate, forecast a majority of 159. Given the final majority of 179, both the broadcasters could feel satisfied, but as Butler and Kavanagh pointed out they, and more particularly the pollsters, had been slightly lucky. The swing Labour achieved would, on a uniform-swing model, have led to a majority of 133, but because both the polls seemd to over-estimate Labour these two factors cancelled each other out.[10]

Table 31 *Effect of weighting in the 1997 general election (%)*

	Raw figures	Weighted figures	Actual result
Conservative	27	29	31
Labour	49	47	45
Liberal Democrat	17	17	17
Other	6	6	7

Having used the estimation method in a general election, I would have no hesitation about using the technique in future exit polls. Because it can always be validated by internal data it has a built-in safety device, and because it is based on actual data rather than extrapolation from other questions, it will still work even if the political climate changes and Labour voters become more likely to refuse.

Notes

1 W. Mitofsky, 'A short history of exit polls', in Paul J. Lavrakas and Jack K. Holley (eds.), *Polling and Presidential Election Coverage* (Sage, 1991).
2 N. Moon and R. McGregor, 'Exit polling: developing a technique', *Journal of the Market Research Society*, 34:3 (1992).
3 J. Curtice and C. Payne, 'Forecasting the 1992 election: the BBC Experience' in I. Crewe and B. Gooschalk, *Political Communications: The British General Election of 1992* (Macmillan, 1995).
4 G. Mathias and D. Cowling, 'The ITN exit poll', paper presented at EPOP conference, Essex, 1992.
5 P. J. Brown and C. D. Payne, 'Election night forecasting', *Journal of the Royal Statistical Society*, A 138 (1975).
6 Curtice and Payne, 'Forecasting the 1992 election'.
7 N. Moon, 'Dealing with non-response with a political component', in *Proceedings of Symposium 97: New Directions in Censuses and Surveys* (Statistics Canada, 1997).
8 P. J. Brown, D. Firth and C. D. Payne, 'Forecasting on British election night 1997', *Journal of the Royal Statistical Society*, forthcoming
9 *Ibid.*
10 D. Butler and D. Kavanagh, *The British General Election of 1992* (Macmillan, 1992).

8

Private polling

You don't need a weather man, to know which way the wind blows

In Chapter 7 it is argued that exit polling deserves to be treated as a special case, and thus deserves a chapter of its own, because exit polling is strikingly different in methodological terms from predictive polling, and serves a much more narrow function. This is true, but there is another type of polling which, it can be argued, is even more different from the pre-election polling discussed in most of this book, and thus even more deserving of a chapter of its own.

As explained in Chapter 7, exit polling has almost no methodological similarities to pre-election polling, but its purpose, while limited, is broadly the same. Exit polls set out to predict, a few hours in advance of the announcement of the actual result, who has won the election. Pre-election polls do the same thing, but from anything from three weeks to a day in advance of the election, instead of a few hours before the result. Exit polls also set out to illustrate why voters behave the way they did, and thus to establish the issues which may have won or lost an election. Pre-election polls have a similar function, though again with the critical time difference that they are collecting data in advance of the vote rather than after it.

Private polls conducted for political parties themselves may or may not be methodologically similar to the prediction polls, but their purpose is very different from that of prediction polls. In terms of purpose, the differences between private polls and pre-election polls are even greater than the differences between pre-election polls and exit polls.

There is far less information available about private polls than prediction polls, as their very name makes it clear. Even after an election has finished, the parties may well be extremely reluctant for any information about their polling to enter the public domain, for fear that their opponents may be able to benefit from it either during the life of the Parliament, or certainly at the next general election. Once they have been published, and thus lost any exclusivity, media clients do not generally insist on any degree of client confidentiality. Indeed, one of the features of opinion polling in Britain, as in many other countries, is the openness of the whole process. Full details of methodology are available to anyone who asks, and it is almost invariably the case that once results of a poll have been published the full tabulations, and even the raw data themselves, can be accessed by anyone, whether in the media, in a political party, or merely a member of the public. In writing this book I cannot think of any work which has been done for a media client which I was not able to discuss in the book, for reasons of client confidentiality. On the other hand, having been the Labour Party's pollster for two general elections, I am very conscious of the fact that not just the information they collect, but the methods they use to collect it, are as confidential to them as data on a new product launch, or a new research technique for testing advertising, would be for my commercial colleagues and their clients.

In this chapter I have concentrated on information already in the public domain, though I am very grateful to the Labour Party for agreeing to the inclusion of some information not previously published elsewhere.

As with so much of the research described elsewhere in this book, the history of private polling begins in the USA, from where it spread not just to Britain but to virtually the entire democratic world. With prediction polling, although there are differences of technique, there are many similarities between election polling in Britain, in the USA, and in other democratic countries. Despite the very different sizes of the British and US electorates, there are similar numbers of national polls conducted during an election campaign, and they have similar sample sizes.

With private polling, however, there is a vast disparity. Kavanagh states that in the 1992 general election the Conservatives spent £250,000, and Labour £200,000.[1] At the 1997 election the parties were obviously slightly more coy, for Butler and Kavanagh give no sums for total spend, merely noting that Labour's total spend was 'certainly a record for Labour'.[2] In stark contrast, Clinton pollster Stan Greenberg revealed that the Clinton campaign spent $125 million in 1992, with a very large (but unspecified) proportion of that spent on polling and focus groups.[3]

In Britain, the two main parties each conduct research on a substantial scale, while the minor parties do so to a very limited extent. For the two main parties most of their spend is typically on nationally representative samples, though there may be concentrations in groups of marginals, and occasionally polls in individual marginal seats. In the USA, the individual presidential candidates may well have their own pollsters as well as those pollsters funded by the national party. As well as the vast sums spent on the national campaigns, there are also senators, congressmen, state governors, and myriads of candidates for less significant office, all of whom spend very large sums on their election campaign, and all of whom spend part of that money on private polling.

In Britain there are only five polling companies that do significant volumes of political opinion polling of any kind, and at any one time only two who do significant amounts of private polling. For all of these, political opinion polling is only a small part of their total business. In the USA, there are dozens of firms, some of significant size, that derive all their income from conducting polls for parties and candidates.

The differences are not just those of scale, but in the kinds of polling carried out, and in the relationship between pollster and client. The pollster is an integral part of any American political campaign, and the nature of campaigning in the USA gives far more scope for the conduct of private polls. In Britain, apart from leaflets dropped through people's letterboxes and small posters put in windows and on fence posts, political advertising during elections is entirely at the national level. Indeed the rules on election expenditure make this inevitable. No matter what constituency they live in, all electors will have the opportunity to see the same party broadcasts and the same poster campaigns. The parties do not have the money to run significant campaigns at local level, and the nature of the broadcasting system is such that it would be very difficult even if they did.

In the USA, the national party can run different advertisements in each state, or even at the level of different television markets within states. Each candidate for Governor, the Senate or the House will almost certainly run their own local television advertising campaign, and many candidates for state- or city-level office will also do so. If large sums are being spent on television advertising, it makes sense to spend money evaluating that advertising, both during the process of making it and after it is shown. Because they are not restricted by state control on a number of advertisements, as British parties are with their party political broadcasts, US candidates may well make a whole series of different advertisements during the course of the campaign.

This is facilitated by the fact that, again, freed from the restrictions affecting British parties, candidates' advertisements on US television may be as short as thirty or fifteen seconds. If something happens during a campaign the candidates can have an advertisement on air that same evening in relation to that particular issue. Having shown it once, they may well wish to do research to test its effectiveness before deciding whether to show it again. Depending on the results from this research, the advertisement may be dropped altogether, showed again in modified form, or shown again in exactly the same form.

In Britain the main parties make around four party electoral broadcasts during the course of the election. Each one lasts either five or ten minutes, and in recent elections have been far more sophisticated and have involved far higher budgets than broadcasts from earlier years. They therefore take quite some time to make, and are thus shown only once, so it is very difficult for them to be tested effectively. There is little point in testing them after they have been shown if they are not to be used again (though reaction to *Kinnock: The Movie* in 1987 was sufficiently positive for it to be shown again as the penultimate broadcast of the campaign). Because they tend to be quite complex constructions, it is also difficult to test broadcasts during the process of making them. By the time they are in a sufficient state to be shown to a test audience, party broadcasts are ready to be shown for real. Labour did once experiment with using party officials to stand in as leading politicians, just reading out the scripts that would be used in the broadcasts so that the wording at least could be tested, but this was not a success.

The first significant figure in private polling in Britain was Mark Abrams, who apart from his role in political polling for the Labour Party, was one of the most significant figures in the development of social research in Britain. During the Second World War the government carried out surveys of morale, and the 1945 Labour government had continued this, although with less than wholehearted enthusiasm. As Abrams wrote, 'Labour leaders, in their role as cabinet ministers, energetically abandoned any research in communication activities that might be construed by their enemies of being of use to the Labour party.'[4]

There is always a danger that the distinction will be blurred between a government conducting research about public opinion on policies it is pursuing, and a political party carrying out polling on a public mood to help it win the election. This was seen in 1997 when the new Labour government announced its intention of setting up a 'People's Panel', a research exercise designed to provide a constant form of monitoring reaction to the government's new initiatives. This was criticised by the Conservative Party as being no more than Labour Party polling paid for out of the public purse.

According to Kavanagh, Labour was the first British party to commission private polling, with a survey conducted by Mark Abrams in 1946. The party was divided on the merits of such polling, however. While party leader Hugh Gaitskell was in favour, deputy leader Aneurin Bevan was opposed, on the grounds that politicians themselves should be finding out what the public thought. Bevan used his role as party treasurer to prevent funds being authorised for further research, and the first significant piece of private polling in Britain, a survey conducted after the 1959 election and which was reported in the book *Must Labour Lose?* by Abrams and Rose,[5] was funded by sources outside the party itself.

In what was to become a precursor of the problems of the use of polling within political parties, and within the Labour party in particular, the results of the Abrams and Rose survey – suggesting that its links with trade unions and commitments to nationalisation were both unpopular with the public – were unpopular with those on the left of the party, who either consequently or coincidentally were the ones who opposed the use of polling; and popular with those on the centre right, who were the supporters of polling.

Whilst for a long time lacking the resources the Conservatives had for large-scale media campaigns, Labour has always had a number of sympathisers within the communications and advertising industries, and since the 1960s there have been informal groupings of such sympathisers to advise the party on communication strategy. This became slightly more formalised for the 1983 election in the Shadow Communications Agency (SCA). In the mid-1980s the advisers subsequently became slightly less important as the Labour Party's growing resources meant it was able to pay for advertising at a similar level to the Conservatives, and employ relevantly skilled professional staff.

In 1962 the then much more informal volunteer group of media experts stressed the need for access to their own survey research, and Mark Abrams was again commissioned to conduct this. This research was very much part of the media strategy, with the results used to help in the design of poster campaigns and press advertisements. It was also used to measure reaction to party broadcasts and politicians themselves, functions which have hardly changed throughout the use of political polling. Butler and King were in no doubt that while it may not of been of huge direct relevance in 1964, when public polling once arrived it was here to stay. 'Whatever its influence in 1964, the use of survey research by politicians seems almost certain to remain a permanent feature of permanent British political life.'[6]

Labour did virtually no polling for the 1966 election but returned to private polling in 1968 with a survey of 1,200 party activists conducted by US researcher Conrad Jameson. Jameson then made the mistake of discussing the research findings with the *Sunday Times*, thus breaching one of the key rules about the difference between public and private polls, and did no further work for the party. Labour returned briefly to Mark Abrams while taking care to ensure that the results were kept under close wraps, but in 1970 Abrams decided to withdraw from private party polling and Labour began its long association with MORI.

The Conservatives meanwhile had also been conducting their own private polling, though on a much smaller scale than Labour. Before 1959 they had made occasional use of surveys by National Opinion Polls (as NOP were then called) and by Gallup, on special occasions such as by-elections. But as with Labour at the same time, there was little or no machinery within the party to manage the conduct of polling or to make efficient use of the polls' findings. Most of what research there was was done by the party's advertising agency to measure the impact of the various advertisements.

Impressed by the work that went into the polling for *Must Labour Lose?*, the Conservatives began polling on a serious scale in 1965 when they too began a long relationship with a private pollster, the Opinion Research Centre (ORC), later known as Harris. The Conservatives also launched a long-running panel study conducted by the British Market Research Bureau (BMRB), which was continued for many years.

The Conservatives were sophisticated in their use of polling in the 1970 election, drawing heavily on the experience of other countries such as the USA and the former West Germany. 'A great variety of polls were commissioned and their conclusions offered significant contributions to almost all aspects of Conservative activity. . . . They appear to have been at least as fully developed and ingeniously applied as those used by political parties anywhere, with the possible exception of Germany.'[7]

Not only did Labour conduct less research than the Conservatives in 1970 – just two surveys during the campaign – they were also less well equipped to make use of it. 'There is no evidence that these surveys had any impact on Labour's strategy. The party in fact seemed to lack the skill to commission polls that would be of much more use to it, still left to digest or give effect to their findings.'[8] This analysis typifies the problems faced by private polls before 1970, and the 1970 election may be seen as a watershed where the Conservatives escaped from the previous problems into more efficient uses of polling, whilst Labour did not do so until slightly later. The general experience of parties before 1970, and, for Labour, even in 1970, was that there were significant barriers between the pollsters and their party clients. The clients were not research-sophisticated, which led to problems in both design and interpretation. In particular, clients were likely to interpret the results to fit their own preconceptions. This, in turn, meant that polls were likely to be drawn into internal office politics, particularly if they seemed to lend support to the view of one faction over another. It was fear of their use in this way that lead to the results of polls being treated with such secrecy, so that only a select few were in a position to be able to make use of the information.

The 1974 elections saw a further stepping-up of the use of private polling, and daily polls were used by both parties for the first time in October 1974. As the parties increased their alliance on private polls, so the influence of the pollsters themselves increased. During the October 1974 election, MORI's Robert Worcester produced written comments daily on the MORI poll findings, and these were delivered each evening to Prime Minister Harold Wilson and Party Secretary Ron Hayward, and were subsequently used the next morning in the daily strategy meeting, which Worcester also attended. However, Labour politicians and campaign advisers were insistent that private polls were not important in deciding policies, or even party strategy. Whilst the pollster and the politicians may have been sitting at the same table, the fact they came from very different starting points inevitably caused some problems. According to Butler and Kavanagh, 'The inevitably imprecise relationship between a commercial pollster and a political party which employs it not surprisingly led to misunderstandings.'[9] The danger is always particularly intense when the poll findings conflict with the views of at least some politicians, and the more involved the pollster becomes, the more danger there is of this form of conflict. On the one hand Worcester himself complained of being left in the dark, while for some politicians at least he was overstepping the mark. After Worcester wrote in MORI's *Public Opinion Digest* about the unpopularity of nationalisation, and warning against upsetting the floating voter, he was 'instructed to refrain from making comments on the ground that he was employed as a pollster, not a policy advisor'.[10]

According to Kavanagh, MORI had to face three problems: the lack of a single, clearly defined client; the fact that many of the poll findings were unpalatable, especially to the left wing; and general suspicion amongst many politicians and officials about polling. He cites two particular examples to make this point. As Chairman of Publicity Committee, Tony Benn instructed MORI to stop asking questions about the popularity of individual politicians. (The poll findings showed that Benn's own individual ratings were poor, but there was very little doubt that he would have argued the same way if his own ratings had been high.) Harold Wilson told Worcester to carry on asking questions about individual politicians but to report the results of these questions only to him, and not to other members of the Labour campaign team.

Kavanagh's second anecdote concerns Party Treasurer Norman Atkinson, who in 1979 told Labour's National Executive Committee: 'Twenty members of my general management committee and I can do a better job [than polls] of assessing public opinion.' Young left-winger Neil Kinnock intervened: 'Norman, why do you need the other twenty?'[11]

While tensions such as this are almost inevitably present because of the pollsters' semi-detached relationship with their party clients, the fact that they are outsiders means that the pollsters are able to take a more dispassionate view. As Butler and Kavanagh wrote, 'In one way the value of having private pollsters in full daily contact with the party strategists lies in the objectivity they bring to essentially partisan gathering.'[12]

Arrangements were little changed in the succeeding elections, with the Conservatives continuing to use ORC (renamed Harris in 1983) and Labour continuing with MORI. By 1983 spending was fairly equal between the parties. According to Butler and Kavanagh the Conservatives spent £80,000 in the year before the election and £96,000 during the election itself,[13] and were prepared to have spent more if their position looked in any danger. Labour spent a similar amount during the election – around £100,000 – but only £40,000 before it. One major difference between the parties was in the period between elections, since Labour did virtually no polling between 1979 to early 1983. As before, many in the National Executive, mainly on the left wing of the party, were suspicious about polling and continued to be suspicious about Bob Worcester's own role in interpreting poll findings. MORI did conduct twenty polls for Labour during the 1983 election, but much of the pre-election work was qualitative rather than quantitative in nature. Because this book is about opinion polls it concentrates entirely on quantitative research, but qualitative research plays a significant role in private political work by the parties.

While the basis of quantitative work is the size and representativeness of the sample, which allows a survey sample to speak for the entire population, the basis of qualitative research is far smaller numbers, not seeking to be representative of the whole population, but whose opinions are sought in much more depth. The aim of quantitative research is to show how many people in the country hold certain types of opinion. The aim of qualitative research is to establish what sorts of opinions are held within the population, and, more importantly, the reasons why those opinions might be held. Thus quantitative research is very good at answering the question 'what?', while qualitative research is very good at answering the question 'why?' Qualitative research may take the form of in-depth interviews, where an interviewer follows a semi-structured questionnaire with a respondent, asking much more probing questions than on a typical quantitative survey, and then following up to try and establish the reasons why certain answers have been given, in an interview often lasting over an hour. The more common form of qualitative research, however, is that of the group discussion, often referred to in a political context as a focus group. (This nomenclature is, however, misleading since a successful group discussion will tend to be unfocused rather than focused.) A typical group consists of eight to ten participants, with a researcher acting as 'moderator' to start the discussion and ensure that it doesn't deviate into blind alleys.

The parties use qualitative research to examine their own and the opposition's party images, and also to measure the effectiveness of slogans or advertising. A typical exercise in a group discussion would be for the moderator to hand round a whole series of cards with descriptions on them such as 'hard-working', 'understands people like you', 'indecisive', 'doesn't really stand for anything', and asks the group participants to choose which of these words they think apply to Tony Blair, and which they feel apply to William Hague.

Qualitative polling is an important part of the parties' private research strategies, but it does not fall within the classification of 'opinion polling' and is not further discussed in this book, other than to note its increasing importance for the parties.

Party spending on private polling continued to increase, with each party spending around £120,000 during the 1987 election, having spent comparable sums in each year – around £100,000 for the Tories, and £80,000 for Labour – during the lifetime of the Parliament. The 1987 election was the last one in which MORI polled for the Labour Party, and after the Labour contract ended Bob Worcester offered advice to the Tories before the 1992 election. Whilst still using Harris as their main researchers, the Conservatives also appointed US private polling guru Dick Wirthlin as a part-time adviser. This was part of a general increase in contacts between the British Conservative Party and campaigners for the US Republican Party. Wirthlin was a strong believer in the importance of research to measure people's values. The argument is that although people's opinions on politicians and individual policies may well change quite considerably in the short term, their underlying values are much more stable. This is a principle widely used today in marketing research, particularly for market segmentation, and generally known as psychographics.

There are many competing methods for creating a classification of consumers, or voters, on the basis of their values. In the commercial world the claim is that, since social class is too crude a measure to be a good discriminator, being able to describe people as members of a particular group in a much more detailed form of classification creates much more meaningful analysis. Because it is a different approach from traditional research, there is sporadic press interest in this form of classification, and it is not uncommon to read newspaper articles describing these value-based groups such as 'belongers', 'inner-directed', and so on. The disadvantage of this approach is the very considerable cost of collecting the initial data by which respondents can be classified, and Harris carried out very large-scale surveys to provide data for Wirthlin's analysis. As the classification is based on combinations of answers to a very large range of attitudinal statements, the questionnaire is very long, and the sample size needs to be large to permit breakdown into the large number of groups. The Conservatives spent £500,000 in 1990 alone on Wirthlin's research, but once John Major replaced Margaret Thatcher as party leader there was no further work of this kind, although Wirthlin did continue to give the Conservatives advice.

The spend on Wirthlin's polling dwarfed that in the election itself, although election spend continued to increase compared with the previous election. In 1992 the Conservatives spent £250,000 during the campaign, with Labour close behind on £200,000. As in most elections, the Liberals simply did not have the resources to conduct significant volumes of private polling, although in 1992 they did spend as much as £40,000, considerably more than previously.

Within the Labour Party, responsibility for polling lay with the Shadow Communications Agency (SCA). The SCA was one example of the modernisation of party communications brought about by Peter Mandelson, who became Labour's Director of Campaigns and Communications in 1985. The creation of the SCA was one of the recommendations made by advertising consultant Philip Gould, who was invited by Peter Mandelson to make suggestions about the way the party should use its communications more effectively. Similarly to some of the more informal bodies that existed in the 1960s, the SCA was made up of full-time Labour staff, plus volunteers from the communications industries. One reason for the use of volunteers was financial, but it was also the case that, particularly following the debacle of 1983, advertising agencies were unwilling to be publicly and formally associated with the party. In practice the advertising input for the SCA came almost entirely from the BMP (formerly Boase Massium Pollitt) agency, but this was on an unofficial basis. Other members of the SCA were the party's pollsters, and the qualitative researchers who carried out the group discussions. While in many commercial research campaigns, the qualitative and quantitative research are carried out by the same agency, Labour has always used qualitative specialists separate from its pollsters. NOP replaced MORI as the Labour Party's quantitative pollsters in

1990, and my colleague Richard Glendinning and I became regular attenders at the SCA meetings as a result, but as with MORI we were responsible only for quantitative polling.

NOP conducted a number of by-election polls for the Labour Party, and a series of large political-attitude surveys in the run up to the 1992 election. During the election we were conducting polls almost daily, with samples of around 600 by telephone. There was also a weekly panel conducted by telephone of around 700 people interviewed each weekend. Each evening results were reported by NOP to Deborah Mattinson of the SCA, who wrote a report each evening for Patricia Hewitt to give to the media monitoring group the following morning, and which Philip Gould presented to the main campaign management team in the evening.

Labour continued to invest heavily in research throughout the 1992 to 1997 Parliament, at a time when the Conservatives were doing little research. Several surveys were conducted each year, with sample sizes of around 1,500 and lengthy questionnaires concentrating particularly on tracking and image questions to do with the economy. During the election itself we conducted 1,000 sample telephone polls twice weekly with results being reported to Philip Gould. Gould was also conducting his own focus groups three or four nights a week, and there was a major series of group discussions in the Pennine marginal band conducted by Deborah Mattinson.

The Conservatives did virtually no polling from 1992 to 1996, when they appointed ICM as their new pollsters following on from Harris. Unlike Labour's policy of splitting the different types of work, ICM were responsible for both quantitative and qualitative research for the Conservatives. From October 1996 they conducted monthly polls, with the frequency being increased to weekly from January 1997, and then daily during the campaign, with a sample of 500 each day.

Dick Wirthlin conducted another survey for the Conservatives in 1996, and Labour had its own US expertise in the form of Clinton pollster Stan Greenberg, who acted as an observer during the Parliament, and was closely involved throughout the 1997 campaign. At the start of this chapter it was noted that private polling is far more advanced and on a larger scale in the USA than in the UK, and in recent years there has been a conscious attempt by the British parties to bring some of the American techniques back for use in Britain. The SDP were actually the first to do this, using Sarah Horack, formerly of the US agency Yankelovitch, in the 1983 election.

On Labour's side Philip Gould has had for a long time close connections with the Americans and was present as an observer at both of Bill Clinton's presidential election victories. During the 1987–92 parliament, Gould visited the USA on behalf of the party to meet a number of US polling consultants, in a search for approaches which might successfully be used in Britain. As a result of this a relationship developed between the Labour Party and Democratic polling house Mellman Lazarus, whose principals visited the UK on a number of occasions and advised on a polling strategy.

Melman and Lazarus also introduced to the Labour Party's political campaigning strategy the use of 'people metering'. This is another technique widely used in the USA, particularly for the use of campaign advertising. A number of respondents – typically around fifty or sixty – are gathered in a hotel room or hall, and shown visual-stimulus material such as party advertising, news items, or debates between politicians. Each respondent has a small handset wired to a central computer which they can use to register their opinion continuously during the stimulus. This is typically done by the use of a dial which respondents may be asked to turn to the left if what they see is making them less inclined to vote for a particular party, and turn it to the right if they are more inclined to vote for that party. It can also be used to establish whether respondents think that claims made in the party broadcast are believable or not.

The computer to which the handsets are attached produces a immediate output of the average of all respondent's handsets, in the form of a constantly moving line, which can be superimposed over the stimulus and viewed by party officials sitting in an adjoining room. In this way they can see instantly which parts of the stimulus material are successful and which not. In the USA this is used very heavily to fine-tune party advertising, but for the reasons stated earlier in this chapter, the possibilities for amending party broadcasts in this country are much more limited, and Labour used the technique much more to obtain general feedback on the strengths and weaknesses of different slogans and claims.

The response graph is useful in its own right, but to get full value out of a people-metering session it is common for there to be follow-up qualitative research. This can be done either by keeping all respondents in the hall as an oversized group discussion, or simply by selecting eight or ten to form a more normal-sized group discussion. The stimulus material can then be played back to the respondents with the response graph overlaid on it, and the party researchers can then point to occasions at which the line moves sharply upwards or downwards, and ask respondents what it was about that particular part of the stimulus which made them react in that way.

The relationship with Mellman and Lazarus did not continue beyond the 1992 election, but some of the techniques which they had introduced continued. The SCA effectively ceased to exist after 1992, when the Labour Party appointed an advertising agency, but a polling advisory group continued to exist and meet regularly. This was led by Roger Jowell, a long-time Labour supporter who is head of the independent research institute, Social and Community and Planning Research. Philip Gould continued to be involved, as did members of the party's advertising agency, BMP. The party itself was represented by polling co-ordinator Greg Cook.

Because of the concerns about the part that quota sampling may have played in the failure of the polls in 1992 (see Chapter 6), the tracking series of polls conducted during 1992 and 1997 were all conducted using random samples, although it is interesting to note that the voting-intention figures produced were very similar to those found in the published quota polls at the same time. The main features of the tracking series were the concentration on economic issues, seen as being key to the chances of Labour winning the next election, and the use of a core of constant items which were repeated on every survey in order to establish whether any change in opinion was taking place.

The results of each survey were presented by Roger Jowell and me to Shadow Cabinet meetings. Unusually, because of the very large lead Labour enjoyed in the public opinion polls, we were encouraged in our presentations to stress any of the negative aspects of each survey, because the party leadership was particularly keen to avoid any overconfidence among politicians or party officials.

During the election itself we switched from face-to-face to telephone interviewing, but preserved the random sampling technique by re-interviewing people who had previously been interviewed on NOP's Random Omnibus Survey, and who had said they would be prepared to take part in a further interview. We recognised that there was a possibility that those who had agreed to be re-interviewed might be a politically biased sub-set of the original respondents, and there was also a possibility that those we succeeded in interviewing a second time would be a biased sub-set of all those we tried to interview, for the reasons to do with response bias discussed in Chapter Six. To combat this we drew on information from the original omnibus survey. In the omnibus every week respondents are asked how they would vote if there were a general election tomorrow, and also how they had voted in the previous general election. We thus knew the voting behaviour pattern of the sample at the time of the first interview, and so were able to manipulate the reissued sample to ensure that it had the same balance. If, for example, it were the case that Conservative supporters were more likely to refuse a second interview, this could be corrected for simply by drawing a higher proportion of Conservative supporters than Labour supporters from the pool available to second interview. The approach appears to have been successful, for in our final poll conducted on 26–27 April the voting figures were Conservative 29% and Labour 46% compared with an actual election result of 31%:44%.

Of course, as with all party polling, the voting intention was not the reason for conducting the survey, but voting-intention questions are always included as a means of analysing the results. The impetus for the questionnaire content came from Philip Gould, and from Stan Greenberg, who was based in the USA for the early part of the campaign, but spent the last weeks at Labour Party headquarters in Millbank Tower. As well as suggesting questionnaire content, Stan also imported a number of American questioning styles, such as the use of ten-point rating scales rather than the five-point one traditionally used in British opinion polling.

As is generally the case, the polls were used to establish the points at which Labour was vulnerable to Conservative attack, and also to establish the areas where attacks could most successfully be made on the Conservatives. Considerable use was made of split-sample techniques, with half the respondents being asked one version of the question and the other half another, with the intention of seeing if one form of wording had more of an effect on respondents than another.

For each poll, on the night interviewing finished the data were sent by modem across the Atlantic to Greenberg Research in Washington. Stan Greenberg and I then examined the data and discussed any weighting we felt was necessary. Once this was agreed NOP produced weighted tables which were supplied to Greg Cook at the Labour Party first thing the following morning, whilst Stan supplied written reports analysing the data.

It seems likely that the US influence on the manner of private polling in the UK will continue to be important, but the very significant differences in the nature of campaigning between the two countries mean that it is unlikely private polling in Britain will ever achieve the influence and status it currently has in the USA. There are, indeed, signs in the USA that the role of the private pollster in determining strategy is being questioned by many some political activists. Even Frank Luntz, a political pollster very closely associated with the Republican Party (and, indeed, censured in 1997 by the American Association for Public Opinion Research for blurring the distinction between research and political propaganda) suggested that the politicians themselves were being diminished by the process: 'dependent on professional consultants, candidates have become less involved in decision making in their own campaigns, sometimes appearing more like spectators in electoral process'.[14]

The same point was made by Peggy Newman, not a pollster but a speechwriter for Presidents Reagan and Bush: 'Polls are the obsession of every modern White House and every political professional. In every political meeting I have ever been to, if there was a pollster there his words carried the most weight because he was the only one with hard data. . . . I felt that polls are driving more than politics, they are driving history.'[15]

As we have seen above, this was very different from the role of pollsters within British elections, and Kavanagh points out this distinction. On the US side, he makes a similar point to Luntz. 'American pollsters are really campaign consultants to many candidates and expect to have an influence on the campaign, deciding which issues and themes are to be promoted and how the candidate is presented. Indeed candidates are often kept at length from campaign decisions and only marginally involved in strategy.' On the British side he notes that Mark Abrams was very closely involved in the preparation of the Labour campaign publicity in 1964, and the same was true of Humphrey Taylor for the

Conservatives in 1974, but since then no Labour or Conservative pollster has been part of the inner strategy group.[16] The parties will continue to need private polling, and the private polling will become more sophisticated, but the information from the polls will merely be one item of a mix influencing the party professionals managing the campaign.

Notes

1 D. Kavanagh, *Election Campaigning – The New Marketing of Politics* (Blackwell, 1995).
2 D. Butler and D. Kavanagh, *The British General Election of 1997* (Macmillan, 1997).
3 S. Bauman and S. Herbst, 'Managing perceptions of public opinion: candidates' and journalists' reactions to 1992 polls', *Political Communications*, 11:2 (1994).
4 M. Abrams, 'Public opinion polls and political parties', *Public Opinion Quarterly*, 27:1 (1963).
5 M. Abrams and R. Rose, *Must Labour Lose?* (Penguin, 1960).
6 D. Butler and A. King, *The British General Election of 1964* (Macmillan, 1965).
7 D. Butler and M. Pinto-Duschinsky, *The British General Election of 1970* (Macmillan, 1971).
8 *Ibid.*
9 D. Butler and D. Kavanagh, *The British General Election of October 1974* (Macmillan, 1975).
10 *Ibid.*
11 Kavanagh, *Election Campaigning.*
12 Butler and Kavanagh, *The British General Election of October 1974.*
13 D. Butler and D. Kavanagh, *The British General Election of 1983* (Macmillan, 1984).
14 F. Luntz, *Candidates, Consultants and Campaigns: The Style and Substance of American Electioneering* (Blackwell, 1988).
15 P. Newman, *What I Saw at the Revolution* (Random House, 1990).
16 Kavanagh, *Election Campaigning.*

9

A time of flux –
1997 and beyond

As the present now will later be past, the order is rapidly fadin'

Inevitably, after the problems in 1992, the pollsters started thinking about ways in which they should change their methodology to try to avoid the same errors recurring in the next election. The first stage of this process was obviously to try to find out what had gone wrong in 1992, and as well as co-operating fully with the MRS committee, the pollsters also carried out examinations of their own. Chapter 6 has discussed in some detail these investigations into what might have caused the problems of 1992. Some of these problems, once isolated, were easier to solve than others. There have been a number of changes which all pollsters have agreed on as being the correct strategy, while there are other more tentative approaches which have been tried by one polling company but not by the others.

One change common to all the pollsters has been the revision of the quota controls and weighting targets. Having relied too heavily on commercial research sources in 1992, the pollsters now draw on the large-scale government surveys such as the GHS.

One further modification made by NOP in their quota controls was an attempt to account for the differences between the demographic make-ups of the population and the electorate. Using information from the OPCS census/electoral register check,[1] we reweighted census data to allow for the fact that people in some demographic groups are much less likely to appear on the electoral register than others. The quotas set by NOP are thus slightly more upmarket than the population as a whole, to try to take account of any differences between the population and the electorate.

This is not a change which is set in stone, for there is no guarantee that the differences between the two universes will always be the same. As the memories of the poll tax recede it may be that more people reappear on the electoral register. There will be no sure way of knowing until another electoral-register validation exercise is carried out, and once that is done then NOP will again look at the quota controls being used.

Secret ballots

Although one of the hardest things to prove as a definite cause of the error in 1992, the overwhelming weight of circumstantial evidence suggest that differential refusal rates played a significant part, with Tory supporters simply less likely to take part in polls than Labour supporters. A clue to one approach to dealing with this problem can be seen in Chapter 8. During NOP's development of an exit-polling technique on behalf of the BBC, the level of refusal and the tendency to overestimate the Labour vote were both reduced by switching from an interview technique to a self-completion technique. The theory is that if people know that they can answer the question without anybody else – either the interviewer or, in the case of an exit poll, someone else walking past – knowing how they have voted, they will be less worried about admitting to supporting an unpopular party, and therefore more likely to answer the survey question. There is no doubt that this approach is the correct one for exit polls, and indeed it is used all round the world. The question then arose as to whether a similar approach could be put into practice for opinion polls as well.

On the surface this seems a very attractive idea – if it works for exit polls, why shouldn't it work for opinion polls? However, there is a critical difference in methodology between exit polls and opinion polls which means that it is much harder to operationalise a secret ballot in an opinion poll, and in particular it is harder to persuade respondents that it really is secret. In an exit poll the interviewer hands the respondent the ballot form and simply leaves them to get on with it. The interviewer cannot see what the respondent has marked on the ballot paper, and the respondent puts the paper in the box without the interviewer having any immediate access to it. The only way the interviewer could actually know what the respondent had done would be by opening the box immediately after the ballot paper had been put in, taking it out and reading it. However, because of the flow of voters and the constant process of approaching respondents, and then putting ballot papers in the ballot box, this is not only impossible but it is also obvious to the respondent that it is impossible. Respondents therefore can be in no doubt that the answers that they give are genuinely secret.

For opinion polls an approach has to be designed which is able to cope with interviews being conducted either in the street or in the home. It would be possible with street interviewing for an interviewer to station themselves somewhere with a ballot box, and to give respondents self-completion questionnaires as on the exit poll. However, since it would not be necessary on an exit poll for an interviewer to attempt to have several respondents completing questionnaires at the same time, it would be physically possible for the interviewer to open the ballot box and take out the questionnaire as soon as the respondent has put it in. Even if the interviewer is not doing this the respondents cannot be sure it will not be done once they are out of sight. As for in-home interviewing, there is clearly no question of the interviewer turning up carrying the ballot box. When such a method has been tested it has been by means of an envelope. The interviewer gives the self-completion questionnaire to the respondent along with an envelope in which they seal the ballot paper, having marked their choice upon it. However, they then give the envelope back to the interviewer who leaves the house with it. The interviewer clearly knows which house the questionnaire has come from, and the respondent has no means of knowing whether the interviewer is going to open the envelope immediately after leaving the house.

An intelligent respondent will realise that the secret ballot is in practice a sham in an ordinary opinion poll, and this means that if people do have severe reservations about anybody else finding out how they intend to vote it is unlikely that they would regard the 'secret ballot in an envelope' approach as being safe enough to justify taking the risk of completing the questionnaire. Indeed, their suspicions will be well justified, for the interviewer does take the questionnaire out of the envelope immediately after leaving the house. The reason for this is not nosiness, but a function of an essential difference between an exit poll and an opinion poll.

In the predictive exit poll all we are trying to find out is the party respondents have just voted for. We also ask the party they voted for in the previous election as a means of validating the sample, but we need to know no more about each respondent. If we are particularly keen on analysing the results separately for males and females the interviewer could mark a code for this on the question-naire, and if necessary the interviewer could also estimate the respondent's age and even the respondent's class. However, with an opinion poll, there are almost invariably up to a dozen other questions on political topics of the day. In making use of the results of these questions the client will want not simply to look at the total answers, but will almost inevitably want to analyse how Conservative voters differ in their opinions from Labour voters.

This means that it is essential for each person's answer to the voting ques-tion to be matched up with their answers to all the other questions. With an interview technique this is obviously not a problem: the voting question is there on the questionnaire along with all the other questions. With a secret-ballot technique it is thus essential for the interviewer to remove the ballot form and copy the answer from it on to the questionnaire, so that each respondent's voting intention can be matched up with the answers given to other questions.

Despite these very real disadvantages of using a secret-ballot approach in an opinion poll, several of the pollsters experimented with it in the months after the election. Indeed, ICM, renowned for their use of innovation as a marketing tool, made a very early decision to switch over to use of the secret ballot after only a couple of experiments. They and their media client, the *Guardian*, explained in considerable detail in the newspaper why this approach was con-sidered by them to be superior, and how the problems of 1992 would have been greatly reduced had secret ballots been used. However, the other agencies which carried out tests on the secret ballot were less convinced.

In NOP's case we carried out three experiments using our Random Omnibus Survey. In each case half the sample – around 900 people aged eighteen and over – were asked the question in exactly the normal way, while the other half were given a self-completion questionnaire and an envelope to put it in. There was no clear pattern of results across the experiment of the kind found by ICM in their tests. Although on one occasion the secret ballot did produce a more Conservative result, on another it produced a more Labour result, and on the third there was no difference between the secret-ballot approach and the standard-question approach. NOP therefore decided not to make a switch to secret ballot, though we announced that we were prepared to experiment further in the future should any evidence suggest that we might expect to find a different result. Almost exactly the same was true of MORI, who conducted their own internal experiments. They too failed to find any consistent effect from the use of secret ballots and they too decided against putting them into practice.

Aside from any issue of whether the respondent believes it really is secret or not, another difficulty with the secret ballot is that it is impossible to use questions in exactly the same way as in an interview survey. Chapter 4 has shown that the traditional voting question is in fact two voting questions, with all those who initially refused to answer or who said they were not sure which party they would vote for being asked a supplementary question on which party they would be most inclined to support. This is done because experience has shown that a more accurate result is achieved by doing so than by asking the single question. With the secret ballot, however, there is no real opportunity to do this in the same way. Obviously the interviewer cannot open the envelope, look at it and say to the respondent 'I see you are not quite sure which party to vote for, so which party are you most inclined to support?'

The double-question approach *can* be incorporated into a self-completion question – all that is needed is for an instruction at the end of the question: 'if you are not sure which party to vote for please fill in the party you are most inclined to vote for' – but this has less effect than an interviewer-administered interview using the two-question approach. A respondent who really is having severe doubts about who to vote for may well look at the question and think that, having not really decided who to vote for, they should still just record it as don't know. There is a difference between this simple opting-out, and having actually to answer a question twice.

The secret-ballot approach will therefore always tend to have more 'don't knows' who might have been 'squeezed' into one party or another using a traditional questioning technique. Where the secret-ballot approach suffers even more is with refusals. If someone doesn't want to answer the question they will just write 'refused', tick a refusal box, or even just leave the question blank, before putting it in the envelope and handing it back to the interviewer. In this way they can avoid having to commit themselves without having to confront the interviewer. With an interview-based approach the respondent is again forced to stick to his or her guns in a reiteration of the question, and many of those who initially refuse do then go on to give an answer to the voting question.

While superficially attractive in theory, the evidence does not exist to support the widespread use of secret ballots in opinion polls. ICM themselves no longer use a secret ballot, having now found another new approach which, they believe, solves the problems of 1992 (discussed below), and no other pollster has started using secret ballots.

Dealing with non-response

As explained in Chapter Six, the 1992 election raised serious doubts about the standard approach used by opinion polls to deal with those people who are still undecided or refuse even after the squeeze question is effectively to ignore them altogether. By simply taking out any respondents who are undecided or who refuse after the squeeze question, and repercentaging the levels of party support based just on those who do name a party, the pollsters had made a false assumption that these non-responders were just like the rest of the sample, when in fact they were more likely to be Conservative supporters.

The analysis made by NOP after the election was based on the answers given by those who were undecided or who refused the voting question, to other questions in the questionnaire. The logical progression was to use these other questions in future surveys to predict the voting intention of non-responders. One question commonly asked for analysis purposes is how people voted in the previous election, and this correlates very strongly with current voting intention. However, this is perhaps too 'obvious' a question, and most of those who refuse to answer the voting-intention question also refuse to answer the past-voting question, which limits its usefulness.

Less directly connected to voting, but for that reason easier to answer, are other questions which seek to measure respondents' favourability towards the different parties. Another common question is to ask how satisfied people are with the way the Prime Minister is doing his job, and possibly also how well the Leader of the Opposition is doing his. Alternatively a question may ask which of the party leaders respondents think would make the best Prime Minister.

Another question which correlates well with voting intention is economic competence. It is widely accepted that most people make their decisions on how to vote on the basis of economic factors, and few will vote for a party which they feel will be less competent at running the economy than the alternatives. Therefore a question along the lines of 'Which party do you trust more to make you and your family better off?' or 'Which party do you think will be best at running the economy?' will be answered by many people who refuse or say they don't know at the voting intention question.

By looking at those who do answer the voting question and comparing their answers to that with their answers to these more peripheral questions, it is possible to measure the extent of the correlation between these various indicators. The post-1992 investigation made it fairly clear that those who refused the voting question or who were undecided were more likely to be Tory sympathisers. The question was, how could something be done in the opinion polls to counteract this? Again, all the main pollsters carried out their own experiments, leading to what is now known as the process of 'adjustment', and which all of the pollsters except MORI used in some form in 1997.

ICM's approach was based on analysis of the 1992 British Election Study (BES). They took past vote as the most powerful of all the other indicators, and relying on an assumption that the relationship between variables found in the 1992 BES will hold constant for all surveys, used a process whereby 60% of 'don't knows' and 'refusals' are given a current vote equal to their claimed 1992 vote and added back into the voting-intention figures.[2]

NOP's approach has been similar in principle but different in practice, particularly because it calculates all the relationships afresh with every survey. One main difference is that instead of simple copying across a proportion of claimed 1992 vote into current vote, NOP relies on a change matrix, and uses the question on underlying party identity rather than past voting. If the figures from those who do answer the voting-intention question show that 80% of all of those who say they basically consider themselves Conservative intend to vote for them, then we can assume that of those undecideds and refusals who identify with the Conservatives, 80% of them also will be current Conservative supporters. Thus if loyalty levels of any of the parties change over the course of time the allocation of current vote based on party identity will change along with it.

To give an example of how this works in practice, let us assume that out of a survey of 1,500 people, some 100 either refused to answer the voting question, or said they were undecided how to vote. (It is fairly standard practice to assume that those who say they won't vote at all will indeed not vote, and they can be safely ignored.)

We begin by examining the answers to the party-identity question for those respondents. Let us first suppose that, of those 100, 20 said they felt they were basically Conservative, 10 said Labour and 10 said Liberal Democrat (for the sake of simplicity I will ignore other parties in this example). The remaining 60 did not identify with any party.

The first stage then is to decide for these forty people what their current voting intention should be. This is done by reference to the cross-analysis of claimed party identity against current voting intention from those who have answered the voting question. In this example, of all those who said they identified with the Conservatives and did answer the voting question, 70% intended to vote Conservative, 20% intended to vote Labour and 10% to vote

Liberal Democrat. So if 70% of Tory identifiers are still Tory, we can assume that for those twenty people who refused the current voting question or did not know, but who told us they identified with the Conservatives, then 70% of them also – fourteen people – will vote Conservative. Similarly, four can be assumed to be Labour voters, and two Liberal Democrat voters. The same calculations can be done to estimate levels of support for the other two main parties as well, as Table 32 shows.

Table 32 *Adjusting the methodology of the polling process, stage two*

Party identity of undecideds/refuseds	No.	Current voting by past voting category (%)			Votes allocated to each party (%)		
		Con.	Lab.	Lib. Dem.	Con.	Lab.	Lib. Dem.
Conservative	20	70	20	10	14	4	2
Labour	10	10	80	10	1	8	1
Liberal Democrat	10	10	30	70	1	3	7
Not stated	60	–	–	–	–	–	–

As can be seen, not all of those who refuse or are undecided at the current voting intention name a party that they identify will. We therefore have to go through a further stage to try to allocate a current vote for them based on some other question. In 1997 NOP used the economic competence question – 'Who would you trust most to make you and your family better off, the Conservative party under John Major or the Labour party under Tony Blair?' – as the next stage. Looking only at those undecideds and refusals who also fail to answer the party-identity question (sixty people in the example above), we look to see how many would trust the Conservatives more, how many would trust Labour more, and how many would trust neither.

The same process of allocation is then gone through, as with the party identity. That is to say, we look at all those who did answer the voting question to see what proportion of those who thought the Tories were best at running the economy were actually Conservative voters. Then the percentages and base sizes are multiplied together in just the same way to produce an absolute number of Conservative and Labour voters as a result of this adjustment.

Adding together the 'new' voters for each party generated by the calculations from the party identity, and the 'new' voters generated by the economic competence question, we have a total number of extra votes for each party to go in to the tables. However, this is still not quite the end of the story, for not all of those who refuse the voting question or say they don't know then go on to answer one or other of the two questions used in our calculations. In our fictional example, at the end of the process only 79 of the 100 'don't knows' and 'refuseds' had been allocated to a party. To deal with this we simply take the 'new' voters and multiply each of them up by a factor of 100/79. This means that we have now effectively estimated a current party support for every single one of our undecideds and refuseds. Adding these figures to the original voting-intention figures from those who did answer the first question produces the final overall adjusted figure, as shown in Table 33.

Table 33 *Adjusting the methodology of the polling process, final stage*

Party identity of undecideds/refuseds	No.	Current voting by party identity category (%)			Votes allocated to each party (%)		
		Con.	Lab.	Lib. Dem.	Con.	Lab.	Lib. Dem.
Conservative	20	70	20	10	14	4	2
Labour	10	10	80	10	1	8	1
Lib Dem	10	10	30	70	1	3	7

Economic competence answers of undecideds/refuseds	No.	Current voting by economic competence category (%)			Votes allocated to each party (%)		
		Con.	Lab.	Lib. Dem.	Con.	Lab.	Lib. Dem.
Conservative	30	74	2	10	22.2	0.6	3.0
Labour	5	5	76	19	0.25	3.8	0.95
Neither	15	8	12	31	1.2	1.8	4.65
Sum of the above					39.65	21.2	18.6
Total votes allocated 79.45							
Total votes weighted to total number of undecideds/refuseds (i.e. 100/79.45)					49.9	26.7	23.4
Votes from original voting question					414 (33%)	623 (49%)	233 (18%)
Final vote totals					463.9	649.7	256.4
%					34.0	47.0	19.0

This approach is quite a complicated one but it has been designed to be the most justifiable in theoretical terms. Although we went through the full process of recalculation, as shown in Table 33, for every one of the monthly polls we conducted for the *Sunday Times* from June 1995 until the 1997 election, the impact of the adjustment was almost invariably the same – it added 1% on to the Conservative vote and took 1% off the Labour vote.

Weighting by past voting

Perhaps the most contentious of all the various adjustments made by the pollsters to try to improve their performance since 1992 is the use of weighting by past voting to try to correct for imbalances in the sample. In theory, past voting is the ideal variable to use to correct for response bias. If supporters of one party are more likely to refuse to take part in a survey or are harder to get hold of, then the profile of past voting amongst the achieved sample will show a shortfall for that particular party. Thus if the Conservatives win an election by 40% to 30%, but their own supporters are much less likely to take part in surveys, then one might find a past-voting distribution in the achieved sample showing 35% having voted for the Conservatives and 35% having voted for Labour. (Again, for the sake of simplicity in these examples we will ignore the rather complex issue of dealing with those who did not vote in the previous election.)

Since we know what the levels of support achieved by each party actually were in the previous election, these figures would seem to show clearly that we have interviewed an unrepresentative sample, and that corrective weighting is needed. If in our polls we find that we have only 40% ABC1s when we expect to have 45%, we can correct for this by weighting up all the ABC1s in our sample by a factor of 45/40. To the extent that being ABC1 correlates with voting, then this corrective weighting should remove any resulting bias. In the same way, if we weight those 35% Conservative voters back up to the 40% who did actually vote Conservative in the last election, and weight the 35% Labour down to the 30% who actually did, then we should remove any source of bias resulting from differential response amongst supporters of the different parties. Because of the very high correlation between past and present voting, this would seem to be a highly efficient way of checking that a sample is representative.

When ICM switched their polling for the *Guardian* from face-to-face to telephone interviewing (as is discussed further below), they cited as evidence of the superiority of the telephone method the fact that the claimed 1992 recall vote in the telephone poll exactly matched the actual 1992 election result, whereas it was common in opinion polls conducted face to face for the results to show a much closer election result than there had actually been. At first sight this would seem to be a vindication of their new methodology, but in fact almost all commentators have always argued that past voting is a very unreliable measure, starting with Himmelweit *et al.* in 1978.[3] It is a classic example of what is sometimes described as 'opinions masquerading as facts'.

It seems on the surface to be a perfectly simple question. The last election was not that long ago, and voting is a reasonably important act, and one might therefore suppose that people would remember how they had voted. However, there is more to it than a simple question of memory. People's memories are selective in a number of different ways, and when it comes to their recall of voting behaviour their memory may well be coloured by their present opinion, or by events since the election. Many people like to appear consistent in their views, and if they have switched from the party they supported in the last election to another party they may well succeed in persuading themselves that they have not switched at all, but have always voted for their current party. Alternatively, it may not be their memory that is at fault, but merely that they have a desire when asked by an interviewer to appear consistent. For whatever reason, there is no doubt that answers to the past-voting question are less than wholly reliable.

There has been circumstantial evidence to support this argument, but until recently, little of any substance. However, in part sparked by the discussion over the error of the polls in 1992, 1996 saw two surveys published which provided reasonably solid evidence that even if one were able to question every single elector in the country, one would still get a past-voting recall which differed from the actual election result. The most important evidence comes from the British Household Panel Study (BHPS). This is a very large social survey, funded by the Economic and Social Research Council (ESRC) and managed by the Research Centre into Micro-Social Change in Britain at the University of Essex. It involves annual interviews with nearly ten thousand adults in nearly five thousand households in Great Britain. It covers a very wide variety of issues and always includes some questions each year on politics.

In the second year of the survey, in autumn 1992, respondents were asked how they had voted in the previous general election. This showed a recall very close to the actual election result. Because NOP carry out the fieldwork for the BHPS, I was able to ensure the inclusion in the 1995 wave of the survey of a repeat of the past-voting question.

This time the recall vote showed results quite different from the actual election result. To some extent, of course, there will be change caused by differential drop-out during the life of the panel, but this has already been corrected for in the weighting carried out by the research team. There is plenty of information available about those who are interviewed early on in the life of the panel but then drop out, and weighting factors can be calculated from this. The panel represents the first time that a very major survey, conducted using random sampling, and with a very high response rate, has asked a past-voting question some years after the actual election. My main purpose in placing this question was to answer the question 'What answer would you expect to get to the past voting question if you asked it of a very high quality sample?'

The idea was, that by finding out what answer you would expect to find from a very large, very high-quality random sample we would have a benchmark against which we could assess our much smaller, faster turnaround quota polls. We have always been unhappy with the idea of weighting back to the actual election result, but had no firm evidence that we should be weighting to anything else. The panel study provided us with the evidence of what we should be weighting to.

We would have gained this from any high-quality, large sample survey, but we gained even more because of the panel element. Not only did we find out what the sample as a whole said in 1995 that they had actually done in 1992, but we were able to see on a person-by-person basis how the answer given in 1992 had changed by 1995. This is unaffected by any changes in differential panel attrition, and what it showed clearly is that many of those who in 1992 said that they had voted Conservative a few months previously were claiming by 1995 that they had not voted at all, or even that they had voted for a different party.

Similar evidence is obtained from the British Election Study (BES), another, although much smaller, panel survey. This too involved interviews with the same respondents at one-year intervals, though the past voting question was only asked on one occasion since the election. Because neither the BHPS nor the BES got the election result 'right' in their first recall just after the election (the BES in particular had quite a strong pro-Conservative bias), allowance needs to be made for this as well. This means that it is difficult to come up with a firm answer – Peter Kellner estimated a 1% Labour lead from the BHPS,[4] while John Curtice estimated a 2% Conservative lead from the BES[5] – but there is no doubt that a perfectly conducted survey in 1996 would come up with a claimed past voting somewhere around these two figures, and certainly nowhere near the 8% lead that the Conservatives actually got in 1992.

Even without being able to be exact about the figures one should expect, this evidence gives us much more confidence to make at least some use of past voting as a corrective measure. Because it has always been suspected to be an unreliable measure, pollsters have fought shy of using past voting, and certainly if they had done so fully then almost all polls in the 1980s would have overestimated the Liberal or Liberal Democrat vote. Now that we have a better idea of what recall should be it can play a major part in the process of validating any opinion-poll sample. In particular, Curtice and Sparrow have argued that past voting can be an indicator of an unrepresentative sample, and weighting can then be used to correct it.[6]

Indeed, past-vote weighting was used by several of the pollsters in 1997, but not by all, and those that did use it did not agree on targets they should be weighting to, but where it was used, it led to improved estimates.

Random sampling and telephone interviewing

The debate between the proponents of quota and random sampling is rendered somewhat academic by the sheer unfeasibility of carrying out random surveys during an election campaign itself. A random sample with a poor response rate has few advantages over a quota sample, and to achieve a higher response rate a fieldwork period of at least two weeks is really required. Only by making continued call-backs on people who are out at the first call can the number of non-contacts be brought down to a satisfactory level. However, a media client is unlikely to be satisfied with a methodology which allows him only one or at the very most two polls during the campaign, and which are two weeks out of date by the time they are published.

This would seem to rule out any use of random sampling for election polls, and yet random sampling is commonly used in other countries. The explanation for this apparent discrepancy is that in other countries, particularly in the USA, these random surveys are conducted by telephone. British pollster Humphrey Taylor, now running Harris in the USA, has shown that there is a huge diversity of methods used for telephone surveys around the world, with around half the firms he surveyed using random-sampling methods and half not.[7] Partly because of the sheer size of the country, which makes national face-to-face interviewing very expensive, and partly because of a different telephone system and a different attitude to the use of the telephone, research conducted over the phone has been far more common in the USA than it is in Britain.

As discussed in Chapter 6, the first use of telephone sampling for opinion polling in this country, by ASL in 1983, was a failure, but they then succeeded in the following election in producing results over the telephone which stood up well against the results from the other face-to-face polls. The principal original problem with telephone interviewing was a built-in bias because those on the telephone were more middle class than those who were not. Any telephone-only poll would therefore underrepresent the more working-class part of the population.

The first stage towards correcting for this was obviously to upweight the more downmarket respondents so that the profile of the achieved sample matched the social-class profile of the country as a whole. However, simple corrective weighting by class failed to solve the problem, and closer examination revealed that within any one class group, those on the phone were likely to be different from those without. Phone-ownership was lowest among DEs, but DEs on the phone were disproportionately likely to be running their own small business in a semi-skilled trade, such as window-cleaning. It is well known that the self-employed are considerably more likely to vote Conservative than are employees, and so the achieved DE sample on a telephone interview was likely to be biased towards the Conservatives. Upweighting these DEs to try to compensate for the overall shortage of their numbers merely made matters worse.

What was needed was not so much simple weighting as some means to compensate for these imbalances. The first steps in this direction were taken by Bill Miller from Glasgow University, who came up with the concept of 'super-weighting'.[8] The principle behind super-weighting is that lack of telephone-ownership is a downmarket social indicator on a par with other social indicators. If it were possible to find another group who were on the telephone but were similarly downmarket, then oversampling this group would go a long way towards compensating for the telephone biases.

Miller's theory was that there were three key indicators of relative depriva-
tion. Not having a telephone was one, being a council tenant was another,
while the third was not having a car in the household. At the very bottom of the
scale were those who were living in council houses, with no car, and no telephone. Such a group was never going to be covered in a telephone-poll because
obviously they are not on the telephone. However, just above this are a number
of groups who fit two of the three criteria. Thus there are council-house tenants
with no car who do have a telephone, people with no car and no telephone but
living in non-council accommodation, and those living in council accommodation with no car but a telephone. Of these three groups only the second would
not be included in a telephone survey – both the other two would. Miller argued
that by not so much upweighting as by originally oversampling the two downmarket groups who were on the telephone, this would compensate for those
who were not.

Miller's own experiments backed up his theory, and the pollsters themselves
carried out experiments. These experiments were normally done by taking
surveys that had already been conducted face to face, extracting those people
who were on the phone, and then establishing ways in which they could be
weighted in order to replicate the whole of the original sample. The results of
these tests were somewhat inconclusive, for although super-weighting was
shown to work, in many of the experiments simple demographic weighting
worked just as well.

In the 1987 general election the Market Research Development Fund commissioned NOP and ICM jointly to carry out an experiment to test the effect of
different weighting schemes in a general election. This too suggested that
simple weighting could work just as well as super-weighting, and although the
results were not published until after the election, the simple-weighted eve-of-
poll telephone survey proved to be the most accurate of all the 1987 election
polls.[9]

Closer examination revealed that the problem lay not so much in finding a
means of weighting telephone-owners so that they looked like the whole population, but rather the problem of finding a representative sample of telephone-
owners in the first place. Weighting schemes could be found which would take
the telephone-owners out of a face-to-face sample and make them look like the
total sample, but when these same weighting schemes were applied to surveys
conducted purely by telephone the results still showed biases compared with
other polls at the time. As the proportion of people in the UK with a telephone
rose to well over 90%, the impact of excluding those without a telephone
became trivial, but the problem of sampling remained.

Originally most telephone surveys were conducted just by drawing names at
random from the telephone directory to form the sample. However, as the proportion of subscribers who were ex-directory increased there became more and
more worries about this as a method of sampling, and it became apparent that

biases amongst those who were ex-directory explained the differences between telephone and face-to-face polls.

Various approaches have been attempted to try to rectify this problem. Most of these involved some semi-random element, such as drawing a sample from a telephone directory and then adding one or two to the final digit to produce a new number. This increased the coverage of ex-directory numbers, but still fell a long way short of removing the bias. The problem is that people who are ex-directory tend to cluster together in certain areas. This means that in an areas where only one in ten are ex-directory, any individual subscriber has nine times more chance of being selected by a directory plus one method than some other subscriber living in an area where nine in ten are ex-directory.

The Americans solve this problem by using pure random sampling – known as random-digit dialling (RDD). The standard original approach was something known as the Mitofsky–Waksberg method – after its two progenitors.[10] Mitofsky–Waksberg is a two-stage sampling process intended to ensure that the resulting sample is with a probability proportional to size. The main problem with RDD of any kind is that there are far more numbers in existence than are actually used by subscribers. The US 3-3-4 standard telephone number system allows for a possible ten billion telephone numbers, though there are fewer than five hundred million in existence. Selecting numbers purely at random would lead to an enormous amount of time wasted calling numbers which simply do not exist.

The first stage of any RDD sampling process is thus to narrow down this huge range of possible numbers into blocks of numbers which are known to exist. The US telephone authorities are far more co-operative than BT in making this information available, and this is a significant reason why RDD sampling was used far earlier in the USA than in Britain. Within any three-digit area code it is a simple matter to find out which three-digit exchange codes exist, and which blocks of numbers within that have been allocated and which remain unused.

Mitofsky–Waksberg starts by identifying all blocks of 100 telephone numbers known to exist – achieved by removing the last two digits from the full telephone number. A simple random sample is drawn of these blocks of 100 numbers, and within each sample block a random subscriber is identified by generating a number between 00 and 99. These telephone numbers are then rung not with the intention of conducting an interview, but merely to establish whether they are actually numbers in use, or numbers unobtainable.

If the sample number within a block of 100 proves to ring, then that whole block of 100 is treated as a possible sample member. If the one sample number does not ring, the whole block of 100 is excluded from the sample. The chance of the sampled number ringing is in direct proportion to the number of working numbers within that block of 100, and so what this method achieves is a sample of blocks of 100 numbers in proportion to the number of subscribers within those blocks.

Because this sampling of primary sampling units has been conducted with probability proportional to size, the survey must then seek to carry out the same number of interviews in each primary sampling unit. This is where the Mitofsky–Waksberg is somewhat complex because it requires numbers to be generated at random within that block of 100 until a certain number have been found which are working numbers. This process will obviously vary also according to the penetration of numbers within the block. If all 100 numbers are operational, and the target is to get 15 working numbers within each block, then the first 15 numbers will all ring and will then form the sample. However, if only 20 of the possible 100 numbers are actually in use, then 75 calls will need to be made before 15 working numbers have been identified. Once these 15 numbers have been found they are then the sample and cannot be replaced. Large numbers of recalls are made on them in order to maximise response and no replacement can be made for refusals.

Mitofsky–Waksberg is a very elegant method in theoretical terms but it has practical difficulties. It is difficult for the telephone centre to manage the interviewers since it is impossible to issue a constant size sample. Close watch must be kept on the number of working numbers reached within each block of 100 to ensure that the sampling proportions are kept correct. In order to try to remove these problems whilst still maintaining the advantages of sampling of probability proportional to size, an alternative approach known as list-based RDD has been developed.

The theory behind this approach is that rather than using the first-stage dialling to ensure that blocks of 100 are selected with probability proportional to their size, other information can be used to establish whether each block has a high or low density of numbers. Although, as in Britain, not all US subscribers are in the directory, the directory listings provide a useful surrogate for the distribution of numbers. Thus if one were to count the number of directory listings within each block of 100 numbers one would end up with a number which is lower than the actual number of subscribers, but which may well give a relatively close approximation to the relative densities.

What has made this approach easy to administer is the now widespread availability of complete sets of US telephone directories on CD-ROM. These can be purchased in almost any computer store in the USA for less than $100. They are freely accessible databases and allow US research agencies to construct patterns of numbers across the whole telephone system. Based on this advanced knowledge it is possible to draw samples, including both directory and ex-directory subscribers, where constant numbers per area are issued to the field.

As with the directory plus-one method, anybody living in a block of 100 which is entirely ex-directory has no chance of getting into the sample at all under this method, and this represents therefore a potential bias. There has been a considerable amount of experimental work in the USA looking at the profile of surveys interviewed by means of list-based RDD, and comparing with the known population parameters of the country as a whole. Most of these surveys have indicated that the bias that results from using list-assisted RDD is not significant, and is more than justified by the savings which the method can produce in survey costs.[11]

In Britain there have been attempts made to try to establish whether RDD sampling could be carried out on a commercially sound basis, but until now the verdict had always gone against it. Collins and Foreman were among those to study the theoretical and practical issues in detail, and concluded that at that time RDD was not cost-effective in Britain.[12] The main problem is that far less information about the structure of the telephone-number system is available in this country than in the USA. Even without attempting to go as far as list-based RDD, it is extremely inefficient even to try to replicate Mitofsky–Waksberg because of the lack of available information about which blocks of numbers are in existence and which are not. Lepkowski has shown that using a two-stage approach such as Mitofsky–Waksberg it is possible to increase the incidence of working residential numbers from 25% at the first stage to 60% at the second stage.[13] In the Foreman and Collins experiment, however, stage one also produced a residential number rate of 25%, but at stage two this was increased only to 39%. In comparison, the directory plus-one method produced 61% working residential numbers.

The UK telephone regulator Oftel publishes lists of exchange codes and sub-codes within use which helps to refine the sampling process, but the number of potential telephone numbers is still far greater than the number of actual ones. Even if one allows for the fact that the opening 0 and 1 in British telephone numbers can be ignored because at the moment all except a small number of special services begin with 01, the number of potential telephone numbers in Britain is also over one billion – enough for every household in the country to have fifty telephone lines each!

BMRB made some attempt to bridge between directory plus *n* and RDD by using the BMRB omnibus survey as the seed for plus *n* rather than the directory,[14] and it was this work which sparked the idea for a programme of experiments by NOP, described by Moon and Noble.[15] The starting point was that, although no detailed 'map' of the British telephone system is available, if one had a large enough list of working telephone numbers it would be possible to establish which blocks of 100 numbers were in use and which were not. Our original idea was to use NOP's Omnibus cumulated over two years, or else samples used for other surveys, but a larger list proved to be available from a list-broker.

This list had over twelve million numbers (there are around twenty-nine million telephone lines in the UK), and the broker supplied an analysis showing each 100-number block within the whole list, and the number of numbers on the file within that block of 100. Although we could not be sure, it was reasonable to suppose that the distribution of the remaining seventeen million numbers was broadly the same, and we could treat this list of blocks as an approximate map of the UK telephone system, from which RDD samples could be drawn using Mitofsky–Waksberg.

Tests using this method were conducted at a by-election and a local council election. In each case the demographic profile of the achieved sample was reasonably close to the profile for that area given in the census data, and the predicted election result was close enough to the actual result to make the experiment worth continuing with.

The next step was to find funding for a larger-scale experiment on a national scale. There is an understandable reluctance on the part of major survey-research users to fund experimental research in survey methods, but in the UK the Health Education Authority (HEA) has been a notable exception to this. We approached the HEA and obtained their agreement to part-fund a larger experiment with RDD methods. (NOP effectively funded part of the work themselves by charging the HEA only their direct costs.) The survey, conducted with the same Mitofsky–Waksberg sampling approach, was a replication of the Health Education Monitoring Survey (HEMS) – a large survey conducted by the HEA using a random sample and face-to-face interviewing.

The achieved sample had fewer elderly people than the population as a whole, but this is a common phenomenon in telephone surveys, and to a lesser extent in face-to-face ones. Once this was corrected by means of weighting, the achieved sample broadly matched population estimates obtained on the face-to-face HEMS and on the GHS. Comparison of other variables, such as whether people currently smoke or have ever smoked, also revealed similar figures on the RDD survey to the face-to-face surveys.

This does not prove that RDD used in this way can produce a true random sample in the same way that samples drawn from PAF or the Electoral Register can, but it shows that in many cases it can provide estimates of population characteristics that are either in or are close to the range of values found in high-quality surveys using unequivocally established probability samples. With this evidence behind us, we went on to conduct a national opinion poll in election week, using RDD. This was not for any client, and was funded internally by NOP, so was not published at the time. The results are discussed below with the other results of the 1997 polls.

Despite the various problems with telephone sampling, two pollsters – Gallup and ICM – switched over to telephone interviewing before the 1997 election, and at NOP we carried out a number of experiments into the use of RDD, though still used face-to-face interviewing for our published election polls. ICM made the switch to the telephone purely for methodological reasons, though in Gallup's case the move was prompted by the closure of their face-to-face interviewing field force. ICM use a directory plus n system, while Gallup use a form of list-assisted RDD, buying numbers in from another broker.

The five main pollsters who had polled in 1992 all polled again in 1997, though in some cases for different media clients. Although the names were the same, the period between 1992 and 1997 was characterised by great diversity between the pollsters, allowing those with little imagination to produce endless headlines of 'POLLS APART'. The greatest gap came in November 1995, when Gallup showed a Labour lead of 39.5%, and ICM a Labour lead of only 17%. Gaps such as these between the polls have been common, and it is not because the polls are becoming much more variable month on month, but because there were consistent and systematic differences between the different polling organisations.

The 1997 general election

The preceding part of this chapter has shown how the pollsters tried to deal with the problems identified in 1992, but while there was agreement between them on some – the quotas to be used, for example – there has been divergence on others. Perhaps the most obvious is the split between the two using telephone interviewing and the three remaining with face-to-face; but there were also differences between those who adjusted and those who did not, and between the different uses of weighting by past voting.

The MRS Committee encouraged this kind of variety: 'We would encourage methodological pluralism; as long as we cannot be certain which techniques are best, uniformity must be a millstone – a danger signal rather than an indication of health. We should applaud diversity; in a progressive industry experimentation is a means of development.'[16] However, whilst all the pollsters agreed with this, I think we all hoped that one method (preferably our own) would prove the most accurate in 1997, and would then become best practice.

However, at the end of the election no one was very much the wiser. The performance of the polls in 1997 proved very difficult to interpret. Whereas in 1992 everyone knew the polls had got it wrong, no one seemed to agree whether they were right or wrong in 1997. Just looking at the titles of articles written by the pollsters themselves makes this clear. On the one hand there is NOP with 'A Reputation Restored'[17] and MORI with 'They got it right this time';[18] while on the other there is ICM with 'The failure of the polls in 1997'.[19]

So why should it prove so difficult to decide if the polls were right or wrong? There are two separate issues here – whether the final prediction polls were accurate or not, and whether one can generalise about the polls on the basis of the final poll from each organisation.

In fact the final election polls, shown in Table 34, had average errors which were not much lower than they had been in 1992, but they escaped the opprobrium they had suffered last time out. Partly this is because when one party is 13% ahead of its nearest rival, errors of 3% or so on each party are not going to change the overall story. The polls said Labour would win by a landslide; Labour won by a landslide; ergo, the polls were right.

Table 34 *Actual and predicted results, 1997 general election (%)*

Pollster	Harris	NOP	ICM	Gallup	MORI	
Newspaper	Independent	Reuters	Guardian	Telegraph	The Times	**Actual result**
Fieldwork	27–29 Apr.	29 Apr.	29–30 Apr.	30 Apr.	30 Apr.	1 May
Sample size	1,154	1,093	1,555	1,849	2,304	
Conservative	31.0	28.0	33.0	33.0	28.0	31.4
Labour	48.0	50.0	43.0	47.0	48.0	44.4
Liberal Democrat	15.0	14.0	18.0	14.0	16.0	17.2
Others	6.0	8.0	5.0	8.0	8.0	8.0
Labour lead	17.0	22.0	10.0	1.0	20.0	13.0
Error on lead	+4.0	+9.0	−3.0	+1.0	+7.0	
Average error on share	2.1	3.0	1.7	1.9	2.1	–

Also, and I believe more significantly, the polls throughout 1997 were subject to almost constant criticism on the grounds that Labour could not possibly be that far ahead, and that the polls were going to be even more wrong than they had been in 1992. When it emerged that the polls had been basically right all along, criticism of errors of 3% seemed irrelevant. Journalists who had written things like the following were hardly in any position to complain about the final polls not being quite right.

> The result of the last election revealed the limitations of opinion research . . . The evidence on the ground is that the Conservatives are far closer to Labour than the polls suggest. (*Daily Telegraph*, 28 April 1997)

> Victory on May Day is by no means in the bag for Tony Blair, and there are no signs of the Labour landslide suggested by the opinion polls. (*Independent*, 21 April 1997, writing up a straw poll conducted by journalists)

> I do not believe Tony Blair will win by a landslide. On the contrary, I believe that John Major, who has fought brilliantly, is on course for a majority of around 30–40. (Woodrow Wyatt, *The Times*, 29 April 1997)

One of the reasons for the different interpretations is that analysts have been looking at different things. A very crude measure, as mentioned above, is just to compare the broad outcome predicted and achieved – in each case, a Labour landslide. However, to assess the polls properly, we need something rather more precise. The traditional method is to compare the estimate given by each pollster for each party with the share of the vote actually achieved, and by averaging those to produce an average error for each pollster, and then an overall average across all the pollsters. Both Crewe[20] and Curtice[21] stressed the fact mentioned above that the average errors, while much better than in 1992, were still much worse than in the other elections since 1970.

Curtice attempts to strengthen his case by stressing the size of the error on the gap between the two main parties, rather than the individual errors, although Worcester has long argued that it is wrong to concentrate on the lead rather than party share, since the latter is what polls actually measure.[22] Curtice also seizes on the variation between the pollsters, which I return to below, then undermines much of his case with an eccentric 'what if' analysis, which concludes that if the Conservatives had been three points ahead rather than thirteen points behind, then 'No less (*sic*) than four of the six polls would have apparently have picked the wrong winner.' The first reaction to this is a resounding 'so what?', with a more measured response being to point out that if the Conservatives had been three points ahead the whole nature of the election would have been different, and the factors affecting the polls would almost certainly have worked differently.

Even the errors on party share can be interpreted in more than one way. Curtice argues for the continued existence of pro-Labour bias, and points out that 'No less (*sic*) than five of the six polls put Labour's strength at more than it proved to be in the ballot box. And no less than three polls did so by more than could be accounted for by the conventional three point margin of error. Prima facie this looks like evidence of bias rather than sampling error.' Strangely, he doesn't point out that two polls put the Conservatives' strength too high and three put it too low, suggesting the presence of error rather than bias.

This is not just nit-picking about whether we all try to find figures which back up our own argument, for I believe that the single most important thing about the polls in the 1997 election was their success or otherwise in measuring the Conservative vote. While some of the faults of the polls in 1992, such as the quota errors, acted on both the Labour and Conservative vote directly, the key problem of differential refusal – the 'spiral of silence', or the 'shy Tories' – acted directly only to depress the Conservative vote, with all the other parties seeing their share increased as a result.

The acid-test of whether the pollsters had solved this problem was whether they were able correctly to measure the size of the Conservative vote, and in the event they were. As stated above, the final polls were scattered either side of the true value of the Conservative vote. Furthermore, in forty of the forty-two polls conducted by the main pollsters the Conservative vote was $31\% \pm 3\%$.[23] Whilst these figures are open to more than one interpretation, the most plausible one is that the Conservative vote barely changed during the election and that the polls measured it correctly, with the expected level of sampling error around it.

The 1997 election was certainly one where much of the country turned against the Conservatives, as their massive defeat on election day eventually attested. The dominant mood was one of 'time for a change', and it appears that there were many voters whose primary aim was to get the Conservatives out, and who were less worried about exactly how it should be achieved. One consequence of this was that despite winning a lower proportion of the total vote than in 1992, the Liberal Democrats more than doubled their number of MPs. What the pollsters agreed on was that the Conservatives were well below the level of support where they had a hope of holding on to power – the main story of the election. What they tended to disagree on was the distribution of the anti-Conservative vote between Labour and the Liberal Democrats.

The fact that all the pollsters but one overestimated the Labour share of the vote, and the average error on the Labour share was as high as 3% is still a cause for concern, and the pollsters would be unwise to be complacent following their performance in the 1997 election. However the performance of the polls in 1997 was much better than in 1992, and better than some critics have implied.

As stated earlier, the other problem in determining best practice from an analysis of the polls is that commentators almost inevitably concentrate on the last poll conducted by each pollster before the election, and yet, particularly in terms of drawing conclusions about methodology, the final polls are misleading because in several cases they told a different, and contradictory story from the earlier campaign polls. I am clearly biased, since NOP's final published poll was just about our worst of the campaign, and it is galling to be remembered perpetually for this when NOP performed very creditably throughout the election. LSE statistician Colm O'Muirchearteaigh made the point as eloquently as only he can when he wrote: 'There seems to be little or no evidence of a late change in voting intention and therefore to judge the pollsters by their final poll in those circumstances would be like using proximity to a chair when the music stops in a game of musical chairs as a measure of skill.[24]'

Of the final polls, the two which came closest to the actual result were Gallup and ICM. This would seem to suggest a triumph for telephone over face-to-face polling, and yet Gallup and ICM came to their final poll from very different starting points. Despite having just argued against it, I will use the Labour lead as the measure here, precisely because it is the easiest shorthand. ICM's final poll predicted a lead of just 10%, while Gallup had 14%, compared with the actual lead of 13%.

However, if we compare the final poll with the previous poll from the same organisation we get two very different stories. ICM's previous poll had a lead of only 5%, suggesting a swing of 2.5% to Labour in the last week. Gallup, on the other hand, had a lead of 20% in their previous poll, and so they suggest a 3% swing to the Conservatives in the last days. They cannot both have been right about this movement, and so at least one of the telephone polls must have been inaccurate. The point of my argument here is not to try to criticise one pollster compared with another, but simply to suggest that despite initial impressions, the 1997 election provides no evidence as to the superiority of telephone polls over face-to-face ones.

Over the whole campaign, there was a consistent difference between ICM on the one hand, and the other four pollsters on the other, with ICM having consistently lower Labour vote shares. So of the two companies using telephone interviewing, one had the same results as those using face to face, and one had very different ones. NOP's own RDD poll lends weight to the argument in favour of telephone interviewing.

To maximise comparability with other opinion polls, exactly the same demographic weights were set for NOP's RDD poll as for the NOP polls for the *Sunday Times* and Reuters. As Table 35 shows, the results of the poll, with these weights, were very close to the actual election result.

Table 35 *NOP's RDD poll, with demographic weights, 1997 general election (%)*

	RDD poll	Election result
Conservative	33	31
Labour	45	44
Liberal Democrat	17	17
Other	5	8

This would at first sight appear to be a massive vindication of the RDD method, but detailed examination of the result produced a few caveats. Chief amongst these was the whole issue of claimed past voting. As discussed above, one would expect a good sample to have a claimed past voting showing the two main parties almost neck and neck. In fact, the demographically weighted RDD sample produced a recall of 1992 vote of 36% Conservative and 29% Labour,[25] well outside the acceptable range, and suggesting a sample biased towards the Conservatives. For this reason, the data were weighted by past voting, using both the NOP and ICM target weights. As Table 36 shows, this did not improve the figures, and in the case of the 1% Conservative lead actually made them worse.

Table 36 *NOP's RDD poll, weighted by past voting 1997 general election (%)*

		Weights used		
	Demographic only	Con. 33 Lab. 32	Con. 33 Lab. 30	Election result
Conservative	33	31	31	31
Labour	45	48	46	44
Liberal Democrat	17	17	18	17
Other	5	5	5	8

Critics of the traditional face-to-face polls have tended to centre their criticism on the use of the quota-sampling method, but on this point again there is no evidence either way from the 1997 election. Indeed, there is some counter-evidence. The argument made by Jowell *et al.*[26] is that, because of availability bias, quota polls interview fewer Conservative supporters than do surveys with random samples. However, in the 1997 election Gallup was the only organisation using true random sampling for its published polls, and yet it produced some of the highest Labour vote shares of the campaign, and was overall no different from the quota pollsters. There undoubtedly are still difficulties in using quota samples, but it would appear there may be other difficulties with random samples.

Curtice and Sparrow suggest that the differences between the figures obtained by ICM and Gallup, using broadly similar sampling methods, lie in questionnaire wording, and more particularly the wording of the survey introduction.[27] They argue that the introduction is critical in determining the level of non-response, and with it the level of response bias, and that ICM's introduction wording is less likely to deter Conservative supporters from taking part.

They may well be right, and this is one of many areas where there is still room for further research. The performance of the polls in 1997 was far from perfect, and it would be unwise simply to assume that using exactly the same methods in the next election will guarantee success. It would seem that, for the next election at least, methodological pluralism will still be the order of the day.

As well as the questions of reliability discussed above, the polls face two other, partly related problems, as they approach the next, and future, elections. Following almost every election, especially ones where the performance of the polls is less than perfect, there are calls for opinion polls to be banned. While polls remain perfectly legal in Britain, there are many countries where they are banned for all or part of an election campaign. One of the reasons cited for the banning of polls is that they influence voters, and thus affect the election result. Both of these issues, banning and influence, are discussed in more detail below. Because the latter is a possible reason for the former, it is discussed first.

Do polls influence voters?

The simplest answer to this question is that if polls had any significant influence on voters, it would never be possible for the polls to be correct, and yet in many elections, as we have seen, they have been remarkably accurate. This itself is proof that there is no consistent, significant, influence.

There are three ways in which it is said that polls might influence people. The first argument is that voters are likely to support whomever the polls show to be in the lead, so they have the satisfaction of voting for the winning side. This is known as the bandwagon effect, as people jump on the bandwagon of the leading party. However, it is also possible that people will react against the party in front, particularly if they are a long way in front, as they do not wish to see a government with a very large majority. This is called a backlash effect. The final theory has the same effect as the second, as the entire opposite of the bandwagon effect, but for different reasons. This theory argues that people are inclined to support whomever is trailing – an underdog effect, much as is often seen in the field of sports, where the crowd roots for the team or player who is losing.

Let us suppose that a poll is published a few days before an election, showing the Conservatives ahead by 43% to 36%, and let us further suppose that the poll is broadly correct. If this poll does have an influence on voters, for example, a backlash or underdog effect, then the Conservative lead will decline, and the national mood will be less Conservative on polling day than it was when the poll was conducted, and the poll will thus appear to be wrong.

As we have seen, polls do not always get it right, but they do often enough to show that there is no widespread habit of people changing their minds as a result of seeing an opinion poll. This is evidence that polls do not always influence people, but it does not address the question of whether they may sometimes do so.

Apart from the fact that polls are right more often than they could be if they had widespread influence on voters, other evidence cited for the lack of any influence is the behaviour of the US electorate. Because of the time differences between the east and west coasts, people living on the west coast know the result of the election in states on the east coast while their own voting stations are still open. If knowing the result merely of an opinion poll had an effect on people's behaviour, then one would expect knowing the result of the actual election should have an even greater effect. However, exit polls have shown that voters on the west coast who were aware of the results on the east coast did not vote any differently from those who were unaware.

This would seem to be conclusive evidence that polls do not influence voters, but Marsh and O'Brien argue that this is too simplistic approach, and similarly criticise other experiments carried out to that date. 'Unfortunately, the large majority of experiments which have attempted to investigate bandwagons in this way have manipulated the experimental very crudely: they have attempted to alter people's perception of the state of public opinion at one point in time, rather than alter their perception of the trend in which it was moving.'[28] In an earlier article, Marsh had argued that experiments in which people were merely told that recent opinion poll had shown a certain finding, and then asked for their own opinion, did not really address the issue.[29] Marsh argued that being told what opinion was at any time was far less powerful than being told that opinion was moving in a certain direction. Since election results only concern opinion at one time, the same criticism applies to the evidence from the US exit polls. In two experiments, one concerning abortion and one the Common Market, Marsh was able to show that people who were told that the trend was moving in favour of a particular position were more likely to declare themselves in favour of that position than those who were told the trend was moving the other way.

This is not conclusive proof, but it suggests strongly that polls *can* affect people's opinions, without implying that they necessary *will*. For example, the Marsh theory will only hold outside experimental conditions if people are aware of what the current trends are.

One of the criticisms voiced of polls is not merely that they affect people in general, but they affect them in particular ways and can thus have an effect on the election result. This is particularly the case with tactical voting. However, in most cases it is impossible for polls to have a direct influence on the result of an election, and before discussing this, it should be noted that it may not necessarily be a bad thing if polls did influence voters' behaviour.

The critics argue that people change their vote because of what the polls say, and thus cause election results to change. However, even supposing enough people were open to influence in this way to change the result in more than a small number of seats, there are practical problems to be overcome.

Let us suppose that the polls show a trend away from a Conservative government, and some people are motivated as a result to vote the government out. If the trend is towards Labour this may encourage people to vote Labour, but many of these will live in constituencies where Labour will not have a realistic chance of winning the seat. The voter in such a seat who wants to get the government out would achieve that aim better by voting Liberal Democrat rather than Labour. In the case of seats where Labour came a very distant third in the previous election this will be quite apparent to most people, but the same is not true of three-way marginals, or seats where the Labour vote was quite close to that of the Liberal Democrats in the previous election. In such seats the voter who wants to change the government needs to know which of the main opposition parties stands the best chance of winning.

A national poll will not contain any analysis at constituency level, and so the only polls which are capable of affecting election results are constituency-based ones, and here there definitely is evidence that polls can have an effect on occasion.

From my own experience, the by-election in Bermondsey in 1983 is a prime example of this. Bermondsey was a Labour stronghold, held by the very traditional Labour MP Bob Mellish, who resigned as MP when the left wing took over the constituency party and he anticipated being deselected. The local Labour Party selected as its candidate Peter Tatchell, a gay-rights activist seen as being on the far left of the party. Angered by this choice, and supported by Mellish, traditionalists in the local party put up a right-wing candidate, John O'Grady, who stood as the 'Real Labour' candidate.

Seeking to discomfort Labour, the national press reported the by-election at great length, in particular drawing attention to Tatchell's position in what they called the 'Loony Left', and to his role in the gay-rights movement. (Although he 'came out' subsequently, Tatchell was not at that time openly gay himself.)

NOP conducted a poll in January 1983, before Tatchell was formally endorsed as the Labour candidate, but when it was apparent that he would be. This showed him well in the lead, with almost half of the votes, and the two plausible opposition candidates – O'Grady and Simon Hughes of the Liberal SDP Alliance – with just under 20% each.

By the time of the second poll a month later, the gap had narrowed considerably, with support for Tatchell down below 40%, and both Hughes and O'Grady above 20%. More importantly, and much stressed by NOP's client, the *Daily Mail*, the figures based on those certain to vote showed Hughes only 6% behind Tatchell, with O'Grady well behind in third place. A few days later an ORC poll showed the gap closer still, and on their certain-to-vote figures Tatchell and Hughes were neck and neck. Support for O'Grady had fallen considerably, and it fell still further in a *Sun* poll the day before the election, which showed the Alliance in front. In the election itself, Hughes won comfortably, with well over half the votes cast, and O'Grady's vote had fallen to just 7%, slightly ahead of the Conservatives.

Looking across the whole campaign, it is easy to see the polls having an impact in a particular way. The starting point is an assumption that there were many people – possibly a majority of voters – who didn't want to have Peter Tatchell as their MP, for whatever reason. For these people their main aim was to find the candidate who had the best chance of defeating Tatchell. The Tories were clearly not an option, so it came down to a choice between O'Grady and Hughes, each of whom seemed equally plausible challengers at the start of the campaign. What the polls did was to show that of the two, Hughes had the better chance. Although the second poll showed him merely half a percentage point ahead, there was a psychological value to this far greater than its statistical value, and the point was strengthened with his greater lead among those certain to vote. The anti-Tatchell voters thus coalesced around Hughes, and the gap between him and O'Grady continued to grow. Although it was only in the final poll that Hughes appeared ahead of Tatchell, the more important gap was the one between him and O'Grady.

The polls thus almost certainly had an effect in showing anti-Tatchell voters how bets to use their votes, and that was probably also an element of bandwagon effect at the very end, leading to Hughes's runaway victory. Following Bermondsey, a Ten-Minute Rule Bill was introduced in Parliament seeking to ban opinion polls in elections. The issue of banning is discussed in more detail below, but there is a point of principle which I would like to address here.

My own view is that the polls definitely had an effect in Bermondsey, but it was an entirely beneficial effect. Voters' motives for wanting to defeat Tatchell may not have been laudable, but defeating him was their main desire, and what the polls did was to give them objective information which they could use to help them achieve their aim. This seems to me to be far more of a good thing than a bad one.

Similar effects, though on a much less dramatic scale, can be seen in another by-election – Ribble Valley in 1991. Here NOP conducted a poll for the *Independent* the weekend before the by-election, which showed the Conservatives ahead of the Liberal Democrats by 11%. More importantly, the poll also included a question asking people if they would change their vote if it became apparent that Labour had no chance of winning, but that the Liberal Democrats did have a reasonable chance. This question produced a revised voting intention showing the Liberal Democrats 5% ahead of the Conservatives, and on this basis Peter Kellner wrote in the *Independent* article on the poll that, while the raw figures showed the Conservatives ahead, he predicted a Liberal win.[30]

In the event the Liberal Democrats did indeed win with a majority of 10%, and the poll can be seen as a self-fulfilling prophecy. The publication of the poll showed that Labour had no chance of winning, and that the Liberal Democrats did, and people who had said they would change their vote under those circumstances duly did so.

The two examples quoted so far are both from by-elections, and these offer the best opportunity for poll-influenced voting. Because of the concentration of media interest in by-elections there are often polls conducted there, while in a general election polls tend to be national, and as argued above, offer little useful information for the voter wanting to vote tactically. In most general elections there are usually a small number of constituency-based polls, but these are selected for a variety of reasons – for example, because a key politician is standing, or it is a bell-wether seat – and not necessarily because they are prime targets for tactical voting. In the 1997 election, however, a series of constituency polls were conducted in seats ripe for tactical voting, with the express aim of encouraging it.

The *Observer* commissioned ICM to conduct polls in thirteen constituencies where the Tories were at risk, but where it was not immediately obvious whether the Liberal Democrats or Labour had the best chance of defeating them. The *Observer* stated that it had commissioned the polls 'to give the electorate a guide on how to vote tactically',[31] and many voters seem to have followed their lead. The polls showed the Conservatives trailing in ten of the seats, and they went on to lose all but two of these.

My own constituency, St Albans, provides a good example of the *Observer's* exercise in action. St Albans had long been a Conservative-held constituency, with the Liberals in second place. The Liberal Democrats controlled the local council, but Labour had recently won many seats on the County Council, and were gaining in support locally. It was not at all clear who offered the best chance of defeating the Conservatives, but the *Observer* poll showed Labour far ahead of the Liberal Democrats. Local Labour supporters ensured a leaflet containing the results of the *Observer* poll went to every home in St Albans, and Labour duly won the seat comfortably.

The *Observer* exercise set out to do what happened in Bermondsey by chance, and I would again argue that by helping voters to achieve their main wish of defeating the Conservatives, the polls performed a useful and in no way anti-democratic function. Understandably, the Conservatives are likely to be less enthusiastic, and this brings us to the whole question of whether polls should be banned.

Should polls be banned?

In many countries the publication of opinion polls is banned for varying lengths of time before an election. The situation is subject to constant flux, but according to a survey conducted in 1996 by the Foundation for Information, an independent organisation set up by the European Society for Opinion and Marketing Research (ESOMAR), thirty-one of the seventy-eight countries surveyed had some restrictions on publishing polls.[32] The restrictions varied from a mere twenty-four-hour embargo to as long as thirty days in Luxembourg and Turkey.

In Britain there are no restrictions, though there have been periodic attempts to introduce them. In 1967 a Speaker's Conference recommended a seventy-two-hour ban, but was met with opposition from both Harold Wilson's government, and from the press, and was never enacted. Subsequent attempts to ban polls, for example through Private Members' Bills, have similarly failed.

While banning polls is a gut response of many defeated politicians, there are a number of arguments against it. One of these has been discussed above, concerning the influence of polls on tactical voting, and this raises a slightly wider point. During an election campaign voters are exposed to a vast amount of political material, most of it extremely partisan. The parties advertise widely in various forms, and the newspapers have their own political agendas. Although the broadcast media have regulations to avoid bias, their output still consists heavily of reporting equal amounts of partisan information from the parties. The polls represent one of the few areas of non-partisan information available to voters, and as such it would seem undemocratic to deny voters access to it. Even in the case of a series of polls commissioned for a partisan purpose, such as the *Observer* polls in 1997 discussed above, the polls themselves were entirely impartial, and set out to support no party rather than another.

It should be noted that almost all of the restrictions placed around the world on opinion polls concern the publication rather than the conduct of opinion polls. This leads to a further moral argument against banning polls, and has recently led to an even more powerful practical one. Governments by and large do not enact laws to ban the *conduct* of opinion polls, because they usually want to conduct private polls of their own to assist in their election campaigns. This means that polls are still conducted, and because of the contacts between politicians and the press, journalists get to find out what the polls say. They in turn pass the information on to their contacts in business and industry, and soon almost everyone in the connected elite knows what the polls say, while the ordinary public do not.

This is a morally indefensible situation, made worse by the fact that, safe in the knowledge that the polls are not subject to any public scrutiny, politicians can say whatever they want about their polls, regardless how true it is. Thus a party which was trailing before the campaign began will insist that its own polls show it catching up quickly, even if they do no such thing.

Bob Worcester of MORI, a passionate advocate of the case against banning polls, makes the same point.

> In a free society polls cannot effectively be banned: if they were, the political parties would do even more polling than they do now – and leak it even worse than they do now. Secondly, stockbrokers, jobbers and other City 'gents' would do private polls and leak them (or make them up as they do now). Thirdly, foreign media would commission private polls in Britain and publish them overseas, and of course the results would be transmitted and reported subsequently in this country.[33]

While the first of Worcester's arguments address the moral aspect, his last gives a clear foretaste of the practical problems that currently exist in trying to ban the publication of polls. Writing in 1991, Worcester envisaged polls being effectively 'exported' from one country to another, and then 're-imported' by means of secondary reporting. Certainly this has happened in more than one country, but what Worcester could not anticipate was the impact of the Internet on the process.

Today a newspaper in a country with restrictions on the publication of polls can commission a poll, not publish it in its paper, but give a reference in the paper to a Web site – probably based outside the country – where any interested person can read the results. This is still less than universal access, since not everyone has access to the Internet, but it means the results will be available to a much wider cross-section than the previous limited elite, and will then spread further by word of mouth.

Recognising the impossibility of rigidly applying a ban on polls, a number of countries have simply turned a blind eye to publishers who break the embargo. The laws have not been repealed; they have simply ceased to be enforced.

Looking to the future

It seems almost inevitable that bans on the publication of polls will become completely impossible, and polls will spread around the world as democracy does so. They will continue to influence voters, but only some voters, and only in some circumstances.

All around the world, pollsters will continue to seek new ways of improving the quality of the data they produce. In Britain this may well mean more polls being conducted by telephone, and possibly more using random samples.

One of the criticisms of the pollsters in Britain in 1992 was that they had become complacent because of the long run of success they had enjoyed in predicting election results. Following the disaster of 1992, and the less than total recovery in 1997, it is unlikely that the pollsters will be complacent again for a while. This is as it should be, and it means that the polls will continue to be a major part of the electoral process the world over, and will continue to be closely scrutinised by poll-watchers, both professional and amateur.

Notes

1 A. Dale and C. Marsh (eds), *The 1991 Census User's Guide* (HMSO, 1993).
2 J. Curtice and N. Sparrow, 'The failure of the polls in 1997: learning the lessons for the future', paper presented at the MRS Conference, 1998.
3 H. Himmelweit, M Biberian and J. Stockdale, 'Memory for past vote: implications of a study of bias in recall', *British Journal of Political Science*, 8 (1978).
4 P. Kellner, 'Why the polls still get it wrong', *Observer*, 15 September 1996.
5 J. Curtice, N. Sparrow and J. Turner, 'The missing Tories in opinion polls: silent, forgetful or lost?', in C. Pattie, D. Denver, J. Fisher and S. Ludlam (eds.), *British Elections & Parties Review, Vol. 7* (Frank Cass, 1997).
6 J. Curtice and N. Sparrow, 'How accurate are traditional quota polls?', *Journal of the Market Research Society*, 39:3 (1997).
7 H. Taylor, 'The very different methods used to conduct telephone surveys of the public', *Journal of the Market Research Society*, 39:3 (1997).
8 W. L. Miller, 'The British voter and the telephone at the 1983 election', *Journal of the Market Research Society*, 29:1 (1987).
9 C. T. Husbands, 'The telephone study of voting intentions in the June 1987 general election', *Journal of the Market Research Society*, 29:4 (1987).
10 J. Waksberg, 'Sampling Methods for Random Digit Dialling', *Journal of the American Statistical Association*, 73 (1978).
11 J. M. Brick, J. Waksberg, D. Culp and A. Starer, 'Bias in list-assisted telephone samples', *Public Opinion Quarterly*, 58 (1995).
12 J. Foreman and M. Collins, 'The viability of random digit dialling in the UK', *Journal of the Market Research Society*, 33:3 (1991).
13 J. M. Lepkowski, 'Telephone sampling methods in the United States', in R. M. Groves *et al.* (eds), *Telephone Survey Methodology* (John Wiley 1988).
14 S. Deakin and M. van Staveren, *Random Digit Dialling crosses the Atlantic* (BMRB, 1982).
15 N. Moon and I. Noble, 'Forty-eight red white and blue shoe strings – implementing random digit dialling for telephone surveys in the UK', paper presented at the American Statistical Association InterCASIC conference, San Antonio, TX,1996.
16 Market Research Society, *The Opinion Polls and the 1992 General Election*, (Market Research Society, 1994).
17 N. Moon, 'The opinion polls in the British general election of 1997 – A Reputation Restored', – WAPOR Newsletter, 1 (1998).
18 R. M. Worcester, 'They got it right this time', *New Statesman*, May 1997.
19 Curtice and Sparrow, 'The Failure of the Polls in 1997'.

20 I. Crewe, 'The opinion polls: confidence restored?' *Parliamentary Affairs*, 50:4 (1997).

21 J. Curtice, 'So how well did they do? The polls in the 1997 election', *Journal of the Market Research Society*, 39:3 (1997).

22 R. Worcester, 'Rescuing pollsters from their bad press', *UK Press Gazette*, 7 March 1997, p. 451.

23 Gallup carried out a rolling poll for the *Telegraph*, interviewing around 500 people each day, and every day publishing results based on the last 1,500 interviews. To avoid the whole analysis being swamped by Gallup findings, I have followed the BBC's lead and taken each three days as a separate poll with a discrete sample. I have also ignored second and subsequent waves of panel surveys.

24 C. O'Muircheartaigh, 'Election 97: a triumph for the polls', *Research Magazine* (Market Research Society), 373, June 1997.

25 Unlike the actual election result, these figures are percentaged on all respondents, including those who did not vote or did not answer the question.

26 R. Jowell, B. Hedges, P. Lynn, G. Farrant and A. Heath, 'The 1992 British general election: the failure of the polls', *Public opinion Quarterly*, 57:2 (1993).

27 Curtice and Sparrow, *The failure of the polls in 1997.*

28 C. Marsh and J. O'Brien, 'Opinion bandwagons in attitudes to the Common Market', *Journal of the Market Research Society*, 31:3 (1989).

29 C. Marsh, 'Back on the bandwagon: the effects of opinion polls on abortion', *British Journal of Political Science*, 15:1 (1984).

30 P. Kellner, *Independent*, 6 March 1991.

31 *Observer*, 27 April 1997.

32 Foundation for Information, *The Freedom to Publish Opinion Polls* (ESOMAR, 1997).

33 R. Worcester, *British Public Opinion: A Guide to the History and Methodology of Political Opinion Polling* (Blackwell, 1991).

Index

Page numbers in *italics* refer to figures and tables.